THE THIRTY YEARS WAR 1618–1648

G. PAGÈS

THE THIRTY YEARS WAR
1618–1648

ADAM & CHARLES BLACK
LONDON

THIS EDITION FIRST PUBLISHED 1970
A. AND C. BLACK LTD
4, 5 AND 6 SOHO SQUARE, LONDON WIV 6AD

© 1939 PAYOT, PARIS
ENGLISH TRANSLATION © 1970 A. AND C. BLACK LTD

ISBN: 0 7136 1177 4

Translated by David Maland
and John Hooper from the
French, *La Guerre de Trente ans* by
G. Pagès, published by Payot, Paris

PRINTED IN GREAT BRITAIN
BY R. & R. CLARK LTD, EDINBURGH

CONTENTS

FOREWORD

Teachers who have to guide students through the complex diplomatic and political developments of the first half of the seventeenth century have long known that they are best advised to rely on the clarity, insight and soundness of Georges Pagès' *La Guerre de Trente ans*. But for many the book has been of limited use because it was written in French. The present translation should bring it the wider English readership that it deserves.

Georges Pagès was born in Paris in 1867 and spent most of his career as a school teacher, an activity reflected in two excellent books on French history intended for schools. However, from an early age he was interested in original research, and was almost alone among his countrymen in the amount of time he spent in German archives. The result, *Le Grand Électeur et Louis XIV* (1905), has remained the standard work on the relations between France and Brandenburg-Prussia during the first half of Louis XIV's reign. It was largely on the strength of this contribution that in 1922 he was appointed Professor of Modern History at the Sorbonne, where he remained until his death in 1939.

His interests at the Sorbonne were divided between French and German history during the early modern period. *La Monarchie de l'ancien régime* (1928), his first book after he attained his professorship, was a superb, lucid analysis of France's administrative structure in the sixteenth and seventeenth centuries. It has not been superseded as a brief survey of this complex topic. His student, Victor-L. Tapié, completed another book on this period of French history which he never quite finished. As *Naissance du grand siècle*, it appeared posthumously, in 1948. Again, Pagès provided students with the best short account of an important subject, this time the political development of France from 1598 to 1661. In this book, as might be surmised from the dates, he put forward the thesis that absolutism was created during the reigns of Henry IV and Louis XIII. In his view, Louis XIV merely took over a system that had already been fully elaborated by his predecessors.

Although this approach has been much disputed, Pagès' interpretation has continued to influence studies of France's government and administration in the seventeenth century.

La Guerre de Trente ans, published in the year of his death, was the fitting climax of his life's work. It combined his interests in France and in Germany, and allowed him to make a major statement about the importance of the seventeenth century in European history. His outlook is proclaimed on the very first page: 'It was [in Germany] at the cost of thirty years of warfare that modern Europe took its final form.' Pagès saw the war as the climax of a process, reaching back into the fifteenth century, whereby feudal society and the unity of Christendom disappeared, to be replaced by strong national states and a variety of religious beliefs. For him this was the essence of the transformation from medieval to modern, and it was accomplished by the time of the Peace of Westphalia.

Germany had the longest way to go in this development at the beginning of the seventeenth century, and the war had its greatest effect on her. But the consequences embraced all of Europe largely, in Pagès' view, because of the intervention of France. His final sentence is a striking affirmation of the decisive impact made by Richelieu on the entire continent: 'By widening the frontiers of the Thirty Years War, French policy, the policy of Richelieu, created the modern Europe which emerged in all its essential characteristics from the Peace of Westphalia.'

Considering the time when it was written, this was a remarkable statement. With a new German conflict looming, a Frenchman could assert that war had helped Europe to plunge into modernity. One can hardly imagine a more startling contrast to the conclusion of C. V. Wedgwood's history of the war, which, in the previous year, had captured so much of the atmosphere of the late 1930's: '[The war] need not have happened and it settled nothing worth settling. . . . The dismal course of the conflict, dragging on from one decade to the next and from one deadlock to the next, seems to me an object lesson on the dangers and disasters which can arise when men of narrow hearts and little minds are in high places.'

In the 1970's it would, of course, be C. V. Wedgwood who would capture the approval of a young audience. And yet it is clear that Pagès was especially successful in giving a sense of the period, in conveying the motives of the participants, and in setting the war within a broader context. One is aware, as even the chapter titles indicate, that it is a Europe-wide war, settling European issues. The traditional concentration on the Empire, evident even in C. V. Wedgwood, is consciously abandoned, and the book gains a breadth of perspective that is essential to its thesis. Since Pagès' work, no scholar has been able to write about the Thirty Years War as a conflict whose importance was restricted to Germany or the Empire. Its Europe-wide significance has almost become a truism. For this reason C. V. Wedgwood's insistence on the total pointlessness of the fighting has found few echoes among recent historians of the seventeenth century.

Pagès also has the advantage of having found a more even balance between detailed narratives of events and broad analyses of general tendencies than any other student of the war. This is the first book that anyone seriously interested in the period should read. He will neither flounder in swamps of minutiae nor feel wafted to impossible heights of abstraction. He will receive all the fundamental information he needs, and be guided judiciously and sensibly through such intractable problems as the intentions of Wallenstein. The main interpretative difficulties will be laid before him, and he will gain a sense of why these three decades were a decisive era in European history.

None the less, he should be aware that a number of new schools of thought have sprung up since Pagès wrote. It is conceivable that a straightforward 'History of the Thirty Years War' may not be written again for a long time, at least until historiographic fashions have changed drastically. For there are few scholars investigating the seventeenth century these days who are much concerned with the fluctuations of diplomatic history that were still for Pagès, as for all his predecessors back to Ranke, the essence of the story of the war. Some of Garrett Mattingly's students are working in the field, but mainly in an earlier period. For those doing research in the 1620's, 1630's and 1640's, it is social, demographic, economic or internal administrative history that seems to hold the main appeal.

In Pagès' own terms, the only changes that would have to be made as a result of recent work would be matters of detail. He might have to reshape his interpretation of Gustavus Adolphus in the light of Michael Roberts's magisterial two-volume biography of the king (1953 and 1958), which suggested that Swedish policy was more a matter of day-to-day practicality than long-range ambitions. He might also wish to accept Dieter Albrecht's new assessment of Maximilian of Bavaria (1962) as a mixture of Counter-Reformation prince and bureaucratic administrator, and he would certainly rewrite the account of the Diet of Regensburg (1630) in the light of Albrecht's proof that the imperial princes, not Father Joseph, brought about Wallenstein's dismissal. And, finally, he could have taken advantage of the many new insights intothe diplomacy of the 1630's and 1640's to be found in Fritz Dickmann's massive investigation of the background to Westphalia (1959).

But it is not at this level that our view of the mid-seventeenth century has changed radically in the last few years. It is an entire shift of focus that would now be required of a historian of the age of the Thirty Years War. Above all, he would have to come to terms with an issue that is still the subject of heated debate—the so-called 'crisis' of the seventeenth century. The very elements of this crisis reveal how very different the concerns of scholarship have become.

In the first place, diplomacy and international relations are almost totally absent from the debate. They are not considered to have been in crisis, and thus this essential dimension of Pagès' book is virtually ignored. What interests the current generation of scholars is the evidence of economic difficulty, of demographic slowdown, and of trouble between subjects and governments that appears throughout Europe between the 1620's and the 1670's. Only one year before *La Guerre de Trente ans* appeared, Roger Merriman had dwelt upon the coincidence of unrest in the 1640's in a book entitled *Six Contemporaneous Revolutions*, but he had been unable to suggest any pattern underlying the revolts that threatened governments in Portugal, Catalonia, Naples, France, England and the Netherlands. During the last decade, however, difficulties in Sweden, Poland and Russia have been added to those he cited, and by drawing on concurrent social, economic and demographic problems some historians have begun to perceive the era as one of general and widespread crisis.

The emphasis has varied from writer to writer. Eric Hobsbawm has stressed the economic setbacks of the century, caused to a considerable extent by the disruptions of the Thirty Years War. Hugh Trevor-Roper has pointed to the strains between parasitic, extravagant central courts and the traditional élite in the countryside. A Russian scholar, Boris Porchnev, has highlighted evidence of class struggle in France, and in response a French historian, Roland Mousnier, has traced the origins of disorder to tensions within the ruling élite. A whole school of demographic historians, active for little more than twenty years, has uncovered signs of a halt in the growth of Europe's population at the very time that these economic and political troubles were most apparent.

The one vital shortcoming that hampers the advocates of the 'crisis' is that they agree so little among themselves. No two concur in the timing, nature or effect of the phenomenon. Did it start in the 1620's or 1640's? Was it political, economic or both? Did it make any difference? The discord has laid them open to devastating criticism from those who deny that there was a crisis at all, but the influence of their viewpoint has been considerable none the less. Studies have appeared seeking evidence of the crisis in other countries, such as Denmark, or in other activities, such as scientific work. More and more scholars are writing about the mid-seventeenth century as if it were a great divide, the principal watershed between the Reformation of the early sixteenth century and the Revolutions of the late eighteenth century. And naturally the question arises: where, in all this, is there room for Pagès' *Thirty Years War*?

One of the characteristics of a crisis is surely to be found in what follows it. Regardless of how one defines the phenomenon itself—and it has to be admitted that the medical terminology, indicating a very short but very acute deterioration, does not really fit—there can be little doubt about the meaning of 'the crisis has passed'. And the sense of relaxation, of calm, of settlement that this denotes is precisely what is conveyed by almost every aspect of European history in the late seventeenth century. In every country political forms took on the shape they were to keep for a hundred years; economic advance resumed; and in intellectual life the triumph of science was assured by the founding of the English and French Royal Societies and the work of Newton.

Remarkably enough, the very same progression towards a resolution can be perceived in the realm of international affairs. It takes no special point of view to see the anarchy of the Thirty Years War, the most brutal and destructive conflict in European history up to that time, as a crisis in the relations between states. The military ran amok, agreements were broken with impunity, and sheer chaos reigned for thirty savage years. With religious partisanship to excuse the worst perfidy, it seemed that all the traditional rules and courtesies of war had been abandoned to burgeoning armies, which by the 1630's had reached a size (some 200,000 Swedes alone) not seen since the Roman legions. Where, out of all this, could order come?

The solution was found in the first of the great congresses of European history, which sat for seven years in two separate conclaves in the German province of Westphalia. This was an entirely new device—not a negotiation between two or three warring parties, as had been the normal procedure in arranging a peace treaty in the past, but an attempt to solve all the major disputes throughout Western Europe at the same time. The outcome in fact left much unresolved—for a start, the two principal protagonists, Spain and France, remained at war for another eleven years—but everyone *believed* that a new, permanent, ordered system had been created. When, more than sixty years later, another all-embracing peace re-drew the map of Europe, diplomats still considered it merely an adjustment, a rounding out, of what had been accomplished at Westphalia. The persistence of wars—though less severe ones—notwithstanding, there was common agreement at the time that the international crisis had passed and that a stable settlement had been achieved.

In terms of actual results, Westphalia was not without its importance. It brought to an end the influence of religion on international affairs, a change hastened by the Pope's denunciation of the peace. Henceforth, the interests of the state, not the faith, determined foreign policy. Moreover, the gains by the Netherlands, France and Sweden, and the losses by Spain, signified that the centre of power in Europe had shifted north from the Mediterranean for the first time in the continent's history. And yet these tangible evidences of a new situation were not as important as the conviction held by the diplomats of the seventeenth century that they had created a new and settled structure for conducting international relations. In this regard their realm of activity fits perfectly into the 'crisis' thesis.

To anyone familiar with the literature on the 'crisis' it will quickly become apparent that Pagès's work accords closely with the framework that has just been outlined. In fact it was he far more than Merriman who first made historians look at this period in terms of its European-wide significance. He refused to see the Thirty Years War as a stage merely in the history of Germany or the Empire. Instead, it took its place as a decisive event affecting all of Europe. The recent disclosure of its ramifications in economic and demographic developments has served only to reiterate and extend the case Pagès made for interpreting the war in the broadest possible context. *La Guerre de Trente ans* thus remains, not only the best available history of three crucial decades, but also a work highly germane to the interests of contemporary scholarship.

THEODORE K. RABB

Princeton University
1970

Works by historians other than Pagès referred to in this Foreword are:

C. V. Wedgwood: *The Thirty Years War*, London, 1938.

Michael Roberts: *Gustavus Adolphus*, London, 1953 and 1958.

Dieter Albrecht: *Die auswärtige Politik Maximilians von Bayern*, Göttingen, 1962.

Fritz Dickmann: *Der Westfälische Frieden*, Münster, 1959.

R. B. Merriman: *Six Contemporaneous Revolutions*, Oxford, 1938.

Trevor Aston (ed.): *Crisis in Europe, 1560–1660*, London, 1965; especially the essays by Hobsbawm and Trevor-Roper.

A. D. Lublinskaya: *French Absolutism: The Crucial Phase*, Cambridge, 1968; for the 'crisis' and Porchnev's and Mousnier's views.

D. V. Glass and D. E. C. Eversley (eds): *Population in History*, Chicago, 1965; recent work in demography.

THE THIRTY YEARS WAR 1618-1648

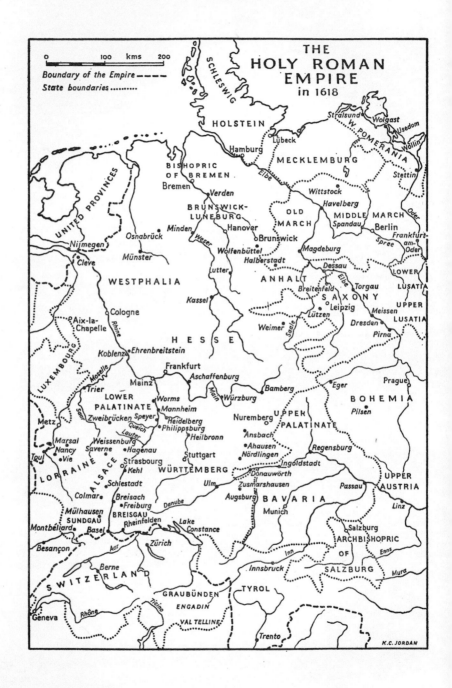

THE
HOLY ROMAN
EMPIRE
in 1618

0   100   kms   200

Boundary of the Empire ----
State boundaries ....

SCHLESWIG

HOLSTEIN

Hamburg

Lübeck

Stralsund

W. POMERANIA

Wolgast
Usedom
Wollin

MECKLEMBURG

Elbe

Stettin

Oder

BISHOPRIC
OF BREMEN

Bremen

Verden

Wittstock

Havelberg

OLD
MARCH

Spandau

MIDDLE MARCH

Berlin

Frankfurt-
am-Oder

Spree

BRUNSWICK-
LUNEBURG

Minden

Hanover

Brunswick

Magdeburg

Osnabrück

Nijmegen

UNITED PROVINCES

Cleve

Münster

WESTPHALIA

Wolfenbüttel

Halberstadt

Lutter

ANHALT

Dessau

Breitenfeld

SAXONY

Torgau

LOWER
LUSATIA

Kassel

Weimer

Leipzig

Lützen

Meissen

Dresden

UPPER
LUSATIA

Pirna

Elbe

Saale

Cologne

Aix-la-
Chapelle

Rhine

HESSE

LUXEMBOURG

Koblenz

Ehrenbreitstein

Frankfurt

Moselle

Trier

Mainz

Aschaffenburg

Bamberg

Eger

Prague

BOHEMIA

LOWER
PALATINATE

Worms

Würzburg

Pilsen

Metz

Saar

Mannheim

Speyer

Main

Nuremberg

UPPER
PALATINATE

Zweibrücken

Queich

Heidelberg

Philippsburg

Lauter

Heilbronn

Ansbach

Ahausen

Regensburg

UPPER
AUSTRIA

Marsal

Weissenburg

Nancy

Saverne

Hagenau

Stuttgart

Nördlingen

Ingoldstadt

Vie

Strasbourg

Kehl

WÜRTTEMBERG

Donauwörth

Passau

Linz

Toul

LORRAINE

ALSACE

Schlestadt

Ulm

Zusmarshausen

BAVARIA

Colmar

Breisach

Freiburg

Danube

Augsburg

Munich

SALZBURG
ARCHBISHOPRIC

Salzburg

Mülhausen

SUNDGAU

BREISGAU

Rheinfelden

Lake
Constance

OF

Enns

Montbéliard

Basel

SALZBURG

Mura

Besançon

Aar

Zürich

Inn

Berne

Innsbruck

SWITZERLAND

Rhône

Ticino

GRAUBÜNDEN

TYROL

Geneva

ENGADIN

VAL TELLINE

Trento

K.C. JORDAN

CHAPTER I

GERMANY AND EUROPE BEFORE THE CRISIS

The Thirty Years War cannot be fully understood if it is studied in isolation since it was merely one of the final symptoms of a much greater crisis—the transition from medieval to modern times in western and central Europe. This crisis was slow to evolve and lasted for a long time. In different countries its successive phases unfolded at different rates, so that if we could draw a graph of its development it would reveal many an unexpected turn, many checks, many reversals and from time to time a sudden swift upward curve. It was a crisis which endured for several centuries, and cannot be contained within a precise chronological framework, but let us say, broadly speaking, that it began somewhere in the fifteenth century and ended in the seventeenth. Politically it was characterised by the formation of the first modern states; from the religious point of view it witnessed the destruction at the hands of Protestantism of the united Christendom which the Catholic Church had established in the Middle Ages.

At the start of the seventeenth century, therefore, this evolution of a new society which had almost taken place in the west had only begun to take shape in central Europe, that is in Germany where the medieval powers of the emperor still survived, and where the struggle between Catholics and Protestants still continued with no end in sight. It was here at the cost of thirty years of warfare that modern Europe took its final form.

In order to understand what Germany was like at this time we must remember that it lay at the very centre of a Europe which was considerably more advanced than itself, and that here the relics of the Middle Ages survived longer than anywhere else. Germany can only be defined in terms of its relations with the new Europe which had already emerged around it, and we might even say that it was precisely the very part of Europe where the Middle Ages had not given place to modern times. Nor can we define it in ethnic terms for it is as impossible to include all Germans within the definition as it is to exclude the other races which had settled there. Usually we equate it with the Empire and, in fact, this approximation is the only convenient definition even though there were Germans outside the Empire and non-German populations within it. But this does not really solve the problem of defining Germany since it is just as difficult to define the limits of the Holy Roman Empire itself—nor do I propose to do so at this stage.

Before tackling the question of Germany itself I intend to make a brief examination of its neighbours. Imperial authority was essentially a universal authority and originally the Empire and Christendom had been one and the same thing. When, however, a great section of Christendom had broken away from it, it became the Holy Roman empire of the German Nation, a meaningless expression which indicated the total incompatability between the traditional claims of the emperors and their real powers. Thus the 'terrain du Saint-Empire', an expression which I think was first used by Lavisse, was reduced in size to one area of central Europe. Subsequently it was further reduced as new regions broke away from the loose federal structure and the confusion to become centralised states of the modern type, while the Empire continued to group under its outdated authority the areas in which particularism and confusion remained.

So what had become of the Europe which existed outside the Holy Roman Empire at the start of the seventeenth century?

Three modern states had been established and since they are well known we need not linger over them. I would only like to remind you of the stage which they had reached in their evolution and how the conflict between Catholics and Protestants had been resolved to date.

The France of the early seventeenth century was the France in which Henry IV had restored royal authority and implemented the Edict of Nantes. The political and religious crisis which had nearly brought about the downfall of absolute monarchy and Catholicism and which had lasted for forty years (much longer than the German crisis was to last), seemed to have ended. The divine right of kings had been restored by the former Huguenot king, Henry IV, and the Catholic Church had recovered its authority throughout France, but the religious settlement acknowledged its co-existence with the Protestant Church which was henceforth to be protected by the law of the land. In fact, internal order was not yet as safely established as it appeared. The long civil wars had shaken society to its foundation, transformed its customs and created hazards for the absolute monarchy from which it was to emerge triumphant only a full half-century later. The Edict of Nantes satisfied neither Catholic nor Huguenot since it guaranteed the advances already made by Calvinism but made its future extension more or less impossible. But these political and religious difficulties, which only served to delay, without ever seriously compromising, the progress of absolute monarchy and Catholicism, did compel French kings to keep a close watch on foreign affairs in order to avoid any repercussions within the kingdom. Henceforth, the monarchy, which increasingly united the forces of the nation, had to deal with the outside world and to intervene when the interests of France seemed at stake.

England was still only a small country out of which the Tudors, and Elizabeth in particular, had made one of the states which counted in seventeenth-century Europe. After the death of Elizabeth in 1603 it was united to Scotland by a personal tie, since James I of England was at the same time James VI of Scotland. But the creation of a state Church which was half Protestant and strictly controlled by the sovereign—that is to say the Anglican Church—had aroused resistance which still continued in the time of the Stuarts and made the seventeenth century in England a century of revolution. England's political and religious constitution was thus not yet settled and English policy at the time of the Thirty Years War was to be paralysed by internal unrest. She could never remain aloof from the continental crisis because a complete victory by Catholicism would have presented a threat to her national existence; but her interventions were only to be indecisive and short-lived.

Spain's position is more difficult to define. It was in the fifteenth century, in the time of the so-called Catholic Kings, Ferdinand and Isabella, that a modern state, the kingdom of Spain, was created in the Iberian peninsula by the union of Aragon and Castile and by the annexation of the kingdom of Granada to Castile and of Valencia to Aragon. Subsequently, Portugal too was annexed by Philip II. But in addition to this there existed the overseas territories whose importance and extent were so great that the kingdom of Spain was no more than the controlling agency of a vast Spanish Empire. The kings of Spain ruled over the whole of South America including Brazil which had been brought into the Spanish Empire when Portugal was annexed. They also governed Central America and Mexico, which at that time included California and the great plains of Texas and Florida. They controlled the islands of the western Mediterranean, the Balearic

Islands, Sardinia and Sicily, and within the Italian peninsula they held the kingdom of Naples and the duchy of Milan. They still ruled over Franche-Comté and the Netherlands as part of the old Burgundian kingdom. Nor was this all. When Charles of Spain became the Emperor Charles V the destinies of the young Spanish Empire were momentarily linked with those of the old Roman Empire of the Germanic Nation, and, if the abdication of Charles V separated the two Empires, they remained nevertheless linked by close family ties. After Charles V, his brother Ferdinand was elected Emperor and his descendants, throughout all the succeeding elections, managed to maintain the imperial crown in their house. Thus this new type of modern state which the kingdom of Spain had become remained involved at the beginning of the seventeenth century in the ramifications of a policy which was Imperial rather than Spanish. After the great efforts of Philip II to give back to the Roman Church its universal authority, this policy could not help but be a completely Catholic one, conducted by the Spanish monarchy and by the great spearhead of the Counter-Reformation, the Society of Jesus which had originated in Spain.

If we leave western Europe where the first strong monarchies had been established, we pass to that ill-defined area on the borders of the Holy Roman Empire, where, moving from north to south, we find the three regions of the Netherlands, Switzerland and Italy. None of these had as yet consolidated its territory nor evolved its ultimate political form.

In the North, the Netherlands belonged both to the Holy Roman Empire and to the Spanish Empire and here new destinies were being forged. Within the Holy Roman Empire they constituted the circle of Burgundy, one of the ten circles formerly created by the Emperor Maximilian I; however, they belonged by sovereign right to the king of Spain who had inherited a part of the former Burgundian state. But the northern region of the Low Countries, the seven provinces of the north grouped about Holland, had already broken away from him, having revolted and formed themselves into a republic. At the beginning of the seventeenth century, in 1609, they obtained from Philip III a twelve-year truce recognising their independence. However, since it derived from a truce, this recognition of the independence of the United Provinces was only provisional, and so far as the Holy Roman Empire and the crown of Spain were concerned, it was not formally recognised until the end of the Thirty Years War in 1648.

The ten provinces of the south, unlike their northern counterparts, had not followed their revolt through to its conclusion. Before his death, Philip II detached them from his kingdom to give them to his daughter, the Infanta Isabella, and to his son-in-law, Archduke Albert of Austria, but on condition that they should return to the crown of Spain on the death of Isabella. Throughout the whole of the seventeenth century they were to be known as the Spanish Netherlands. The Netherlands in general provide us with an example of those frontier regions of the Holy Roman Empire which broke away from it as soon as a more modern type of state could be constituted. As for the religious question, it was resolved by the political separation of the Belgian provinces which had remained Catholic from the seven United Provinces where, in spite of a large Catholic population and despite many extremist Protestant sects which repudiated the authority of the state, Calvinism became, and was to remain, the dominant faith.

Switzerland, at the centre of these frontier regions, was one of the oddest political entities of the time. Its name described nothing more than a geographical region. Within it were the thirteen cantons of Zurich, Berne, Lucerne, Uri, Schwytz, Unterwalden, Zug, Glaris, Basel, Friburg, Soleure, Schaffhausen and Appenzell; then there were their allies, including among them the two republics of Geneva and Mulhouse, the Diocese of Basel and the Grisons, which were associations of quasi-independent townships; finally there were their dependencies which might be subject to all or to several of the thirteen cantons, or to a single one, or even to one of the allies of the cantons. One of these dependencies, the Valtelline, controlled by the Grisons, was to be very important in the Thirty Years War. It is easy to see the extreme complexity of this structure. Every part, except the dependencies, enjoyed complete autonomy. Each canton and each ally had its own laws and its own judges, its own councils, its own seal and its own coinage. The only thing which the thirteen cantons had in common was the federal constitution which exercised little or no control over them. Zurich, the most important canton, could, when it chose, convene a diet which met irregularly and which was little more than an assembly of delegates. It was this independence of the cantons which allowed the religious question in Switzerland to be settled by the simple expedient of each canton organising its church as it saw fit. Four of them, Zurich, Berne, Basel and Schaffhausen, were Protestant cantons in which Catholic worship was forbidden. Two, Glaris and Appenzell, were mixed cantons where Catholics and Protestants lived side by side.

The remainder were exclusively Catholic. In this way religious peace was assured, except in a few dependencies which did not enjoy freedom of religion.

In a time of such great religious fervour, the division of the country between the Catholic and Protestant Churches made it impossible to evolve a common policy, so the cantons profited from their enforced neutrality by invoking a series of conflicting obligations. In 1602 they renewed their 'perpetual alliance' with France; in 1611 they contracted a 'union', again perpetual, with the House of Austria. They knew how to take advantage of their geographical situation and, according to the circumstances and always at the right price, they opened or closed the alpine passes which carried the roads leading from France and Germany to Italy. They also exploited the physical qualities of a race which had been hardened among the mountains, supplying the warring nations around them with bands of mercenaries who rarely returned home empty-handed. It should be added that while Switzerland had long been free from the yoke of Austrian domination, it was legally still part of the Holy Roman Empire at the beginning of the seventeenth century, and would only be separated from it by the Peace of West-phalia.

Italy, like Switzerland, was no more than a geographical expression, and the territorial divisions had remained more or less what they were in the Middle Ages. In this respect Italy was like Germany. Further-more, it had long formed part of the Holy Roman Empire and the time when the emperor could only be crowned at Rome had not yet been forgotten. Nevertheless, at the beginning of the seventeenth century, Italy could no longer be included in the 'terrains du Saint-Empire', and although the emperor still retained the right of investiture in a certain number of principalities, his power had been replaced by that of the kings of Spain, successors to the kings of Aragon. Through Sicily and the kingdom of Naples they were masters of southern Italy, and controlled the coasts of central Italy from Sardinia, through garrisons stationed in Tuscany (Orbitello, Piombino, etc.) and, above all, from the Isle of Elba. From the duchy of Milan they dominated the Po valley and held the key to the principal Alpine passes. Even in Rome, they were still able if they wished at the end of the sixteenth century to determine the resolutions of the Curia by the number and authority of the Spanish cardinals or of those in the pay of Spain. Subsequently, by persistent efforts, Henry IV managed to introduce a few French cardinals into the Curia and to buy the support of a few others. The Pope, too, frequently sought to free himself from the Spanish yoke, but did not always succeed.

In the face of Spain's authority, the principalities and republics, then known collectively as the 'Stati Liberi', a name which they scarcely deserved, counted for little. Even a grand-duke of Tuscany could only maintain a precarious independence, obliged as he was to admit Spanish garrisons to his ports. The republic of Venice, which was to a certain extent protected by its geographical situation, still commanded some respect, but was already well into its decline. The republic of Genoa, whose lands lay between Milan and the Mediterranean could not refuse the Spanish galleys access to its coasts, and had to be content with lending to the court of Madrid vast sums which were never repaid. A breach with Spain would have ruined it. One state alone, the duchy of Savoy-Piedmont, was able to remain completely independent because of its position on both slopes of the Alps. It was a dangerous position but one which could be turned to account since the duke of Savoy was courted at the same time by the kings of both Spain and France. Sooner or later he would have to decide whether his ambitions lay in the direction of the Rhône valley or the Po valley, and the neighbouring presence of an increasingly strong French monarchy finally determined his choice. At the beginning of the seventeenth century, however, Charles-Emmanuel had not yet decided. Constantly torn by the rival attractions of Geneva and Genoa, he hesitated between alliance with France or Spain.

It was self-evident that an Italy so fragmented could neither expel the Spaniards nor avoid the unwelcome attentions of their opponents who understood full well that control of the peninsula was an essential part of the imperial policy of the kings of Spain. Once the war had started in Germany it was only a question of time before it extended beyond the Swiss cantons to the other side of the Alps.

The limits of the Holy Roman Empire were no less uncertain on the eastern and northern borders. To the east its neighbours were the Ottoman Empire and Poland; to the north, the Scandinavian states of Denmark and Sweden. At the beginning of the seventeenth century the tide of Turkish power had not yet turned and the empire of the Ottoman sultans represented a considerable force. They were still masters of the eastern Mediterranean in spite of the few possessions that the republic of Venice had retained there, and if they did not dominate, they at least unsettled the western Mediterranean through the sultan's tributaries, the Berbers. To the north, Muscovy and Poland were

separated from the Black Sea and the Danubian Plains by more of the
sultan's tributaries, the Tartar hordes of the principalities of Moldavia,
Wallachia and Transylvania. The Ottomans had even conquered the
greater part of Hungary. Buda was a Turkish fortress, and from Buda
to Vienna, along both banks of the Danube, stretched a plain which was
defended only by a few fortified towns. We can easily understand the
terror that the permanent threat of Turkish invasion inspired in those
Germans who were protected by nothing more than the narrow strip of
royal Hungary which alone remained in Habsburg hands. The Tran-
sylvanians and Hungarians, while remaining Christian, had for the
most part become Calvinists and did not hesitate to enlist the aid of the
Turks against the House of Austria and the Jesuits, who sought to
return them by force to the Catholic fold. This in turn aroused greater
anxiety in Germany, and the Turkish peril was a dominant factor in
the policies both of the emperors and of the German princes.

Poland, further to the north, presented no threat to the Holy
Roman Empire. This vast and ill-defined country seemed to shift
across the great plains between the Black Sea and the Baltic in a vain
quest for permanent frontiers. Moreover, despite its size it was a weak
state and, unlike the states of western Europe, had made no progress
towards royal absolutism. It continued to waver between monarchy
and republicanism and the 'King and Republic of Poland' was a familiar
phrase in the chancelleries of Europe. Poland did have a king, but he
was an elected king. Furthermore, his election was conditional upon his
recognising and confirming the privileges of the nobility. The nobles,
led more or less at will by a few great landowners, the Palatines,
made up a sort of noble commonalty, the Szlachta as it was called,
which included everyone who owned an estate, however small, even if
he worked it himself. The Szlachta was powerless to direct those who
governed, but it could, and often did, prevent them from governing.
The first half of the seventeenth century was the very period when the
Polish nobility established the custom that no decision could be taken
in the Diets if a single member of the assembly were opposed to it.
Sheltered by the liberum veto, anarchy prevailed, and Poland was
reduced to a state of impotence. It was for religious rather than political
reasons that its history was indissolubly linked with the history of
Germany at the time of the Thirty Years War. Protestantism, which
had originally spread throughout the country, had been banished. In
the reign of Sigismund III Vasa (1587–1632), Poland became the great
Catholic country that it has been ever since, and the influence of the

Jesuits met no further opposition. Henceforward Poland was a sort of Catholic vanguard surrounded by Moslems, Protestants and orthodox Christians. Lutheran Germany, as yet unvanquished by the Counter-Reformation, was threatened in the rear.

Finally there were the Scandinavian countries which had always had, especially in economic matters, a close relationship with the German states. The principalities and towns of northern Germany also bordered the Baltic which, far from separating them, was a source of unity. The monopoly of the northern trade which the Hanse towns had exercised for several centuries was still fresh in the minds of the old German houses of Bergen. When Lübeck's trading power declined it was the Danish customs at Elsinore which controlled the trade of the western nations with the coasts of the Holy Roman Empire and the eastern Baltic. From Germany, too, the Scandinavian countries received the Lutheran faith which spread there without meeting much resistance. In matters of religion, Denmark, Sweden and Protestant Germany were closely allied, but the relationship did not stop there: it was also political. Well before the Thirty Years War, the king of Denmark was duke of Holstein and, by virtue of this, a prince of the Empire. He sat and voted in the Diet. Together with the dukes of Brunswick-Lüneburg, he was one of the most powerful princes of the Lower Saxon Circle. He was involved in everything which happened in the northern regions of the Empire. The king of Sweden, who at that time was less powerful, was only bound to Germany by a common faith, but in 1611 Gustavus Adolphus came to the throne. He rescued the monarchy from the control of the nobles and embarked upon a war beyond the Baltic with the czar of Muscovy and the king of Poland. In 1617, Carelia, Ingria and Estonia, to the south of Swedish Finland, were ceded to Sweden by the Peace of Stolbova. Already, perhaps, there had come to Gustavus Adolphus the dream, which for a time he realised, of Swedish domination of the north German coast, transforming the Baltic into a Swedish lake. Like Denmark, Sweden would not be able to stand aloof from the German crisis for long.

We can now pass from the countries surrounding the Holy Roman Empire to the Empire itself and try to understand that ill-defined and complex political entity. To do so we must treat separately of Germany and the emperor, but always bear in mind that we cannot understand one without the other.

At the beginning of the seventeenth century Germany was a nation which was not yet unified, not even as a nation. Its inhabitants spoke different dialects; they formed distinct groups whose individuality was so sharp that it has not yet disappeared in the Germany of today. States hardly count any more but the Gauen still survive. At the time of the Thirty Years War, as in the Middle Ages, it was still possible to talk about 'The Germanies'. Incapable though these German 'nations' were of following a common policy there none the less existed a certain national consciousness, a kind of German patriotism, but it only became apparent when the national soil seemed to be threatened by the foreigner—by the French or the Turks.

Moreover, we should note, and this is of paramount importance, that in this un-unified Germany the natural division of the country into 'nations', or districts, in no wise corresponded with its partition into the political units which had been created in feudal times by the accidents of inheritance or wars and which were known as 'The Principalities and States of the Holy Roman Empire'. These greatly outnumbered the 'nations', and overlapped to such an extent that it is impossible to draw an accurate map of the Germany of that time. They were infinitely varied in extent, in importance and in form of government. They bore so many different names that it is difficult to remember them all. There existed both secular and ecclesiastical principalities: the former included duchies, landgravates, marches (or margravates) and counties; the latter, archdioceses, dioceses and abbacies. Besides the principalities there were the urban republics, known as free cities, and to all these must be added the petty estates which the Imperial Knights (Reichsritter) possessed around their castles, especially in southern Germany.

If this confused mass of 'Princes and States' had any sort of organic unity it was solely because it constituted the Empire, corresponding to that vast unsettled region to which the emperors laid claim and which did not so far contain any one state which was strong enough to assert its independence. In fact, the heads of these 'Imperial States' who were too weak to emancipate themselves none the less endeavoured, whenever the opportunity arose, to acquire new lands by marriage, inheritance or conquest, and to establish their authority over them, thus increasing their independence. This of course could not be done without some anxiety to the emperor, even at times without some open defiance of his wishes, but the princes always hastened to his side whenever Germany was threatened from abroad. Thus the emperor was indeed head of the Empire.

But what was the emperor? Originally he was the elected king of

Germany, crowned emperor at Rome by the Pope. At the beginning of the seventeenth century, and for some time before that, the king of Germany no longer went to Rome after his election to receive the imperial crown. The election itself conferred on him the title of Emperor. For centuries the form of the election had varied considerably and it was only in the fourteenth century that it had been sanctioned by a solemn act, the Golden Bull. The task of electing the emperor was entrusted to seven princes, who were then considered to be the most powerful in the Empire and who were known henceforward as the electors. Three, the archbishops of Mainz, Cologne and Trier, were ecclesiastical princes. The other four were lay princes: the king of Bohemia, the duke of Saxony, the margrave of Brandenburg and the Count Palatine of the Rhine. Although the emperor was elected by seven German princes, he none the less considered himself to be the successor of Otto the Great, Charlemagne and the Roman emperors. The imperial crown conferred upon him a dignity which raised him above all kings, and the concept of the unity of Christendom survived in him. But the emperor was also a prince who was entitled to his own territories, prerogatives and claims just like any other prince, and the origin of his princely rights was quite different from that of his imperial dignity. This was a feudal authority which made him the sovereign power to whom all the territories of the Empire were answerable, either *mediately*, that is to say in legal language through the agency of the other princes, or *immediately*, without the intervention of a third party. And so it was that the free cities of the Empire enjoyed the privilege of immediacy so that nobody could intervene between them and the emperor. As a prince of course, it goes without saying that the emperor, like all the other princes, sought to extend his personal possessions and to establish his prerogatives and claims: as feudal overlord he sought to increase his authority over the princes of the Empire and the latent antagonism between his claims and the ambitions of the princes was a constant source of conflict.

Finally, the emperor, who while he was an elected emperor was also a hereditary prince, quite naturally sought to keep the imperial title within his family. Since tradition would not sanction a legal heir he gradually did his best to ensure what almost amounted to the same thing. By the beginning of the seventeenth century he had almost succeeded. The electors were accustomed to choose the emperor from the House of Habsburg. Not that his right of succession could not be questioned; it often was. But from the beginning of the seventeenth century to the beginning of the nineteenth it was only interrupted once, by the election of a Wittelsbach, the Emperor Charles VII, and only then because the male line of the Habsburgs had come to an end. So the electors' freedom of choice remained intact and the future was always uncertain, but the House of Habsburg always had recourse to one expedient. The reigning emperor would always take advantage of a moment when his authority was well established and, during his own lifetime, arrange to have one of his sons elected as king of the Romans, thus associating him with the imperial title. But for the reigning emperor to anticipate the imperial election in this way required the compliance of the electors and this they would only grant when they had obtained from him the recognition and confirmation of their privileges by a solemn act called an 'Imperial Capitulation'.

Life within the Empire was dominated by the latent antagonism between the emperor and the princes, but the forms which this antagonism assumed and the means it employed were determined by the institutions which held the Empire together. These institutions could hardly have been more complicated and they have spawned a legal literature devoted solely to themselves which we may safely overlook.[1] We need only note, before extracting the essential features, that they did not form a well-ordered system. They had been created gradually, as the need arose, and they had only succeeded in turning the Empire into a shapeless state which bore the features of many types of state but managed to be none of them. It was what one of the great seventeenth-century constitutional lawyers, Pufendorf, was to call some time after the Thirty Years War: 'A sort of unco-ordinated body politic which might well be compared to a monster.'[2]

The basic constituents of the Holy Roman Empire were the 'princes and states', the 'members of the empire', among which we should include the free cities but not the Imperial Knights, belated survivors of the Middle Ages. Theoretically all these 'members of the empire' had equal rights, but they did not exercise them equally. How could some wretched free city which was little more than an overgrown village carry the same weight as an electoral prince? The states of the Empire varied greatly in size. Leaving aside the emperor's personal possessions, the territories of a duke of Saxony, a margrave of Brandenburg, or a duke of Bavaria, to name but a few, compared in size to the duchy of

[1] Details of the works of the German jurists may be found in *La France et le Saint-Empire romain germanique*, by B. Auerbach.
[2] Irregulare aliquod corpus et monstro simile.

Savoy or the kingdom of the Two Sicilies. On the other hand, those of some abbot or count of the Empire might be no more than single cantons with populations of only a few hundred. These states, which were so essentially unequal, very often had opposing interests and the smaller they were, the more jealously they guarded their independence. Who was to preserve public order and peace among them? It could only be the emperor, but he rarely had the means or the desire and he intervened only in exceptional circumstances. He might sequestrate a disputed inheritance[1] or place a prince or city under the imperial ban.[2] Only rarely did he have the forces necessary to carry out his own sentence; more often than not he was reduced to employing the troops of some prince of the Empire, who quite naturally saw to it that he was well paid for his services. To impose a little order on this confused state of affairs the Emperor Maximilian, at the end of the fifteenth century, had created within the Empire large territorial divisions known as the ten circles. All the princes and states of each circle could meet together in an 'Assembly of the Circle' (Kreistag) and take decisions by which they were bound. They accepted one of their own number as their leader, the 'Director of the Circle' (Kreisoberst). The institution of the ten circles of the Empire survived but it was not very effective. The debates of the circles' assemblies, whose members were all equal, did not always lead to general agreement and when any resolution was taken by the directors they rarely had the authority to carry it out.

Another institution which had gradually developed in the Empire was something of an oddity because it had no legal status; this was the electoral union. It was not created by any imperial law. The electoral college had been officially established by the Golden Bull as one of the colleges of the diet which elected the emperor and the king of the Romans, but the electoral union was quite different. It was composed of six, not seven, electors. The elector of Bohemia was never admitted to it because he was none other than the emperor, archduke of Austria, king of Bohemia and king of Hungary. The electoral union was the meeting of all the electors who, with the exception of the elector of Bohemia, met together whenever they thought it useful, and often negotiated as a body with the emperor; this fact alone explained why the elector of Bohemia was excluded. The electoral union had no rights other than the ones it assumed with the tacit consent of the

---

[1] A good example of this is provided by the famous affair of the succession of Cleves and Julich.

[2] For example the proscription of Donauwörth in 1607.

emperor who allowed it to continue because he often needed to make use of it. It was, after all, far easier to negotiate with this body than with all the princes and states. Similarly, the princes and states permitted it to continue because it often defended their common interest against the emperor. And so it was that a tradition was established. At the beginning of the seventeenth century the electoral union had become a powerful force, perhaps the most powerful force, within the Empire, although its powers had never been legally defined.

But the essential federal institution, the one which really held together the confederation that we have termed Germany, was the Imperial Diet, the Reichstag. All the princes and states were represented at the Diet and they sent their ambassadors to it. It was there that decisions were taken which affected the whole Empire and which could be enforced throughout its confines. But the manner in which the Diet met, debated and voted provided complications which resulted directly from the very complexity of the Empire.

All the princes and states were represented at the Diet, but not always in the same way. The number of seats did not correspond to the number of the 'Members of the Empire'. There were some princes who had several seats, and consequently several votes at their disposal, while, on the other hand, there were several princes who shared a single seat and a single vote. When a prince (for example the margrave of Brandenburg) possessed territories which had in the past had a separate political existence, he had at his disposal a seat and a vote for each one. At the other end of the scale, the imperial counts, who often possessed only a minute estate, or the small free cities, shared the same bench at the Diet and had a single common vote. The total number of seats and votes was far less than that of princes and states.

Furthermore, the plenipotentiaries at the Diet did not all sit or hold their discussions together. The Diet was divided into three chambers or colleges: the College of Electors, the College of Princes and the College of the Free Cities. Notice that the ecclesiastical princes did not form a separate college. The Electors-Archiepiscopal sat with the lay electors; the other archbishops, bishops, abbots, etc. were represented in the College of Princes. Decisions had to be taken in the name of all three colleges, and theoretically therefore they had equal rights, but the way in which the discussions were conducted revealed to what extent this theoretical equality was an illusion. All matters submitted to the Diet were first discussed separately by the College of Electors and the College of Princes. Then these two colleges tried to reach an agreement.

If they failed, the matter was abandoned, but if they succeeded their common resolution was then communicated to the College of the Free Cities, which had not yet discussed the matter. The free cities were unable to modify any common resolution taken by the first two colleges; they could only accept or reject it. Theirs was merely the power to obstruct.

In fact there were only two forces which counted at the Diet, the emperor and the electors, especially the elector of Mainz, Archchancellor of the Empire. According to tradition the emperor could not convene the Diet without the assent of the Electoral College, but he, and only he, held the initiative. Moreover, he exercised, not directly but through the intermediary of his ambassador, the chairmanship or, as it was then called, the post of 'Director of the College of Princes'.[1] The director of the college was an office of considerable influence since it was he who introduced the matters for discussion and controlled the debates. The electors had the great advantage of forming a small college on their own and it was thus much easier for them to reach agreements than it was for the princes, great and small, whose interests often differed widely. As for the elector of Mainz, not only was he director of his own college but also of the Diet itself wherein no matter could be discussed if he had not introduced it or, as we would say today, 'put it on the agenda'. In reality it was he who controlled the assembly's debates.

But in the final analysis the emperor's influence and that of the elector of Mainz all too often cancelled each other out, as it were, and resulted in deadlock. Only the emperor could convene the Diet, but the elector of Mainz could, with the support of the Electoral College, oppose the convocation. A common resolution of the three colleges could not be passed against the will of the electors or the director, but it could only become law if the emperor gave his assent and promulgated it, and the emperor was under no obligation to do so. He in turn, however, could not oblige the Diet to reopen discussion on a common resolution. The result was that he too had only the power to obstruct.

The Diet therefore was a complicated body which functioned slowly and with difficulty. It was an assembly where much speaking was done, and even more writing (for the colleges communicated among

---

[1] I have quite intentionally simplified this. In fact the office of 'Director of the College of Princes' belonged alternatively to the emperor and the archbishop of Salzburg. However, as the latter at that period was normally a prince of the House of Habsburg, the emperor's influence nearly always prevailed.

themselves by exchanging written reports), but little was achieved. Questions of precedence and legal quibbles which gave rise to long successions of reports and counter-reports took up a considerable time and indefinitely prolonged debates which were often never concluded. It would be difficult to disguise the Diet's impotence at the beginning of the seventeenth century, and this impotence was shown in another way. We are led to believe, because hardly anybody today would disagree, that the right of majorities has always been recognised. Mr Konopczynski, a Polish historian, has demonstrated that this is not so. The need to arrive at unanimous decisions in representative assemblies had for a long time seemed more natural than the acceptance of a simple majority decision. It was this feeling that had made the custom of liberum veto possible in seventeenth-century Poland. The liberum veto was never practised in Germany but the Diet was not far from accepting something very like it. The idea was often expressed that a member of the Empire was not bound by a common resolution if its ambassador had not voted on it: it was under discussion at the beginning of the seventeenth century and the lawyers hesitated to formulate an opinion about it. In the latin jargon of the Imperial Assembly it was known as the jus singulorum and it is obvious that those who defended it were encouraged in their resistance by the hesitations of the lawyers. Moreover, it was more or less the case that after the Reformation the Diet began to adopt a procedure which encouraged these ideas. When the Diet could not agree on any religious matter under discussion it split into two groups, the Catholics and the Protestants: both groups had equal rights, neither could impose its will on the other, and the Diet would be dissolved without reaching a conclusion. To use the Polish expression, it was 'broken'. Such a Diet was the Diet of 1607. It is therefore clear that the operation of the Imperial diets was not so unlike that of the Polish diets as we have been led to believe.

To understand the Germany of that period it only remains for us to consider a state, or more precisely a group of states, which was almost entirely part of the Empire, but which retained its own individuality. I refer to the territories of the house of Austria. The Austrian Empire as it existed at the beginning of the seventeenth century, was the recent creation of Ferdinand of Habsburg, Charles V's younger brother. While Charles was still alive, Ferdinand was already archduke of Upper and Lower Austria, ruling over the middle reaches of the Danube above and below Vienna, and over a few principalities previously linked to Austria, namely Styria, Carinthia, Carniola and the Tyrol.

In 1526 he had had himself elected king of Bohemia by the Estates of the kingdom of Bohemia and king of Hungary by the Hungarian Diet. In this manner an artificial group of territories was created, peopled by different races and speaking various languages—German, several Slavonic dialects (Czech, Slovak, Slovenian and Croatian), and Hungarian. Such an incongruous collection seemed fated not to last but in fact, as we well know, it survived into the present century. Ferdinand spent his entire reign consolidating and organising it, even after his election as King of the Romans alongside Emperor Charles V, and even after he himself had become emperor. By his death in 1564 the foundations had already been firmly laid.

Ferdinand divided his territories between his three sons. The eldest, Maximilian, whom he had had elected King of the Romans and who became Emperor Maximilian II, received the crowns of Bohemia and Hungary along with Upper and Lower Austria. Of the other two, one received the Tyrol, the other Styria, Carinthia and Carniola. None the less these three branches of the same house remained closely united and it was not long before they became one again. I have already said that in Hungary Ferdinand retained only a narrow sector bordering the Austrian and Bohemian lands. The rest was held by the Turks. These frontier regions were mainly peopled by Slavs, and the king of Hungary had very few Hungarian subjects. Finally, the Slavonic countries, like the Habsburgs' Germanic countries, were included in the Holy Roman Empire. Only the narrow sector of royal Hungary which had escaped the Turkish conquest remain outside.

This combination of territories was a fact of the utmost importance whose consequences I now propose to examine. The first was the new strength which the emperor derived, even as emperor, from such extensive private possessions. Charles V's imperial authority had been backed by his enormous territorial power, but this had been completely distinct from the Empire, and its political centre, Madrid, had been far from the Empire. By contrast the possessions of Ferdinand and his successors, even those which were chiefly peopled by Slavs, were all part of the Holy Roman Empire with the single exception of the tiny kingdom of Hungary. Moreover, one of the crowns that Ferdinand bore, and which the emperors continued to bear after him, that is to say the crown of Bohemia, carried with it an electoral title. The fact that the emperor should at the same time have been head of the most powerful princely house of the Empire was not without its importance. Nor must we overlook the fact that the territories of the House of

Austria formed a continuous border against the Turks to the east of the Empire. Austria, once the eastern march, had returned to its original role. The Habsburg of Vienna, the emperor, was the natural protector of Christendom, and in particular of Germany, against the Infidels, and that is why Germany instinctively gathered about him as soon as the Turkish threat appeared. One final significant fact was that the emperor was in Ferdinand's day the brother, then the uncle, and subsequently the cousin, of the king of Spain. This meant that the same family, if not the same monarch, reigned in Vienna and Madrid, and that the Austrian branch of the House of Habsburg could, more often than not, count on the support of the Spanish branch in time of peril.

From another point of view the House of Austria's position was to have serious consequences for Germany's future destiny. The interests of the House of Austria and those of Germany were not always the same. As head of the House of Austria the emperor had, of necessity, two policies: the one imperial, that is German, the other purely Austrian. It would sometimes happen that his Austrian policy caused him to overlook the interests of Germany. Furthermore, the emperor's German and Austrian policies were complicated at times by a dynastic, one might say purely Habsburgian, policy. As the great crisis which is the subject of this study begins and then develops we shall see how it was aggravated by the links between Vienna and Madrid, and by the influence of Spanish policy on imperial policy. We shall also see how the Empire's neighbours were obliged to intervene so that the crisis became European in character.

So far I have dealt with the political state of Germany at the beginning of the seventeenth century in isolation, but in the developing crisis the religious situation played a major role. Politics and religion were inseparable and should be studied together, if only the human mind were capable of understanding complex realities by any method other than analysis.

Early seventeenth-century Germany was the country where the Reformation, in this case that of the Lutheran churches, had organised itself more swiftly than elsewhere; it survived there in its original form, still closely bound to the political framework. Notice, moreover, that I say Churches and not Church: there was only one Lutheran confession, the 'Confession of Augsburg', but there were as many Lutheran churches as there were principalities and free cities that had adopted the Confession of Augsburg. It is not part of my task to give the reasons, both political and doctrinal, for this, but to state the consequences. A Lutheran Church was a state church, organised within the state by the prince (or within a free city by the mayor). It recognised the authority of the prince not only in temporal matters but also in matters of discipline and worship. In the eyes of his church the prince was the 'external bishop', exercising throughout his territory the 'episcopal authority' (jus episcopale). It was hardly surprising that the prince who had founded the church and who governed it should have imposed his own particular faith on his subjects. It was after all the Lutherans who invented the famous phrase, 'cuius regio, eius religio'; the ruler of a state determines its religious faith. Moreover, these Lutheran churches, exclusive communities each subject to a strict local authority, had little in common but a dogma and a ceremonial which had remained unchanged from the beginning as rigidly orthodox as that of the Roman Catholic Church. By the same token the Lutherans quickly lost their universal appeal and their proselytising spirit. The Confession of Augsburg was adopted quickly throughout Germany and, almost simultaneously, in the neighbouring Scandinavian kingdoms, but immediately afterwards its propagation ceased, and from the middle of the sixteenth century its power to expand seemed to be exhausted. Moreover, it was at about this time that a second Protestant faith began to infiltrate several regions of the Holy Roman Empire, controlled from Geneva, another powerful source of new ideas. This was Calvinism, or, as contemporaries called it, the reformed Church. It was in this form that Protestantism spread throughout a large part of Germany in the sixteenth century, though not everywhere. Indeed it is difficult to show precisely how Catholics and Protestants shared the Empire at the beginning of the seventeenth century, nor should we forget that the Counter-Reformation had not yet achieved its ultimate successes. The positions were not yet fixed.

We may at least say that Catholicism dominated the south and west, Protestantism the north. However, in the territories of the House of Habsburg, the emperor, king of Bohemia, was soon to be forced (in 1609) to recognise the Protestant faith in Bohemia and Moravia and there were still large numbers of Protestants in Austria. The Habsburg dynasty, however, remained Catholic, and southern Germany, Bavaria and Lorraine were Catholic too. In the Rhineland, the so-called 'Priests' Alley', and in Westphalia, the Catholic lands of the three archbishop-electors and of numerous bishops and abbots marched side by side, and the duke of Cleves was also a Catholic prince. But the whole of North Germany, east of Westphalia, was Protestant, and the

free cities of the Empire (except for Cologne, Aachen and part of
Augsburg), had gone over to Protestantism. The two faiths more or
less balanced each other, and the victory of the Roman Church over the
Reformation was still not certain.

It is also important to explain how the two religions operated, for
hteir freedom of action was strictly controlled. In the middle of the
sixteenth century the Empire had been given a religious statute, the
'religious peace' of 1555, commonly known as the Peace of Augsburg,
and the difficulties of implementing this were so closely bound up with
the religious causes of the Thirty Years War that we must examine it
closely.

Its essential provisions are easy to define. It was drawn up and
signed after a long struggle between Emperor Charles V and the
German Protestant princes which had been as much a political as a
religious conflict. At first the emperor had had the advantage, but
subsequently both sides became more equally matched, and Charles V's
inability to impose his will was certainly one of the factors which
caused him to lose heart and abdicate. Before surrendering all his
crowns, he left the government of the Empire to his brother Ferdinand,
who had been elected King of the Romans, and authorised him to
arrange a peace. A Diet was summoned at Augsburg and from its
discussions emerged a peace which the King of the Romans ratified.
This—the Peace of Augsburg—was thus both a treaty made between
the Catholic and Protestant princes of the Empire and an imperial law
to which all were subject.

The essential provisions of the peace reflected its character as an
imperial law, drawn up by a diet in which all the princes and states of
the Empire, and only they, were represented. As there were only
Catholic and Lutheran princes to be found in the Empire at that time,
the only confessions to be recognised were those of Rome and of
Augsburg. All others were excluded, and in particular the Calvinist
confession since no Calvinist prince had taken part in the discussions.
Thus the right, granted to the princes, to reform the Church within
their own states meant only that they might substitute the confession of
Augsburg for that of Rome. It goes without saying that this applied
only to princes. The people, who were not represented at the Diet, had
no such freedom of choice. The principle of cuius regio, eius religio,
was quite naturally accepted, and subjects either had to accept their
prince's faith or go into exile, which almost always involved the
abandonment and loss of their possessions. An important article of the

peace, known as the 'Ecclesiastical Reservation', laid down that in future, when an ecclesiastical prince, a bishop or an abbot, became Lutheran, he would have to give up the administration of his diocese or abbacy. Until this time this had not been so. On the contrary, a bishop or an abbot who became Protestant converted his diocese or abbacy into a lay principality, hereditary within his own house. This was known as secularising the estate and the attractions of secularisation had certainly eased the propagation of Lutheranism. The Peace of Augsburg recognised the secularisations which had taken place prior to 1552, the date of the truce which led to the peace negotiations, but it forbade any new secularisation. Finally the Peace of Augsburg, which was an imperial law, was guaranteed by the institutions of the Empire. They were to extend their protection equally to Catholics and Protestants. And this not only to the princes who were already Lutherans when the Peace was signed and to the Lutheran churches which were already organised, but also to the princes who might declare themselves Lutherans in the future and any Lutheran churches which might be organised in accordance with the terms of the Peace of Augsburg.

Summed up like this, the clauses of the Peace of Augsburg seem simple and clear. But on closer examination, when faced with the material situations in which they were intended to apply, a number of complications, ambiguities and uncertainties come to light.

The Peace of Augsburg was a peace born of weariness, contracted between two parties who had lost hope of victory. It was, like every religious peace, a compromise between two irreconcilable doctrinal extremes. Charles V had only accepted the idea unwillingly and, rather than sign himself, he had transferred his powers to his brother, the King of the Romans. But although the latter was more flexible, at heart he shared his brother's thoughts. He felt that an emperor who undertook to give equal protection to Catholics and Protestants thereby renounced the concept of the close bond between Church and Empire. For the Church had not recognised the peace; if it contented itself with not condemning it dogmatically, and the Pope had bowed, 'although sorrowfully', to the judgement of a commission of Jesuit Fathers whom he had consulted. He had allowed the Catholics to suspend the struggle 'until that day should come when Christ would give them sufficient strength' to triumph. In the eyes of the Church, the peace was only a truce. As for the Protestant princes and states, they too accepted it only as a provisional compromise because they did not think that it was possible to obtain better terms. Neither party was satisfied. And Ferdinand, like Charles V who was still emperor when the peace was signed, refused to include certain of his own territories in it. Many of its articles did not apply to the Burgundian territories, nor was the kingdom of Bohemia allowed to benefit from it.

This attitude of Catholics and Protestants alike, both of whom considered the peace to be a last resort, explains why they should both have introduced ambiguities and reservations into certain of its clauses, thus making its full implementation more or less impossible. We can accept what Maurice Ritter, a German historian who has made a detailed study of the Peace of Augsburg, said of it. In the peace, he wrote, there are two parts: 'a coherent part over which the states of the two confessions were in full agreement, and another part made up of exceptions to the main provisions, whose meaning and value the Protestants and Catholics interpreted in different and totally irreconcilable ways'.

We need not concern ourselves with the details of these exceptions. We should, however, dwell upon the clause which was to be the greatest source of dispute, the 'Ecclesiastical Reservation', and show how Catholics and Protestants interpreted it. At the beginning of the discussions, the Catholics demanded that all secularisations dating from before 1552 should be annulled, and that all secularised lands should be given back to the Church. This would have effectively destroyed the Reformation and the reaction of the Protestant princes was so strong that a breakdown in the peace negotiations seemed imminent. The Catholics then resigned themselves to accepting the earlier secularisations, but would not give ground over the prohibition of any further secularisation, while the Protestants continued to oppose this vigorously. Was the peace treaty, which in spite of everything both parties really wanted, to founder on a single clause, however important that clause might be? The Diet averted this disaster by avoiding the issue in a way which Ferdinand seems to have proposed, and to which the Protestants consented. The Diet did not write the Ecclesiastical Reservation into the text of the peace. The King of the Romans added it on his own authority. The Catholics considered it to be equally binding, but the Lutheran princes, when they signed the peace, added a protest against the Reservation after their signatures. With Ferdinand's consent they declared that the clause had not been officially approved and that in their eyes it could have no legal value. In the future they were to act in accordance with this declaration.

Among the other disputed clauses or those incapable of application,

I shall mention only one which related to the free cities. According to a very general article they were to enjoy the same rights as the princes, but another more specific article stated that if there were Catholics and Protestants in a town, the condition and prerogatives of the two faiths should be maintained unchanged, even in respect of their property. During the latter years of the war, however, the emperor had forced the mayors of the free cities to surrender all Church property to the Catholics, even when they formed only a tiny minority of the population. In the towns, where the Protestants were far more numerous, this article of the peace was considered a gross injustice, and was a frequent cause of disagreement and conflict.

Under these conditions, the Peace of Augsburg, far from ending the religious and political troubles caused by the Reformation within the Empire, marked the beginning of a long period of sporadic armed conflicts leading to the violent crisis which we now call the Thirty Years War. Two facts above all must be borne in mind, for they were to make the crisis inevitable.

The first was a direct consequence of the way in which the peace had been drawn up. The Diet which negotiated it remained its guarantor. It was the court of appeal whenever the Catholics and Protestants were in dispute—and we know that this happened frequently—but here, as elsewhere, the Diet showed its weakness. It soon became only too clear that the imperial institutions could not guarantee the princes, and in particular the Protestant princes, the protection which they had every right to expect. In this way the Empire began to suffer a kind of disintegration which was soon quickened by the outbreak of war. It was during this troubled period following the Peace of Augsburg that there arose the question of the jus singulorum—the idea that a member of the Diet who had not voted on a common resolution was not therefore bound by it—and, for the first time, we see a diet 'broken', that is to say, unable to arrive at a decision. The moment soon came when the German princes stopped believing in the efficacy of imperial institutions and when the recourse to force seemed to many of them to be the only means of saving Germany from chaos.

The second fact was the ever-increasing growth of Calvinism, which continued to spread in the Rhineland, in southern Germany, in Upper and Lower Austria and in Hungary. On the very day after the peace, one elector, the elector Palatine Frederick III, openly declared himself to be a Calvinist. Others followed suit, although it is true that they were only minor princes, but in 1613 a second elector, the elector of Brandenburg, also abandoned Lutheranism. Now the Calvinists had not been included in the peace and the new confession which, for the most part spread to the principalities whose prince was a Catholic, could only do so in violation of the principle 'cuius regio, eius religio'. The members of the Calvinist Church thus formed within the Empire an extraneous body outside the protection of the imperial laws. Early on the Catholics had become worried by this. In 1566, when the elector Palatine was still the only Calvinist prince of any standing, a Papal legate called on the Diet to issue a ban on Calvinism. But the Lutheran princes, while censuring Frederick III's conversion, refused to go that far, and the progress of Calvinism thus remained possible if a little insecure. Consequently, the Calvinist princes took steps to defend themselves, either by uniting or by seeking alliances with foreign princes. They were to be the first to take up arms against the emperor.

Furthermore, they were not the only ones to act outside the limits of the peace. Many Catholics did the same thing. They were led by the great religious orders, the Capuchins or the Jesuits, and were less concerned with respecting the clauses of the peace than with recovering the souls who had been led aside from the paths of the Roman Church by the Reformation. Their campaign, the Counter-Reformation, had been planned by Loyola as early as 1554, before the Diet of Augsburg, and put into action immediately afterwards. The Capuchins preached everywhere. The Jesuits founded colleges everywhere and from these there emerged the new defenders of the faith. The first of these were founded in Prague and in Ingolstadt in Bavaria in 1556, and it was here that Maximilian of Bavaria and Ferdinand of Styria were educated. Catholicism was on the offensive once more. Moreover, it was at about the same period—in 1563—that the Council of Trent finally confirmed its dogma and condemned all Protestant innovations. Shortly afterwards, the Jesuit Bellarmine wrote his commentaries on the decrees of the Council in a series of resounding works which were widely disseminated in Germany and provided inspiration for practically the whole German episcopate.

So it is not surprising that, in a Germany which was so torn by princely ambitions and religious passions, a local revolt, but one which seemed to imperil the very existence of the House of Austria, should have dragged first the whole of Germany and then the Holy Roman Empire's neighbours into one of the most terrible wars of modern times.

CHAPTER II

THE REVOLT OF BOHEMIA

The Bohemian Revolt began the Thirty Years War. It broke out quite unexpectedly on 23rd May 1618, with the famous Prague Defenestration, but to understand its causes and development, we must first of all bear in mind what Bohemia really was in those days.

It formed part of a group of half-Slav, half-German territories known as the 'Crown Lands of Bohemia', and the crown was worn by the emperor, as head of the House of Habsburg. Apart from Bohemia, after which it was named, the group consisted of Moravia, Silesia and Upper and Lower Lusatia. The Slavs formed by far the larger part of the population in Bohemia and Moravia, although there were Germans too, especially in Bohemia on the northern edge of the country and in the towns. By contrast, Silesia and the Lusatias were peopled almost exclusively by Germans. But questions of nationality did not yet present themselves. Far more important were the political and religious problems.

There was no close union between the 'Crown Lands of Bohemia'. Moravia, Silesia and the Lusatias were more like dependencies of Bohemia, and they were called the Incorporated Provinces. Nevertheless they enjoyed complete autonomy. Each province had its diet but there was no overall diet. Even the 'Estates', the social classes whose representatives formed the diets, differed slightly from one country to another. In Bohemia there were three 'Estates', the nobility, the knights and the towns; in Moravia there was one more, the clergy.

It was in his capacity as king of Bohemia that the head of the House of Habsburg governed the whole group, and it was Bohemia, above all, that he considered to be the essential part of the kingdom. After the accession of Rudolph II, in 1576, the king-emperor made Prague his residence. He held his court and councils there, and it was there that he received foreign ambassadors. Thus Prague became something of a capital city for all the territories of the house of Habsburg, as well as being the national capital of Bohemia.

None the less, the kingdom of Bohemia had its own government, headed by a Grand Chancellor of the kingdom who was appointed for life. He acted in the name of the king, but he had to take into account the privileges of the Estates and the traditional powers of the Diet, so he swore allegiance to the king and the Estates at the same time. The Bohemian Diet met only by royal command. It approved constitutional laws submitted to it by the crown, voted taxes and *nominated* the king when the throne was vacant. As we shall see the value and meaning of this *nomination* were never generally agreed upon. Outside the Diet the internal administration of the country was managed by ancient collegial bodies and important officers, such as the Grand Bargrave, the Grand Judge, the Bargrave of Kárlův-Týn, etc. The majority of the old feudal institutions had survived, paralysing the exercise of royal power, but the situation was beginning to change. From the beginning of the seventeenth century, the Grand Chancellery was occupied by a first class administrator, Lobkowitz, whose place in history has been thoroughly studied by a Czech historian Stloukal. Lobkowitz, who belonged to one of the oldest Bohemian families, was a Catholic and completely devoted to the house of Habsburg. He set about the task of simplifying and centralising the administration of Bohemia in order to make the monarchy absolute. Naturally he encountered stiff resistance, especially from the nobility. Though they were few in number they were great landowners, possessing large estates and playing a leading part in the diets. Some of them like William von Lobkowitz, a relative of the Chancellor, Wenceslas von Ruppa, Matthias von Thurn, and Václav Budovec, were, a little later, to be the organisers and leaders of the rebellion. On the eve of the Defenestration, it would seem that considerable progress had been made towards the centralisation of the administration. We can certainly regard it as one of the causes of the discontent which made possible the early successes of the rebels. The knights and townsmen too shared the nobles' dislike of Lobkowitz' policy of centralisation; moreover, despite their attachment to the crown, they were used to following the lead of the great nobles whose privileges and ambitions were incompatible with the new powers sought by the king.

This political unrest was inflamed by religious passions which perhaps were the most important element in the origins of the rebellion, although at the time the personal ambitions of a few lords seemed to be the chief cause. The great Czech historian Pekař thought so: 'The Czechs', he wrote, 'lived only by their religious fears and prejudices;

they rarely displayed the discernment and competence over constitutional matters which was customary among the Hungarians.'

At the beginning of the seventeenth century, the religious situation
was particularly confused. Absence of any statistics makes it impossible
to state the position precisely, but it seems that in the Czech countries
as a whole—Bohemia and Moravia—there were fewer Catholics than
Protestants. In Bohemia especially the Catholics were only a minority,
but in terms of power, they easily had the upper hand. On their side
they had the king, all the royal family, the Grand Chancellor, most of
the holders of high office—in fact the whole ruling class of the kingdom.
Furthermore this tightly-knit, active Catholic minority was hand in
glove with the religious orders behind the Counter-Reformation, the
Capuchins, who preached the Roman faith among the people, and the
Jesuits who chiefly influenced the nobles. Because of this dual activity
by the government and the church, the number of converts increased
rapidly and the Catholic minority was certainly advancing. It is easy to
understand the Protestants' anxiety.

Resistance was difficult because they were divided. Bohemia was
one of the regions of Europe where notions of religious reform
had made their earliest appearance. As long ago as the early years of the
fifteenth century Jan Hus had been condemned by Rome, but his
followers had not surrendered. During the long religious war which
followed his execution they managed to establish a dissident Church,
the Hussite Church, which adopted the name of Utraquist because the
congregation communicated like the priests with both bread and wine,
sub utraque specie. When peace was made, the Holy See authorised
this type of communion in Bohemia, but from that time onwards the
new Church, satisfied by the pope's concession, could scarcely be
distinguished from the Catholic Church. It had no bishops and
Utraquist priests had to be ordained by a Catholic bishop. At the
beginning of the seventeenth century the Hussite confession had no
more than a handful of adherents who were at odds amongst themselves, some inclining more and more towards Catholicism, others
towards the Lutheran or reformed confessions. The Utraquist Church
was no more than a relic and its vitality was gradually dying away.

Another confession emerged a little later from the Hussite revolution, and this had lost none of its vitality at the beginning of the seventeenth century. Its followers were known to each other as the Brethren
and the church took its name from them: the Fraternity of the Brethren.
The Brethren had been reconciled with the Confession of Augsburg

for a short time, but had then abandoned it when rigorous Lutheran orthodoxy was substituted for Melanchthon's conciliatory formulae. Afterwards the Brethren had found themselves closer to the Calvinists, but they retained their independence. It was a precarious type of independence, however, because they had never been recognised by the king. For the time being they were tolerated, but this state of affairs could come to an end at any time.

Finally there were in Bohemia and Moravia, and even more in Silesia and Lusatia, a great number of both Lutherans and Calvinists. This meant that there were four non-Catholic faiths. And the king-emperor, who had excluded the territories of the Bohemian crown from the Peace of Augsburg, remained free to settle the religious problem as he thought best.

Less than ten years before the revolt, it was settled by Rudolph II who, while retaining his imperial powers, had just transferred the greater part of his domains to his brother Matthias, and remained simply as king of Bohemia. It was in fact in 1609 that Rudolph granted a religious statute to his Bohemian subjects, in the form of a solemn act which we usually term the Letter of Majesty. The Letter of Majesty established freedom of conscience in Bohemia (that is Bohemia proper), and a fairly wide freedom of worship, but this was subject to provisions which it is important to specify. The most significant was that there should be only one Czech Protestant Church. The result of this was that the Protestant churches had to come to an agreement. In fact only the Lutherans and the Brethren joined forces. They drew up a common credo which they both accepted. This was the new Czech Confession and its most important article recognised communion in both kinds. This union omitted the Utraquists who were growing closer and closer to the Catholics. Moreover it did not go as far as to amalgamate the churches, for the Brethren maintained a certain degree of autonomy. The Brethren formed, as certain contemporary documents put it, a little church within the large one, ecclesiola in ecclesia. In addition, the king allowed the followers of the Czech Confession to meet in a diet called 'the diet in both kinds', while the Catholics formed another called 'the diet in one kind'. Finally the two diets signed an agreement together which was ratified by the principal officers of the crown. In it the two sides mutually guaranteed each other's churches, their total freedom of worship, their possessions, and their revenues. It was specified that if the Protestants did not yet have a place of worship in the royal towns or the Crown estates they had the right to build one.

It should be added that a little later, the king granted a more or less identical religious statute to Moravia.[1]

A guarantee of political order was added to the Letter of Majesty. The king allowed the Protestants to elect from among their ranks a certain number of 'Protectors' whose task it was to settle any disputes that might arise within their church and to negotiate, when the need arose, with the Catholic diet. Even the conciliation procedure was precisely laid down. In the case of a disagreement which the Protectors were unable to settle, they could convene a limited diet 'sub utraque', and, on its authority, appeal to the king. The king would then submit the dispute to a sort of arbitration tribunal composed half of Protestants and half of Catholics. But the arbitration procedure was only effective if both parties were resolved beforehand to accept the decision. In 1618, nobody thought of turning to it. The time for compromise was long past.

Such was, from 1609, the religious constitution of Bohemia and Moravia. It rested on the Czech Confession, the Letter of Majesty and the agreement drawn up between the Protestants and Catholics. But what were the consequences of the new constitution? Opinions differ on this point, even among the Czech historians. However, the majority considers that the system laid down by Rudolph II was more liberal than the one which the rest of the Empire owed to the Peace of Augsburg, or even than the Edict of Nantes in France. 'On the basis of the Czech Confession', wrote one of them, Mr. Hrejsa, 'the religious freedom which had been so earnestly desired up to that time, was granted to all its followers together with equal rights with the Catholic minority whose possession of privileges and exclusive right to freedom had until recently been maintained by the sovereign power.'[2] But doubts may be cast upon the stability of the new system. It is difficult to forget that the union of the Protestants ordered by Rudolph II had been difficult to achieve. Their only true area of agreement was in their common hatred of the Catholics. As for the latter, the Letter had made them indignant; they only accepted it when it was imposed upon them. Some of the chief officers of the crown—and they were not by any means the least powerful—in particular Lobkowitz, had taken no

---

[1] On the Letter of Majesty, see Kamil Krofta: *Majestat Rudolfa II*, in which the essential texts are published, but in Czech.

[2] In a book entitled *Ceská Konfesse*, Mr. Hrejsa has made a detailed study of the Czech Confession and he gives the text in an appendix. My translation follows V. Tapié: *La Politique étrangère de la France et le début de la Guerre de Trente Ans*, p. 120.

part in the negotiations and refused to sign the royal act. The Society of Jesus condemned it. The result was that it did not put an end to Catholic propaganda. In Bohemia there was not even a temporary cooling of religious passions of the sort that Henry IV had managed to impose on the two Churches in France during his lifetime.

Three years after the Letter of Majesty had been granted, an event occurred which affected not only Bohemia but the territories of the House of Austria and the whole Empire. In 1612, Rudolph died. In Bohemia, and soon throughout the whole Empire, his successor was his younger brother, Matthias. But Matthias's accession left the future unsettled: he was old and sick and had no children. The problem of the succession which had arisen long before under Rudolph II had only been solved provisionally, and Matthias's counsellors urged him to settle it while he was still alive. He refused because he had no wish to think about his own death and because he doubtless felt too weak to overcome all the difficulties which he foresaw. The settlement of the succession was indeed fraught with danger for Bohemia, for the Empire and even for the future of the House of Austria. The latter, as we have seen, was divided into three branches. Of these the least important ruled only in the Tyrol and seemed destined to come to a speedy end, but the Styrian branch possessed a compact group of states between Austria proper and the Adriatic sea, and was ruled by Ferdinand, an energetic sovereign and a cousin of Matthias. Without any doubt it was in the interests of the House that Ferdinand should be appointed as Matthias's successor and elected King of the Romans. This was also in the interests of Catholicism, for at the College of Ingolstadt Ferdinand had been a willing pupil of the Jesuits, and he had demonstrated his obedience to the Church by forcing the Protestants in his lands to accept conversion or go into exile. But two of Matthias's brothers, the archdukes Maximilian and Albert, and even the king of Spain, Philip III, could urge their claims against Ferdinand's, and it seemed difficult to ignore them. For five years Matthias wavered. In 1617 he finally made up his mind, and immediately there took place the series of events which led to the Bohemian Revolt.

Matthias's brothers were persuaded to renounce their claims more easily than he had expected. Neither Maximilian, who was sick and old before his time, nor Albert, who governed the Spanish Netherlands with his wife, the Infanta Isabella, wanted to succeed him. There only remained the king of Spain's claim. In the end he came to an agreement, not with Matthias, but directly and in secret with Ferdinand through

Oñate, the Spanish ambassador in Prague. The settlement was concluded at Graz, in Styria, where Ferdinand had his residence. Philip III agreed to stand aside on condition that when Ferdinand had received his inheritance he should cede the Tyrol and Austria's possessions in Alsace. More than anything else the king of Spain wanted to safeguard the movement of his troops between the Duchy of Milan and the Netherlands. Possession of the Tyrol would have given him access to the Brenner Pass, and Alsace would have served as a kind of bridge between the Spanish bases in Luxemburg and Franche-Comté. In spite of Ferdinand's promise, Alsace did not become Spanish, but the secret agreement of Graz was none the less the origin of a renewed alliance between Vienna and Madrid, and it alone made it possible to unite all the Austrian territories beneath Ferdinand's sceptre. Matthias accepted Ferdinand as his successor. He also undertook to have him recognized in advance by the Bohemian Estates as king of Bohemia, for he realised that the settlement of his succession in Bohemia was the necessary condition for the future election of Ferdinand to the Empire and for the unification of the states of the House of Austria.

But here the difficulties appeared even greater. We have seen that the Diet of Prague had the right to nominate the new king, but this right was vaguely worded and the precedents could be interpreted in different ways. For Matthias's ministers, the diet's nomination was only a solemn ratification of the candidate whose rights were hereditary. After all Ferdinand I, his son Maximilian II, Maximilian's son Rudolph II and finally Rudolph's younger brother Matthias had all worn the crown in succession. The Bohemians, however, were of another opinion, maintaining that the crown of Boehmia had always been elective. But it was not merely a legal question and both parties were well aware of this. Ferdinand, whom the Catholics looked to for the complete victory of their faith, was for that very reason detested and feared by the Protestants. He had grown up under the influence of his masters at Ingolstadt, and his mother, Maria of Bavaria, had trained him from an early age to follow all the Church's precepts without question. When, at the age of seventeen, he had succeeded his father in Styria, he lived more like a monk than a sovereign. The greater part of his days was devoted to prayer, visits to churches or monasteries, and devout books. The only diversions he allowed himself were hunting and music. His recklessness in undertaking to convert back to Catholicism a country in which there was no longer more than a handful of Catholics is staggering. Abroad this was interpreted as a sign of fearless courage, but his action is easily explained by the complete conviction that God would not abandon him. In fact, Ferdinand's education had only taught him obedience. He was incapable of any initiative. Although he attended all the meetings of his Council, he always followed the majority opinion. As soon as he had to take a decision which seemed to him to involve his conscience (and this was the case with all serious decisions) he immediately consulted his confessor, or often a sort of college of theologians which he would seem to have made up almost exclusively of Jesuits. His simple way of life, his natural grace and good humour (for he was a cheerful person) doubtless won over those who came into contact with him. None the less the Protestants had everything to fear from such a prince.

However, the Bohemians consented to his nomination as king of Bohemia, even in the lifetime of Matthias. This act, which had only been made possible through the skill and determination of the Chancellor, was unexpected and was to have serious consequences. In fact the whole affair had been arranged by Lobkowitz alone. Matthias was still wvaering and his minister, Bishop Klesl, who had rendered his master real services in earlier years but who had been overtaken by events and no longer sought to remain in power, avoided all compromising decisions. Lobkowitz knew how to confound Ferdinand's opponents by swift action, arousing a temporary show of loyalty among the Bohemian nobles and profiting from their divisions. The Diet of Bohemia was unexpectedly summoned for 5th June, 1617, after the emperor had had an illness which gave rise to fears that his death would follow shortly. Matthias attended it, accompanied by the archdukes Maximilian and Ferdinand. On the morning of the 5th Lobkowitz received all the grand dignitaries at the Chancellery. He did his best to persuade them that Ferdinand's nomination was assured and that it would be better for them not to annoy the future king by futile opposition. They were already unsettled when they left him. Then the session opened with a degree of pomp and ceremony which could not fail to intimidate the waverers. It was done in the presence of the emperor to whom the Bohemians were grateful for residing in Prague and for embellishing the Hradčany hill with luxurious buildings, which we still admire today. Matthias read a declaration in which he expressed his desire to ensure his succession in Bohemia before he died. He announced that his brothers had renounced their claims and he asked his loyal subjects to recognise his cousin Ferdinand as king. The session then rose and the Diet met once again on the following day,

6th June. A vote was taken. First the great magnates took the floor in turn: all of them, even Ruppa and Budweis voted for Ferdinand, with the exception of Count von Thurn who affirmed that it was the diet's prerogative to elect the king and not merely to ratify him. However, Lobkowitz's trump-card was to change the ancient custom by which a single delegate spoke for each division. He made everyone vote and speak. The majority of the nobles, who had not expected to speak at all, and who had been surprised by the attitude of the great magnates, did not know what to say, and one after another they approved Ferdinand's nomination. The representatives of the knights and the towns, used to following the nobles' lead, voted in the same way. Ferdinand received an almost unanimous vote and had himself crowned on 19th June. In the meantime, for once well advised by his college of theologians and in spite of inner qualms of conscience, he had solemnly confirmed all the country's privileges and consequently the Letter of Majesty which in his heart of hearts he condemned. Now Matthias could die.

And so, less than a year before the Defenestration, there was nothing to presage the Revolt of Bohemia. But in spite of the extraordinary ease with which it had been accomplished, Ferdinand's elevation to the throne could only increase the discontent. The nobles' leaders, who had given in to surprise and fear, certainly lost no time in recovering themselves and in reproaching themselves for their weakness. They were even more annoyed with Lobkowitz who had outwitted them, the more so because Lobkowitz exploited his victory. Before and after Ferdinand's coronation he took a series of measures which seemed to herald a new, bolder and more active policy. Until then, the three towns which together made up Prague, Staré Mesto (the old town), Nové Město (the new town) and Malá Strana (the little quarter), administered themselves: henceforth the royal magistrates there were given greater powers. The Count von Thurn, as Bargrave of Kárluv-Týn, enjoyed the most lucrative office in the kingdom. He was forced to give it up and to take in its place the far less profitable appointment of Chief Justice. A broad enquiry was set up, first of all in Prague, into the origins of the foundations upon which the churches' livings depended, and it was reasonably feared that many of them which had been founded before the Hussite Revolution might be returned to the Catholics under the pretext of respecting the donors' original wishes. Finally, all Protestant literature had to be submitted to the censorship of the royal Chancellery, before being published in Prague, whereas previously it had merely been authorised by the Protectors. The Protestants viewed these measures as just so many attacks on the status quo which the Letter of Majesty had guaranteed.

At about this time the Bohemians, and especially the inhabitants of Prague, were very distressed by an event of quite a different kind, and one which, a little later, had serious consequences. This was the departure of Matthias. The Emperor had summoned the Hungarian Diet which, in its turn, was to recognise Ferdinand as king of Hungary; and Lobkowitz foresaw even more difficulties at Pressburg than at Prague. He hoped very much that Matthias would be able to keep a close eye on the discussions and attend the Diet if his presence seemed necessary. Furthermore, it appears that an astrologer had predicted that some misfortune would overtake Matthias if he remained at Prague any longer. In the Emperor's eyes, this prediction probably carried more weight than the political circumstances. At any rate, at the end of December 1617, on Christmas Day, he left Prague and went by easy stages to Vienna. The Grand Chancellor Lobkowitz left with him. After him the counsellors and foreign ambassadors left. This was a loss of honour for Prague. It also brought isolation. After the departure of the foreign ambassadors, news of the outside world became rarer. The Bohemians were ill-informed about what was happening in the rest of the Habsburg monarchy, and foreign sovereigns were only very badly informed about what was happening in Bohemia. After the revolt, the Bohemian cause certainly suffered from this. The emperor and the new king had appointed as their representatives in Prague a council of ten 'regents', some of whom, unfortunately, had in 1609 shown themselves to be implacably opposed to the Letter of Majesty.

It was then that a long-standing quarrel between the Protestants and Catholics became embittered and provided the immediate cause of the rebellion. We have seen how, under the Letter of Majesty, the Protestants could build places of worship in royal towns and Crown lands where they had no church. But the definition of Crown lands still had to be agreed upon. Back in 1611, the inhabitants of the little town of Braunau had begun the construction of a Lutheran church, availing themselves of what they believed to be their right. Braunau was on Church land and was owned by an abbey. But when the Protectors had been consulted they had declared that the Church lands must be considered as forming part of the Crown's dominions, since the Church only held them in usufruct. They drew their chief evidence for this from the fact that the Emperor had frequently mortgaged church possessions or pledged them as securities. Naturally, the abbot who owned Braunau was not of this opinion: he forbade the building, which was nevertheless begun, then abandoned, then resumed. The dispute was still not settled by the beginning of the year 1618. Another almost similar dispute had arisen about another town, Klostergrab, or in Czech, Hroby. In December 1617 the Archbishop of Prague had ordered that a Lutheran church, which its inhabitants were having built, should be demolished. They sent several notables to the regents at Prague to defend their cause, but the regents, who had no authority to resolve the dispute but had to refer it to the king, made the mistake of arresting the deputation from the little town and imprisoning them in one of the towers of the Hradschin. This senseless piece of violence touched off the rebellion.

It forced the Protectors to use a procedure provided for in the Letter of Majesty—the summoning of an assembly composed of Protestant delegates representing the royal officials, the towns and the circles. This met in Prague on 5th May 1618.[1] It was poorly attended because many of the urban delegates and most of the officials who were personally attached to the Crown stayed away. It merely drew up a formal letter to the king-emperor and asked the regents to convey it to him. It then adjourned until the 21st May in order to allow the sovereign time to take account of all the facts and to ponder on his reply. It seems that the meeting of the assembly was in no way illegal; on the other hand it could be thought that the affairs of Braunau and Hroby did not come within its jurisdiction. This was naturally the opinion of the emperor and the chancellor, who were quick to seize the opportunity of contesting any action taken by the Protectors. This they did. The royal reply, which had probably been drawn up in Vienna on Lobkowitz's orders, stated that the Protectors had exceeded their powers, that the matter was outside the protestant assembly's jurisdiction and that it was forbidden to meet again. It even contained some thinly veiled threats against the agitators. The question of law was, in any case, unimportant. What struck the Protectors, when the reply to the letter was delivered to them, was the speed with which it had come. They became quite convinced that it was not authentic, that it had been drawn up not in Vienna, but in Prague itself and that the regents

[1] On the events which follow, and particularly the Defenestration, I have followed the account of Tapié, op. cit., which corrects or complements those of Ernest Denis and Gindely. I have also made use of contemporary Czech historians, especially Máchaček: *Defenestrace prazská*, and Pekař: *Bila Hora*. Slawata's *Memoirs* are still the essential source, although many of the details are disputed.

were therefore responsible for it. They did not for a single moment consider cancelling the meeting called for 21st May. On the contrary, they made great efforts to see that it should be better organised and urged the royal officials and urban delegates who had not answered their call in March, to turn out in force. Between March and May tempers began to rise.

From 21st May the situation took a more serious turn. In the morning the assembly, which was larger although there were still many abstentions, was summoned by the regents to the Castle to hear a new royal letter ordering its dissolution. The delegates, numbering about a hundred, went in procession up to the Hradschin. Everything passed off in due form and the delegates obtained a copy of the royal letter so that the assembly could study its terms. They promised to reply two days later, on 23rd May. During the 22nd May there was a heated discussion in the assembly about Matthias's letter and, what is more, unrest broke out in the three towns. The narrow twisting streets began to look as they usually did during riots, but as yet there was no violence. Some of the Protectors, however, met secretly at the house of one of their number, Smiřický, and it was there that the events of the following day were prepared. We do not know what was said there, nor exactly which of the Protectors were present, but Budweis, Ruppa and above all Matthias von Thurn were certainly there with Smiřický. No historian would deny that Matthias von Thurn played the leading part and that the decision was taken to bring the protestant Estates of Bohemia into the revolt and to make the breach irreparable by the judicial murder of the most hated regents—a murder which would gain the approbation of the Protestant masses. There can be little doubt that the names of Slavata and Martinitz, who had both protested the year before against the confirmation of the Letter of Majesty, were mentioned.

So the next day, the 23rd May, the procession formed up once more, crossed the old bridge, climbed the slopes leading to the Hradschin and delivered to the regents a letter containing the assembly's reply and their grievances. But this time the deputation was armed, (this had been authorised on the previous day), some were mounted, others were on foot, and a noisy crowd cheered them on. First they were received in the Castle Chancery, the Vladislav room, where the Protectors read their prepared reply to those present. Then the procession went to the upper floor where the regents were waiting in a smaller room, which it has been possible to identify. The doors remained open because not all the delegates could manage to get inside.

There were only four regents there: the grand Bargrave Adam von Šternberk, Diepolt von Lobkowitz, Martinitz and Slavata. Beside them there was a secretary whom the conspirators did not know, called Fabricius. We can gain a fairly accurate idea of what subsequently happened from Slavata's memoirs. The Protectors accused the regents of having written the so-called royal letter themselves, and called on them to admit this. There then followed a long confused argument which was frequently interrupted by the shouts of the delegates who were crowded at the back of the room and outside. The regents defended themselves as best they could, first by legal arguments which were shouted down, and then, when they felt that their lives were in danger, by entreaties, which were no more successful. Šternberk and Lobkowitz were very quickly exonerated and the accusations, which became increasingly violent, were directed at Slavata and Martinitz. The spokesman for the deputation was not Thurn, but another Protector, Rischany. In the end he asked the crowd if it considered the two accused to be guilty of high treason. The crowd shouted that they deserved death and that they should be thrown from the window. And so it was. In spite of their desperate resistance, first Martinitz and then Slavata were hurled out. Although no grievance had been laid against him, the little unknown secretary was sent out after them. As he fell, Martinitz shouted out 'Jesu Maria!' 'We'll see if his Mary can help him', said one of the conspirators. He leant out of the window, and then said in amazement, 'By God, she really has!' He had seen Martinitz at the bottom of the moat get up almost at once and make off. The secretary was safe and sound too. Only Slavata, who had hung onto the rough face of the wall was hurt. He fainted, covered with blood, in the moat. Polyxena von Lobkowitz, the Chancellor's wife, who had stayed in Prague and whose house was beside the moat, gave all three men shelter. It does not appear that the conspirators made any serious attempt to recapture them.

It cannot be denied that, in the legal sense of the word, the defenestration of 23rd May 1618 was a premeditated act. It was discussed and decided upon the previous day by the conspirators who met at Smiřický's house. The Protectors decided in advance on a crime which was to force Protestant Bohemia to seek the salvation of its faith through rebellion, and which would put an end, once and for all, to Chancellor Lobkowitz's Catholic-biased policy of centralisation. After all, the outrage submitted the accused to a sort of ordeal; no blood had been spilt, and in the eyes of those who had passed sentence, it had taken an almost traditional form, since another defenestration, at Prague itself, had marked the start of the Hussite Revolution. But how much more important were the religious grievances than the political grievances? To what extent were unease about the privileges of the nobility or even the personal interests of the Count von Thurn determining factors in the decision taken on 22nd May? We simply do not know. At least it is certain that the rising of the Protestants of Bohemia was not spontaneous. At first it appeared to be the insurrection of a few nobles in league with the Count von Thurn. It was rather like the insurrections of the Prince de Condé in France at about the same period.

If it had not been the result of an impulsive act dictated by circumstances it is difficult to believe that Thurn and those who supported him, for example Budweis or Ruppa, would not have made more preparations for the conflict which they had deliberately provoked. In fact they had done nothing, arranged nothing. The day after the rebellion they did not even seem to have fully realised its consequences. They loftily claimed to remain the king-emperor's 'faithful and devoted subjects'. At least they still had a sort of loyalty towards the old Matthias, and they accused the king's regents, not the king himself. This in fact was the usual attitude of rebels at that time when nobody disputed the divine origin of royal power, but the rebels of Bohemia seem to have been sincere about it. Indeed, their immediate action bore all the marks of improvisation. Thurn took command of the troops. A directory of thirty members, including William von Ruppa, Václav Budweis and Albert Smiřický was set up, under the authority of Matthias, whom they still considered to be king, to replace the guilty regents who were relieved of their offices. At the same time an 'Apologia' was quickly drafted in which the conspirators denied having committed any crime; this appeared in Czech and German and a little later in Latin. Little more was done until the first imperial letters arrived in Prague.

Thus the violence of 23rd May 1618 was followed by a period of waiting which lasted from the end of May to the end of August. During this time nobody could foresee whether some compromise would be reached between the conspirators and the imperial court or whether the rebellion would spread. At Vienna, Klesl, Matthias's Secretary, thought that a compromise was possible. He avoided doing or saying anything which might exacerbate feelings, and the emperor, who was becoming increasingly incapable of taking any personal decisions, left the matter in his hands. Ferdinand, on the other hand, convinced that only vigorous action could avert the danger, became indignant and accused Klesl of treason. But he had promised not to take any action in Bohemia as long as the reigning king, Matthias, was alive. Besides, he was detained at Pressburg where the Hungarian diet, which was to proclaim him king of Hungary, was in session. Further, to make any order effective, he would have needed troops who were prepared for a campaign. There were none. In August, with great difficulty, about six thousand men were assembled under the command of Dampierre, a Frenchman who had been in Ferdinand's service for some years. In the rebel camp there was the same lack of decision, the same helplessness. They did not have any troops either. Thurn only commanded a few thousand men. No sooner had the directory been created than it was faced with the almost impossible task of procuring money and levying troops. From the earliest days it took only one serious resolution which might make a reconciliation more difficult. It declared that the Jesuits were banished from the realm in perpetuity. Those who lived in Prague had to leave the town and cross the frontier. At all events, they left freely, amidst tokens of respect from all the Catholics and without any demonstrations of hostility.

At that time the conspirators were not even certain of the active support of the knights and the towns; they did not even know if Moravia would follow them in revolt. Certainly the Protestants, Lutherans and Brethren, were in the majority in Moravia, as in Bohemia, although it is thought that the Catholics were more numerous in the former. But there were powerful Catholic lords there, such as the bishop of Olmütz or the prince of Liechtenstein. Above all the decision of the Estates of Moravia might depend on one man, who enjoyed exceptional influence in the country because he was universally respected. This was Karl von Žierotin, an engaging character whose full story has yet to be written. He was one of the most famous representatives of the Bohemian Brethren. He was very rich and liked to live in his beautiful estates at Rosice, but he led a very simple life there, completely devoted to study and to the correspondence which he kept up with most of the important Protestants of Europe. In his youth he had travelled in France and Italy and, as a result, he had acquired the reputation of being a humanist. He liked to speak and write Italian. In 1618, although he was only fifty-four, he seemed anxious to keep in the background after a very active life, but he could not remain aloof from the events in Prague. Although he sympathised with the grievances of his fellow Protestants, he believed that their revolt, started on an impulse and totally unprepared, was an insane act which could only

destroy the established liberties and Churches of Bohemia. He thought
that it was his duty to prevent a complete break between the imperial
court and the rebels at any price. He intervened, going first to Vienna
and then to Prague. He was well received, at least in Vienna, but
he only came away with illusory promises, and the only effect of
his intervention was to delay the Moravian Estates' decision to a
point when the success of the revolt was already seriously compromised.

It was compromised when Ferdinand of Styria decided to act as
king of Bohemia, even though Matthias was still alive. In July, after
his return from Pressburg, where he had been proclaimed king of
Hungary, Ferdinand had no qualms about ordering an act of violence,
which the old emperor did not dare to repudiate. He had Klesl arrested
and taken in custody to a castle in the Tyrol. So Ferdinand took
Matthias's place just as the latter had once taken the place of Rudolph.
This coincided with the outbreak of hostilities in Bohemia. Ferdinand
had summoned troops from Hungary and from Friuli where a local
war between the duke of Styria and the Republic of Venice had just
finished, and his cousin, Archduke Albert, sent him a good Belgian
captain called Bucquoy to command them. The little imperial army
reached Bohemia through Moravia where it was allowed free passage.
The government of Prague, meanwhile, had summoned a German
mercenary captain, the Count von Mansfeld, who was then in the
service of the duke of Savoy. Mansfeld, who was recruiting in Germany,
entered Bohemia from the north west and seized the important town
of Pilsen which had remained loyal to the king. However, the opposing
armies were too small for there to be any hope of a military solution.
As was usual in those days, the armies spent more time plundering
than fighting. After a few months, a whole area of Bohemia was
devastated, but the result of this was a state of poverty and weariness
which might favour an agreement. What made it impossible was the
death of Matthias on 20th March 1619.

This posed two formidable questions which were closely bound up
with one another and which were resolved almost simultaneously.
There was the question of whether Ferdinand would remain king of
Bohemia, or be deposed, and the question of the imperial election.
Ferdinand had been crowned king of Bohemia back in 1617 so he
succeeded Matthias without further recourse to the Bohemian Estates;
he merely notified Prague by letter of the Emperor's death. But he
did not withdraw his troops, so he clearly considered that his pre-

decessor's disappearance had not put an end to hostilities. The directors, therefore, sent back to him unopened the letter in which he informed them of his accession. However, neither side burnt all its bridges. When the directors sent back the royal letter, they gave as their reason an error in the wording of the address; they did not question Ferdinand's rights. Ferdinand renewed the promise, which he had already made in 1617, to respect all the privileges of the territories of the Bohemian kingdom. But from then on, nobody in Prague or Vienna could have any illusions that it was still possible to end the conflict. The directors were well aware that Bohemia's freedoms and the future of Protestant-ism were at stake. Ferdinand was convinced that, if he did not crush the rebellion, the loss of Bohemia would mark the decline of the house of Habsburg and the triumph of the protestant faiths in Germany. Already the consequences of that fatal day, 23rd May 1618, were affecting not only the king of Bohemia and his subjects, but the whole Empire, even the whole of Europe and the whole of Christendom.

This is obvious from the attitude of the princes and states of the Empire as well as from that of the foreign sovereigns. At about the time that Matthias had taken his brother's place, there had been an attempt to organise parties in the Empire. Both Protestants and Catholics, feeling that they could no longer rely on the federal institu-tions to guarantee their security, had tried to do so for themselves, by forming leagues. After the 'broken' Diet in 1607, the Protestant princes, or at least some of them, had been the first to do this: on 5th May 1608 they had formed a League called the Union of Ahausen, after the little town where it had been created. It is more commonly known as the Evangelical Union. The Union was mainly composed of Calvinist princes, for the most part minor princes, except for its leader, the elector Palatine, and free cities such as Nürnberg, Regensburg and Strassburg. It included neither the elector of Saxony nor the elector of Brandenburg, who was later to abandon Lutheranism for Calvinism. As for the Catholic princes, their first attempt to form a union had failed because it was almost impossible to imagine a German Catholic League which was not led by the emperor, head of the House of Habsburg, and because another Catholic prince, the duke of Bavaria, of the ancient house of Wittelsbach, refused to give way to him. It was not until June 1609 that the Catholic or Holy League, could be formed under the leadership of Maximilian. The Emperor remained aloof, and apart from the duke of Bavaria, it consisted only of ecclesiastical princes,— the three archbishop-electors of Mainz, Cologne and Trier, the bishops of Augsburg, Constance, Regensburg and Passau, and a few other prelates. Thus both the Union and the League were incomplete. In the face of the deep disagreement between Lutherans and Calvinists the Union had not even dared to make the defence of the general interests of Protestantism its declared aim. It sought only to defend the private interests of the princes who formed it. Moreover the two leagues had very quickly exposed their weakness when faced for the first time with a serious disagreement between Protestants and Catholics over the question of the Julich-Cleves succession. Since that time they had lain dormant. Nevertheless, it was to the Evangelical Union that the Bohemian rebels turned for help while Ferdinand of Styria tried to rally the catholic princes of Germany to Austria's cause by an agreement with the duke of Bavaria, the head of the Catholic League. Neither the Union nor Maximilian of Bavaria completely shirked their responsibilities, but at first neither side committed itself completely. When the princes of the Union met at Heilbronn in May 1619, they decided on a levy of 14,000 men, but only as a precautionary measure and without any aggressive intent. The only service which they agreed to render to the Bohemian directory was to stand surety for a loan which the Bohemians could not have raised on their own credit and which was indispensable if they were to arm. For his part, Maximilian was ready to send the League troops to serve Ferdinand, but only on the condition that he should be free to dispose of them as he wished and in return for guarantees which Ferdinand hesitated to grant. Nonetheless, it can be established that the German princes, Catholics and Protestants alike, kept a close watch on the Bohemian revolt from the start and were ready to intervene at any moment.

Those outside the Empire were already viewing the situation with growing concern. On the eastern borders of Germany and Austria, the battle waged by the great religious orders against all the protestant faiths had either succeeded or was in full swing and the enmities which it aroused had not yet died down. In Poland the victory of the Society of Jesus and King Sigismund III (the Jesuit King, as he was called) was complete. Sigismund had no intention that it should be compromised by a Protestant victory in the neighbouring Empire. He allowed Ferdinand of Styria to recruit troops in Polish lands. On the other hand, in Transylvania, in Turkish Hungary, and even in royal Hungary, Calvinism was holding its own. The Prince of Transylvania, Bethlen[1]

---

[1] He is commonly called Bethlen Gabor, but Gabor is only a Christian name, placed after the surname.

offered to take arms and called the Hungarian Calvinists to rise against
a king who was persecuting them. It was personal ambition which
caused him to side with the Bohemian rebels, and by presenting a
direct threat to Vienna across the narrow strip of royal Hungary, he
could give them decisive help.

To the West, the three great powers of Spain, England and France
had, of necessity, an interest in all that was going on in Germany,
but in different ways.

In the time of the duke of Lerma, Philip III's favourite, Spain had
appeared to lose interest in Austria and to seek peace alone. This period
of withdrawal lasted only as long as Lerma was in favour, and from
1617, under a new favourite, the courts of Vienna and Madrid came to a
closer understanding. After the secret agreement of Graz, Oñate, the
Spanish ambassador who made it, had almost as much influence on
Austrian policy as the emperor's ministers themselves. It might be said
that he had almost as much influence as the confessor, for they
understood each other well. Together they kept alive in Ferdinand's
mind a determination to work relentlessly for the triumph of the
Roman faith; they both urged him to make the energetic decisions
to which he himself inclined; they both promised him Spanish help.
If Philip III sometimes hesitated a little when faced with the consequences of such a thorough-going Catholic policy, and thought
perhaps of the disappointments which it had brought his father, his
cousin from the Netherlands, the archduke Albert, insisted that he
should not allow the Church's victory on heresy's chosen ground to
slip from his grasp. Before Spain intervened, it was Archduke Albert
who was the first to give Ferdinand encouragement and then help.

England's position was very different. Although the Anglican
Church had retained both the hierarchy and certain ceremonies of
Catholicism, England was Protestant. The English hated 'popery'.
Their king, James I, was the father-in-law of the young elector
Palatine, Frederick V, head of the Evangelical Union and the future
'Winter King'. James could not wish for, still less favour, the Roman
Church's triumph in Bohemia and perhaps shortly afterwards through-
out the Empire. However, he did not wish to help the rebels. At the
time he was dealing tactfully with the Catholics, at least outside
England, because he hoped to marry his son Charles to the Spanish
Infanta. Above all he was frightened of committing England to a
conflict which was none of her business and from which she stood to
gain nothing. When, a little later, Frederick V was elected king by the

Bohemian States, James would neither approve his acceptance of the crown nor offer him help to secure it.

French policy at the beginning of the Bohemian revolt is more difficult to define, but it has been thoroughly studied by Tapié.[1] At the time of the defenestration, Louis XIII was still only seventeen. It was only in the previous year, after the murder of Concini and the Queen Mother's exile to Blois, that he had really felt that he was king, and it cannot be thought that he had already developed any ideas of his own on foreign affairs or was in a position to impose them on his ministers. In all probability this was also true of the new favourite, Luynes, who had scarcely begun to get a grasp of the affairs of state. French external policy had to be conducted by the Secretary of State for foreign affairs, Brûlart de Puysieulx, son of the Chancellor and heir to the traditions of Henry IV. Any reproaches directed at Puysieulx for not supporting the Protestant cause against the courts of Vienna and Madrid from the first must be based on the preconceived idea that French policy was necessarily hostile to the house of Austria. In fact it was not, nor would it have been if Henry IV had still been alive. In any case, it is too easily forgotten that the marriage of the king with an infanta had brought the courts of France and Spain closer together and that it required—but at a much later date—the clear-sightedness of a Richelieu to perceive what the great cardinal called the Spanish peril. At that time, Louis XIII only saw a more immediate danger from the way the Bohemian revolt jeopardised the Roman Church, for like Ferdinand he was its obedient and devoted son. Nor could he help thinking that the rising of the Protestants in Prague might encourage the Huguenots of Béarn to do the same thing, at a time when he had made up his mind to re-establish Catholicism in their lands and return to the Catholic church the possessions that the former subjects of Jeanne d'Albret had plundered.

The situation in Bohemia and the Empire was still uncertain in August 1619, but there was no hope of an early peace settlement. The striking thing is that, so long as they did not receive foreign help, both sides were militarily powerless. The only armed incidents of any note were a fruitless expedition made by Thurn into Lower Austria where he camped for several days on the outskirts of Vienna but did not have the necessary artillery to attack the town itself, and a defeat suffered by Mansfeld at Zablati in southern Bohemia. It was an ordinary, unimportant battle, the result of an unexpected encounter, but it did allow

[1] Op. cit.

Ferdinand to go in safety to the electoral diet at Frankfurt. During these months the important thing was not the campaigning of Thurn, Mansfeld or Bucquoy, but the way in which two events were taking shape simultaneously which were to give the Bohemian Revolt its full significance: these were the elections of a new emperor at Frankfurt and a new king of Bohemia at Prague.

There could be no doubt that Ferdinand of Styria's candidature would finally win the day at Frankfurt. It was backed by the established tradition that the imperial crown should stay within the house of Habsburg, and since Maximilian and Albert had renounced their claims, Ferdinand was the only representative of his house. He could count in advance on four votes, those of the three Ecclesiastical electors and his own—for it was also traditional that the king of Bohemia, as an elector, should vote for himself, and Ferdinand was still king of Bohemia. Only a single Catholic candidate could oppose him— a Wittelsbach. But although Maximilian of Bavaria delayed announcing publicly that he would not be a candidate, everyone knew that he had no intention of being one. It is true that another Catholic prince, the duke of Savoy, spread rumours that he might be elected, but he was the only one to take his fantasies seriously. As for the three Protestant electors, they had no illusions about the impossibility of having one of their co-religionists elected. At the last moment they would either have to isolate themselves in fruitless opposition, or rally, whether they liked it or not, behind a Catholic candidate who was assured of success without their support. So convinced were they that they did not try to prevent the election of a Habsburg, but merely to delay it—and even in this they failed. So Ferdinand's accession to the Empire was assured, supported by some, and accepted by others, not only within Germany but even beyond; Philip of Spain had warmly commended it, Louis XIII openly declared that he considered it to be a guarantee of peace, and James I himself made it widely known that he would welcome it with satisfaction.

However, as long as Ferdinand was not reconciled with Maximilian of Bavaria, one doubt still remained, and when he left Vienna on 11th July to go to Frankfurt by easy stages, he headed first of all for Munich. He did not go there only to seek definite support for his candidature from a potential rival, but also to enlist the aid of the League against the Bohemian rebels. The first matter was a foregone conclusion; as for the second, the negotiations could only be tentative: Maximilian's claims were such that Ferdinand could not yet make up his mind to meet them: for the time being he had to be satisfied with a conditional promise which was that if the Evangelical Union came to the aid of the Bohemians, the Catholic League would intervene against them. After this, Ferdinand went on his way, accompanied by a large court, and made his entrance into Frankfurt on 28th July. There, everything went off according to his wishes. The Electoral College refused to receive a delegation from the Estates of Bohemia and then decided to proceed with the election on 28th August. On that day the three ecclesiastical electors were present in person while the other four were represented by plenipotentiaries. The director of the College, the archbishop of Mainz, first turned to the archbishops of Trier and Cologne, who declared themselves in favour of Ferdinand. He then turned to the elector Palatine's representative, who nominated the duke of Bavaria, but added that he would support the majority. When this was assured by the votes of the plenipotentiaries of Saxony and Brandenburg, and when the votes of the elector of Mainz and the elector of Bohemia were added to the four others, the representative of the elector Palatine had to keep his word and Ferdinand was unanimously elected. Henceforward he was the Emperor Ferdinand II.

Now two days earlier (although the news had not yet reached him), the Bohemians had appointed his successor as king of Bohemia. He had not foreseen this when he left Vienna, but, from that moment, the Estates of Bohemia had strengthened their position by the support of the 'incorporated provinces', Silesia and the two Lusatias, which had finally been joined by Moravia. It was not that Karl von Žierotin had changed his attitude; he steadfastly advised submission, but opposition was growing around him, led by one of his relatives, Ladislas Velen von Žierotin. The troops themselves and their leaders were divided; two of these successively defected and declared for the king, trying, unsuccessfully, to take the troops with them. The second of these was none other than Valdštejn (whom we know as Wallenstein), of the great Czech, albeit Catholic, family. It was then that the Moravian diet made up its mind: on 11th May 1619, it concluded a treaty of alliance with the diet of Bohemia. The five provinces of the kingdom were henceforward united in the rebellion; and they thought they could count, if not on the open support of Upper and Lower Austria, at least on that of the strong Protestant minority which was effective there.

Under these new conditions, the diet of Bohemia which met at Prague in July, was able to take a very important initiative whose true nature has been revealed by contemporary Czech historians and which did not escape the attention of Ernest Denis. It brought about a union of the provinces who were thus allied together to maintain their common resistance, and without exception they all pledged themselves to an organisation which accurately reflected popular feeling. The Act of Confederation drawn up at Prague on 21st July made Bohemia, Moravia, Silesia and the two Lusatias not a federal state, which nobody would have wanted, but a confederation of independent states. We cannot help thinking that it had perhaps been modelled on the Union of Utrecht, although the Confederation created at Prague and the Republic of the United Provinces differed in that the former retained its monarchy. Nothing remained of Lobkowitz's centralised administration: each of the five provinces preserved its autonomy, and their only common institution, that of the Protectors, was elected separately and did not even constitute a permanent assembly like the States-General of the United Provinces. They met for discussion only once a year, though in exceptional circumstances the Bohemian Protectors might invite them to meet together. They also had to meet to declare war or conclude an alliance. Another characteristic of this Bohemian Confederation was that it did not separate religious from political matters: it was based on evangelical principles: ecclesiastical matters became affairs of state and, by virtue of this, subject to the Protectors' approval. Nothing in the Act of Confederation of July 1619 involved Ferdinand's deposition, but it nonetheless confirmed the breach: he remained king in name only. It demanded explicit confirmation from him of the Letter of Majesty; it reasserted, for the future, the elective nature of the royal title and laid down the form of the election. It was extremely unlikely that Ferdinand could ever accept such a rejection of all his policy.

Besides, he did not have the time to show what he thought of it. He had left for Frankfurt and the outcome of the imperial election was infinitely more important to him than vain bargaining with rebellious subjects. The events of the preceding months were brought to their logical conclusion in his absence. We must now, however, take account of other developments which had been building up over a long period.

Soon after the Defenestration of Prague the German princes had the feeling that there was likely to be a new election to the Bohemian throne. Two of them in particular—the elector of Saxony and the elector Palatine—took a very natural interest in this. The elector of Saxony was undeniably the most important of the German Lutheran princes and among the Protestants of Bohemia there was a large number of Lutherans; was it not right for him to help them? But that would be to side against the emperor. If the latter emerged victorious what would become of the Saxon princes, who, by their own interpretation of the Peace of Augsburg, had taken over, technically as administrators, a certain number of dioceses in the circle of Upper Saxony? On the other hand, the elector reflected that Saxony shared a long frontier with the Crown lands of Bohemia. If he offered his support to the emperor in defence of the monarch's right against the rebels—an alliance which would be all the more highly prized because he was a Protestant—he might perhaps obtain as compensation for the expense of providing arms, one, or even both, of the Lusatias which would very conveniently round off the inheritance he had received from his ancestors. Throughout the summer of 1619, the elector of Saxony continued to waver between these two desires and his ultimate choice was to depend on the fate of the crown of Bohemia.

As for Frederick V, the elector Palatine, it was this very crown that he coveted. We do not know when the idea occurred to him, but it would seem to have been quite early. He was young and by nature irresolute so perhaps he was egged on by the prince of Anhalt, a minor Protestant prince who was something of a party leader among the German Calvinists and who had been chosen by the Palatine as his counsellor; or perhaps by his wife, a haughty English princess, daughter of James I, who was very proud of her royal blood and considered her current title of electress as something of a fall from grace. Whatever the facts of the matter, there had been secret talks between Frederick and the Bohemian directors before Matthias's death, in July, and again in November 1618, and in December Frederick sent the Count von Dohna to Bohemia with precise instructions. But the Palatine wanted it to look as though the Bohemians had taken the initiative, so the talks dragged on. To bring them to light it needed the mad ambition of the duke of Savoy, who, in order to win the vote of the elector at Frankfurt, had held out the hope of Venetian money which would allow him to maintain a small army. For some time the duke of Savoy's candidature for the Empire and that of the Palatine for the crown of Bohemia fitted well together. In the end, by his very hesitation, Frederick got what he wanted: the crown of Bohemia seemed to have been offered to him without his having openly sought it. On 19th August, the Bohemian diet at Prague pronounced Ferdinand's deposition. On 26th August, Frederick V, the Elector Palatine, was elected king.

Throughout the entire business (and this was not a very happy omen)

Frederick had acted as though he was not at all sure that he wanted the crown, although he wanted to have it offered to him. In July and August he went to Amberg, in the upper Palatinate in order to be closer to Prague, then he returned to Heidelberg, then went back to Amberg. He vainly tried to delay the election in Prague, as he had in Frankfurt. He would have liked to wait for the reply from his father-in-law, whose approval and support he had sought. The reply was a long time coming and he had just despatched a messenger to Prague when he learned that James advised him to refuse the crown. Deep down, Frederick knew the risk he was running by accepting it. He realised that he could not hold out in Bohemia on his own without the support of France and England which would obviously be denied him. Although he was head of the Evangelical Union, he was not even assured of the effective support of the princes and cities of the Union. Clearly he was not the sort of man who takes fortune into his own hands. Still hesitating, it seems, or at least regretting that he could no longer hesitate, he took the road to Prague with his entire Court and made a ceremonial entry on 31st October. He was then twenty-three years old. His youth, his bearing and his charm at first won him the sympathy of the Bohemians, but the new queen, Elizabeth, who could not speak a word of Czech and was not able to communicate with anyone, was isolated among her ladies-in-waiting, who were all English, and showed herself for what she was, haughty and lacking in kindness. She only needed a few weeks to make herself unpopular. The new sovereigns had been crowned immediately after their arrival in Prague, on 4th November 1619, at the beginning of the season which was to earn for Frederick the name given to him by contemporaries and endorsed by history: the 'Winter King'.

So, within two days of each other, on the 26th and 28th of August 1619, the election of Frederick V as king of Bohemia and that of Ferdinand of Styria as emperor had at last created a clear-cut situation. The causes of these two events were very complex and I have tried to give an overall picture without examining them all in detail. Throughout, chance had played its part and so had men like Thurn, Ferdinand of Styria and Frederick, who had no idea where destiny was leading them. History is always like this. In any case, the moment of choice had passed. Thurn, who had been the first to cast the dice, had reverted to his previous role as military commander, and not a very good one at that. Frederick had no option but to defend his crown, and Ferdinand could only set out to dethrone the man who in his eyes was an usurper and to re-establish the prestige of the house of Habsburg by crushing the rebellion.

The next stage seemed almost determined by the two elections of 26th and 28th August. Ferdinand's election to the Empire assured him of the support which promised his future triumph,—above all, it assured him of Spain's support. From the beginning Archduke Albert, who was mindful of the fact that the twelve-year truce concluded in 1609 with the States-General of the United Provinces would soon expire and that then a war in Germany would allow the king of Spain to move his troops more easily to the Low Countries, insisted that Philip III should authorize him to recruit troops and give him the means to do so. At first Philip III had avoided the issue, but after the imperial election he allowed his cousin, in January 1620, to levy 20,000 men who were to occupy part of the Lower Palatinate under the command of Spinola, one of the finest captains of the day.

Another consequence of Ferdinand's election was that agreement was reached between the emperor and the duke of Bavaria. Maximilian had not wished to commit himself as long as he was uncertain that the king of Spain would also intervene; thereafter his mind was set at rest on that point. Besides, there was enough at stake in the war for Ferdinand II to grant the leader of the Catholic League, whose army had become indispensable to him, the guarantees and privileges for which he was asking. Maximilian was to reorganise the League free of any imperial interference, and he alone was to dispose of its troops. The emperor undertook to pay all his expenses and, until such time as he was able to do so, he offered as security the territories that were to be occupied, starting with Upper Austria where the rising had spread. Finally, although there was no question of its being written into the agreement, Ferdinand gave the duke of Bavaria a verbal promise to have the electoral title transfered to him after Frederick V's defeat. As for the Lutheran princes, who had perhaps even less sympathy for the Calvinists than they had for the Catholics, the election of a Calvinist as king of Bohemia caused them considerable anxiety and deterred them from intervening. Moreover, it resolved the dilemma for John George, the elector of Saxony, who offered to help Ferdinand against the usurper. To reach Bohemia, he crossed Lusatia and occupied it until such time as the emperor should be able to meet the costs of his war effort. He had high hopes that that day was a long way off.

The net was thus drawn around Bohemia, threatening the destruction of the Palatine—but this was not all that was involved. It was likely that the intervention of the Catholic League would bring that of the Evangelical Union in its wake. It was also likely that the Lutheran princes of Germany, in spite of their lack of sympathy for Frederick V, would not be able to keep out of a conflict in which some day the very fate of the Reformation would be at stake. Moreover, the projected transfer of an electoral title was in itself enough to provoke a German war. Above all, there was already reason to fear that this war, by renewing the links between the catholic monarchies of Austria and Spain, might force the Empire's neighbours to revise their policies.

But first we must deal with the German war.

CHAPTER III

THE GERMAN WAR

The military operations which decided Bohemia's fate after the election of Frederick V subsequently spread to the two Palatinates and even to a few parts of the Rhineland and Westphalia. To term this the German war is to simplify history a little, just as Michelet did when he invented such titles as the 'Bohemian Period' or the 'Danish Period' of the Thirty Years War. At that time it was, above all, a question of German interests in what was essentially a German Civil War. But already foreign sovereigns were beginning to intervene, for one reason or another, either, like the king of France, with the object of re-establishing peace, or, like the king of Spain, in order to give armed support to one of the sides. We shall see how the very character of the war gradually changed during the years which followed, but if we wish to make the extremely complex German politics of that period tolerably clear, then simplify we must.

It is true that the complications did not occur immediately. In the early stages, until Frederick V was expelled from Bohemia, events took a fairly natural course, more or less as a well-informed and very shrewd observer might have expected.

After his election to the Empire, Ferdinand II was more determined than ever to reconquer Bohemia, but preparations for a war took time in those days. Levies were difficult, especially when money was short, as was generally the case. As Ferdinand could not act without the Catholic League or the Saxon troops, he had to wait until Maximilian of Bavaria and John George of Saxony were ready. In the autumn of 1619, it even seemed that the imperial cause might be in danger. At about the same time as Ferdinand became emperor, Bethlen, the Prince of Transylvania, had entered and crossed royal Hungary. Thurn had joined him before Vienna. But even together, they did not have enough troops and above all sufficient siege weapons to take such a strong town. It was not long before they abandoned the attempt; Bethlen went back to Hungary and Thurn to Bohemia. Then, as usual, winter interrupted operations. At the beginning of the spring, neither Maximilian nor John George, nor Spinola—who was to occupy the Rhenish Palatinate with the Spanish troops from the Netherlands—had opened their campaigns. On the other hand, Frederick V in Prague was encountering more difficulties than he had foreseen. Being completely German, surrounded by Germans who had come from the Palatinate with him, and not knowing the Czech language, he appeared like a foreign king in Bohemia. Back in the autumn he had thought to make the crown hereditary by having his five-year-old son elected in advance to succeed him, but he had not known how to win the affection of the nobility, to whom he owed his election. A contemporary lampoon made this clear enough. It ran: 'You are king only by permission of the nobles ... by their temporary permission, that is.' At first they were charmed by his youth. But it was accompanied by total inexperience and a good deal of levity: 'He thinks that everything is easy and leaves everything to God', wrote one of his ministers, Camerarius. He had no money and hence no troops, and his appeals to the Evangelical Union remained more or less unanswered. He could find no allies outside Germany; his father-in-law, James I, only wanted the restoration of peace and advised him to give up a crown which after all he had hesitated to accept. The position of the 'Winter King' was still precarious on the eve of the decisive operations.

It was then that a French intervention served the imperial cause much more than Louis XIII's ministers had intended. At the beginning of winter, Ferdinand sent an ambassador, the prince of Fürstenberg, to Paris to ask the French king to help him conquer the heretics. He underlined the danger which would threaten the Church if the Protestants were victorious in Bohemia. The pious Louis XIII was moved by this. He too had to fight with rebellious subjects, the Calvinists of Béarn, since he had undertaken to re-establish Catholicism in their lands and to restore the property which had been seized from the bishops. It was natural that he should make a mental comparison between Béarnese resistance to the royal edict and the Bohemian revolt.[1] However, he hesitated to promise the new emperor the troops he asked for. His confessor, Father Arnoux, had to add his entreaties to Fürstenberg's. It is said that Louis XIII was persuaded by a sermon which Father Arnoux preached before the king on Christmas Day, to make Fürstenberg a somewhat vague promise which the ambassador hastened to

[1] This point of view was exposed for the first time by Tapié in the work already quoted.

take back to Vienna. There were even some troop movements towards the frontier, but Puysieulx the Foreign Secretary, good Catholic though he was, was even more reluctant than the king to commit France to a war from which there seemed little to be gained. The troops did not leave the kingdom. Instead, an official embassy, led by a prince of the blood royal, the duc d'Angoulême, was despatched with instructions to negotiate between the Evangelical Union and the emperor in order to ensure that peace was kept before any decisive campaign could be started.

When the duc d'Angoulême arrived in South Germany, where he expected first of all to see the duke of Bavaria, the situation had changed somewhat. The Catholic League and the Union had finished marshalling their troops, and the two armies were almost face to face in the region of Ulm, with the League's army slightly larger than the Union's. At the same time, the princes of the Union were at odds among themselves. The margrave of Ansbach, who commanded the army, was personally resolved not to abandon the king of Bohemia, but other princes, especially the duke of Wurtemberg, secretly wanted the peace to be kept. This fitted in well with the duc d'Angoulême's instructions which were to urge moderation on both sides, and when the Union princes, who had overestimated the size of the League's army, were made to believe that Maximilian of Bavaria was about to attack, they accepted the French offer of mediation. The duc d'Angoulême drew up a draft agreement, the Treaty of Ulm, which was signed by the leaders of both sides on 3rd July 1620.

It is a treaty which has provoked endless discussions, first among contemporaries and then among historians, and its consequences were in fact more far-reaching than the text at first suggested. It was solely an agreement between the two Leagues. It was signed by Maximilian of Bavaria for the Catholic League and by Ansbach for the Union. The duc d'Angoulême's signature did not appear since he had only been a mediator. Besides, as he had no-one he could trust who understood German, it would have been extremely unwise of him to sign a text which he did not understand. In it, both Leagues promised not to take any action in the future which might harm the other ' in any way or on any pretext whatsoever', and to withdraw their troops simultaneously. There was no more to it except a small clause, article 3, under which Bohemia was not included in the agreement. This left the Union princes free to go to Frederick V's aid, but they were much more concerned to defend the Lower Palatinate against the Spaniards who were starting to move into it and who were not affected by the Treaty either, since they had made no alliance with the League. In the long run, therefore, the treaty of Ulm allowed the Catholic League to help the emperor in Bohemia and to some extent neutralised South Germany without closing the Palatinate to Spinola. Consequently the king of Bohemia was isolated and left open to the attacks of all his enemies. The treaty of Ulm made his defeat more or less inevitable.

The duc d'Angoulême did not interpret it this way, but rather as a first step towards the restoration of a general peace. He thought that the emperor would be conciliatory towards his rebellious subjects and that Frederick would be resigned to giving up a crown which he did not appear to be in a position to defend. He left Bavaria and went to Vienna to complete his work. There he was badly received. Ferdinand II no longer had any reason to abandon his attempt to restore his authority in Bohemia by armed force, with the help of the king of Spain, the League, and the elector of Saxony, and he replied to the duc d'Angoulême's overtures that the king of France had promised him military aid and not an embassy. It soon became clear that the duc would achieve nothing and that imperial policy was directed by Oñate, the Spanish ambassador. In a final audience, Chancellor Lobkowitz declared that his master thought that any negotiations were useless, 'there being nothing more to be gained from treaties since he resolved to secure complete obedience from his subjects, and this could only be assured by the sword'. The duc d'Angoulême could only watch helplessly as a succession of events took place quite different from those for which he had hoped. This was the decisive campaign which by November was to reach its climax before Prague at the Battle of the White Mountain.

Like all the campaigns of the Thirty Years War, the campaign of autumn 1620 was rather chaotic and it is only possible to relate it briefly if it is presented in a very simplified form. We may pass quickly over three widely separated theatres of operations. The Rhenish Palatinate, on the left bank of the Rhine, was conquered by Spinola between August and November, except for a few fortified towns which he did not bother to besiege. To the east of Bavaria, the League's army entered Upper Austria; to the north of Bohemia, the elector of Saxony began the occupation of the Lusatias. In this way both Maximilian and John George indemnified themselves since the emperor, who had agreed to pay all their costs, allowed them in the meantime to administer the territories which they occupied. Needless to say, more important than all of these was the offensive directed at Prague.

This was where the two main armies finally met. They were quite different from each other. The king of Bohemia's army had been hastily recruited from all over the place. There were very few Czechs in it, but there were Germans from every region, Austrians, Hungarians and even English. It had very little cohesion, discipline was very slack, and the rebels had been unable to achieve a single command; instead there were three armies, commanded by the Prince von Anhalt, the Count von Thurn and the Count von Mansfeld. The catholic army had only one leader, the Belgian Tilly, who held his command from Maximilian. Although it included soldiers from various nations—Walloons, Flemings, Italians and a handful of Spaniards—it was far better disciplined. Above all, it had a fanatical quality, instilled by the impassioned preaching of the monks who accompanied it, especially the Carmelites of whom one, Father Dominic de Jesus-Maria, was the Pope's special representative. They gave the operation the air of a crusade. Of course neither of the armies was large. It is generally thought that Maximilian's numbered about 25,000 men, and the king of Bohemia's rather less, perhaps 20,000.

The king of Bohemia's troops were not concentrated at the start of the campaign. The Prince von Anhalt's army was in Pilsen, one of the towns which had rallied to the new king, and was preparing to defend it, but Tilly's army passed further to the south and marched straight on Prague. The Prince von Anhalt then left Pilsen and tried to outpace the catholics in order to reach Prague before them and combine with Thurn and Mansfeld. By taking poor roads, and at some cost, he succeeded. During the night of 7th and 8th November, the three leaders established their troops on the hills which dominate the left bank of the Vltava, to the west of Prague, about a central position known as the White Mountain (Bila Hora). In its turn the catholic army arrived before the slopes at first light on 8th November. It had come by forced marches, but Tilly decided to give the enemy no time to fortify his positions. After mass had been celebrated by Father Dominic de Jesus-Maria before the paraded troops, he gave the order to attack. The battle—more of an affray than a battle—hardly lasted more than an hour. At first the Prince von Anhalt and the Count von Thurn achieved some tactical successes but then the Bohemian troops were seized with panic. They broke ranks and fled in disorder to Prague where they crowded into the Lower Town which was already packed with the peasants who had taken shelter there with their carts and livestock. As for Frederick V, he found out too late that the battle had been started and learnt immediately afterwards that it had been lost. The confusion which reigned in Prague convinced him that he could not save his capital. He fled, with all his court, at dawn on 9th November. There can be fewer battles which were shorter or less keenly contested than the Battle of the White Mountain. Few, however, have had such decisive results.

The immediate results became apparent in Bohemia and were worked out there during the years which followed until about 1628. For the sake of clarity, it is better to follow them through and then resume the account of the German war and its extension after the imperial victory.

The day after the White Mountain, Tilly's troops entered Prague along with the last fugitives of the beaten army. The rest of Bohemia did not offer any resistance. Moravia, which was untouched, might not have laid down its arms without a struggle if Frederick V had taken refuge in its territory, but the German king thought only of putting himself under the protection of the German princes. He quickly reached Breslau in Silesia, and shortly afterwards he was in Brandenburg, where the elector was a fellow Calvinist. His subjects, who hardly knew him, no longer had any reason to sacrifice themselves for him and Moravia, following Bohemia's example, submitted to Ferdinand II. Thus the Palatine's foolish and lamentable adventure was over. A song, current in Germany in 1620, drew this conclusion, and tempered irony with a little pity:

Oh! Poor winter king, what have you done?
How could you steal the emperor's crown
By pursuing your rebellion?
Now you do well to flee
Your electoral lands and Bohemia.
You will pay for your mistake with grief
And suffer mockery and shame.
Oh! Pious emperor Ferdinand, grant him pardon!
Do not hold his folly against him.
He's a very young man,
Who did not realise beforehand
How much a crown weighs.
Now it is weighing very heavy on his head.
If he had known, he would not have done what he did.

But Ferdinand, who believed that God had chosen him to exterminate the heretics, was incapable of pity.

The first result of the imperial victory was the complete submission of Bohemia, achieved by terrible reprisals. The Estates had to make due restitution and swear obedience to the emperor. When Maximilian left Prague, where he had held a formal entry with the army, he left a strong garrison under Tilly's command and installed the Prince of Liechtenstein as imperial governor. A little later, in February 1621, an extraordinary court was set up to mete out numerous death sentences. On 21st June, 27 of the leaders of the rebellion, including 12 directors, were beheaded in the square of the old town; 29 were sentenced in their absence, and 18 were imprisoned. In addition, the court ordered wholesale confiscations, appropriating to the crown not only the lands of those who had been condemned but of all those who had fled, despite a statute of Rudolph II which had guaranteed possession to their legal heirs. The operation brought scant profit to the imperial coffers. Ferdinand II allowed those who had served him well to make a handsome profit for their services, and the pressing need for money necessitated the hurried sale of all the sequestrated properties without even the creation of a special body to administer them and initiate the sale. The emperor granted lands to Liechtenstein, Martinitz, Slawata, Bacquoy, to all the colonels and to many others. The imperial court, presided over by Liechtenstein, was commissioned to sell the remainder. When the operation was closed in 1628, it was found that no proper accounts had been kept, and it was impossible to discover precisely what the total product of the sales had been or what had become of the money received. One example will suffice to give some idea of what the emperor's friends had been able to make out of it. The Baron von Trautmansdorf, a Counsellor of State, bought an estate valued at 300,000 florins. He obtained it for 200,000 and to enable him to make the purchase he received 60,000 as a gift and 105,000 in the form of a loan from the emperor. Thus he only paid 35,000 florins for a property which was worth at least ten times as much.

The political reorganisation of the realm was completed at about the same time as this enormous transfer of landed property. A revised constitution was imposed on Bohemia in 1627 and on Moravia in 1628. There were to be no more Protectors in either country, the crown became the hereditary property of the house of Habsburg, and the diet's confirmation of the sovereign was no longer necessary. The king had complete freedom to choose all the high officials, who no longer held their posts for life, but were appointed for five years. The courts lost their independence and became subject to the king's authority. Lastly, a new Estate, that of the clergy, which already existed in Moravia, was created in Bohemia. It included the archbishop, the bishops and the leading clergy and held the senior position in the diet. On the other hand the towns now played only an insignificant role. In this way, Lobkowitz's work of centralisation and the house of Habsburg's political conquest of Bohemia were both achieved.

The religious conquest went hand in glove with the political conquest. At the beginning it was a little less brutal because the emperor wished to humour his ally, the Lutheran elector, John George of Saxony. But this state of affairs did not last. To begin with, the Jesuits returned in the wake of the victorious army. They settled in Prague once more and reopened their College. It was the Jesuits, together with the papal legate, Cardinal Caraffa, who dictated Ferdinand's actions. They persuaded him without any difficulty that to ensure his salvation he should abolish the Letter of Majesty and that his subjects' revolt entitled him to do so. He obeyed. The return of the Jesuits had been followed immediately by the proscription of the Calvinists, who were not protected under any imperial law. The abolition of the Letter of Majesty also allowed the emperor to exile the Bohemian Brethren who were classed with the Calvinists. The Lutherans, too, were associated with the Brethren in the Czech church created in 1609, but for fear of upsetting John George, Ferdinand spared them for some time. It was only in October 1622 that the order was given to the imperial Governor, Liechtenstein, to expel the Lutheran pastors. At the same time communion in both kinds was banned in Bohemia. Subsequently, from 1623, the persecution spread to the Lutheran townspeople and peasants. Protestants of any faith no longer had the right to hold funerals or baptisms in accordance with their beliefs, and were excluded from public office. All the successive measures which had been taken against them were finally codified in the Edict of 24th July 1624, thereby exposing them to the full force of the law. As for the Catholic Church, it was reorganised by the Jesuits and the Capuchins, and replaced the heretical churches throughout the kingdom.

Within a few years the Counter Reformation, backed by the Catholic League, transformed Bohemia far more than its submission to the House of Austria had done. Lutheranism only reappeared there much later as a result of German immigration. The old Hussite Bohemia became one of the most Catholic countries in Europe, and Czech civilisation was impregnated with Catholicism. The Roman Church was responsible for the spread of the Baroque and its extraordinary vigour, which gives Bohemian architecture of the seventeenth and eighteenth centuries its essential qualities, can only be explained in terms of the predominating influence of the Jesuits. The religious reconquest of Bohemia at the beginning of the Thirty Years War was thus fundamental, not only in the history of the Holy Roman Empire, but in the general history of Europe. It had more lasting and more far-reaching consequences than the political conquest of Bohemia by the Habsburgs.

Lastly, to the political and religious conquests must be added the partial Germanisation of the country. This of course was not wholly a result of the war, or at least, it was only one in terms of the small contribution made by the transfer of certain landed property from Czech families to families of German origin. The progress of Germanisation had begun long before the Prague revolt. From the end of the sixteenth and during the first years of the seventeenth century, the knights had become impoverished and decimated by long wars against the Turks. Many of the families who had been famous in the time of George of Podiebrad had become extinct and their vast estates were often bought by foreigners, of whom many were Germans. It is certainly not possible to talk in terms of a German conquest of Bohemia during this period, but contemporary Czechoslovak historians—and Tapié agrees with them—record that 'the truly Czech character of the country was affected' and that 'German spread there at the cost of the national language'.

I have followed the transformation of Bohemia after the Battle of the White Mountain until 1628 or thereabouts, because it forms a cohesive whole and we shall hardly have occasion to return to it. The political and religious constitution of King Wenceslas's realm would not again be challenged. The Bohemian episode of the Thirty Years War was finished. If Frederick V played any further part in the war, it was not as king of Bohemia, for he had definitely abdicated, but as the elector Palatine—and it was precisely in this capacity that he brought about an event of the utmost importance for the German War, which brings us back to our main story.

In January 1621, hardly two months after the victory of the White Mountain, the emperor banished from the Empire the elector Palatine and a few minor princes who had been his allies—the Prince von Anhalt, the margrave of Iaegerndorf and the Count von Hohenlohe.

This action was entirely different from, and altogether more serious than, the most stringent measures taken against the Bohemians by the man who had always regarded himself as their lawful ruler. It was taken by Ferdinand in his capacity as an emperor, dealing with princes of the Empire, and it was done without even consulting the electoral college. Now the banishment of Frederick V entailed the confiscation of his possessions—that is to say the future fate of the Upper and Lower Palatines—and, what was even more serious, his deposition as an elector. Ferdinand had hesitated before passing sentence because he foresaw the consequences clearly enough, but he was bound by the talks he had held with Maximilian of Bavaria in Munich, in 1619, on the eve of the imperial election. The promise of the title of elector and the right to occupy the Upper Palatinate which bordered Bavaria had been the secret price of the Catholic League's intervention against the heretics of Bohemia and the usurper of the crown. Although the emperor feared the increase in power and prestige which the elevation to the electorate would bring to the Wittelsbach family, he had to keep his word, especially as the Bavarian's troops had already occupied the Upper Palatinate and Upper Austria as sureties. Moreover, Ferdinand's conscience was being constantly prompted by his intimates, the Jesuits and Capuchins of Vienna, not to mention the Pope's special envoy, Father Hyacinth. The difficulties of putting this plan into action still remained to be solved.

The settlement of the Bohemian crisis might well have been the occasion for a reorganisation within the Empire. The emperor could have summoned a diet to settle the fate of the Palatinate and the electoral title and also to renew the Peace of Augsburg, revising it in the light of Catholic opinion—but Ferdinand dared not grasp the nettle. He remembered the 'broken' Diets of 1608 and 1613 and merely summoned a 'deputation', which was a partial diet without power to pass imperial laws. To it he called the electors (except, of course, for the elector Palatine), three Lutheran princes, the duke of Brunswick Wolfenbüttel, the duke of Pomerania and the landgrave of Hesse-Darmstadt, and, among the Catholics, the duke of Bavaria, the archbishop of Salzburg, the bishop of Bamberg and the bishop of Würzburg. In this way he hoped to rally around the head of the Empire, along with the Catholic princes, the Lutheran princes who had displayed the most hostility towards the Calvinists.

In the event, he failed. The expulsion of the Lutheran pastors from Bohemia and the initial persecution of the adherents of the Confession of Augsburg had annoyed and disturbed all the Lutheran princes, especially the elector of Saxony. At the beginning of 1622, a packet of letters from Father Hyacinth had the misfortune to fall into the hands of the Count von Mansfeld, who sent them to Dresden where they were made public. They provided ample proof that the transfer of the electoral title to the house of Bavaria had been negotiated a long time before by the Catholic princes in the interests of Catholicism and that it was an accomplished fact. The emperor had in fact signed Maximilian's act of investiture in September 1621 and had had it taken in great secrecy to Munich by Father Hyacinth. Besides, whether they were Calvinists or Lutherans, the Protestant princes could not approve the abandonment of parity, that is the equal distribution of the votes, in the Electoral Union (from which the Elector of Bohemia was excluded). It would mean that in the future, instead of being three against three, there would be only two—Saxony and Brandenburg—against four Catholic electors. The result of all this discontent was that neither John George of Saxony nor George William of Brandenburg came to Regensberg in person; they merely sent ambassadors to represent them. The 'deputation', therefore, being almost exclusively composed of Catholics, was even less qualified to take the serious decision which was expected of it.

Nevertheless, it met on the appointed date, 7th January 1623, and the emperor obtained its approval for the transfer of the title, but it imposed a condition which could not have pleased Maximilian: this was that electoral powers would only be conferred upon the duke of Bavaria as a personal title for life and would then revert to the Palatine branch of the house of Wittelsbach, that is to one of Frederick V's heirs. The investiture ceremony took place none the less on 25th February 1623 in the presence of the 'deputation' which then dispersed at the beginning of March.

The elector Palatine's deposition and the transfer of the electoral title to the duke of Bavaria marked the triumph of the Catholic cause. This triumph was celebrated in Munich with lavish feasts and in Rome with a ceremonial Te Deum in Saint Peter's, but no Protestant prince was present at the investiture ceremony. Those who had more or less come out in support of the Palatine, like the margrave of Baden or the landgrave of Hesse-Cassel, began to fear for themselves: would not they too, in their turn, be banished from the Empire? At the same time many secularised lands were returned to the Church in accordance with the Catholic interpretation of the Peace of Augsburg, and Catholic canons were introduced into the chapters where the Protestants had gradually acquired a majority. It became increasingly obvious with each day that passed, that the Roman Church, which dictated Ferdinand II's decisions, would not allow him to restore peace to the Empire. The emperor seemed resolved to exterminate heresy outside as well as within Bohemia, by continuing and widening the scope of a war which had already brought him such resounding success. Thereafter it was the very existence of Protestantism in the Empire which was at stake.

In truth, the war had not completely ceased outside Bohemia after the campaign in 1620. It would be tedious to recount it in detail. It is enough to outline its chief features and to show how it spread, step by step, within the Empire during the few years for which it remained a German war, despite the help which the house of Spain gave to the house of Austria.

To understand it, we must always bear in mind the nature of the Holy Roman Empire in those days. For this reason, I have already devoted a whole chapter to describing it. We must remember the extreme subdivision of land, the confusion over rights and possessions, the territorial ambitions and the religious dissensions which turned one prince against another. Nor must we forget the ambivalent attitudes of princes to the emperor's authority: though they regarded its protection as indispensable, if only against the Turks, they also feared it because it threatened their independence, the liberty of the German nation as they were already calling it. In an Empire so partitioned and divided, where the princes' ambitions outran their strength, and where their desire for action was constrained by fear, warfare was bound to be sporadic and piecemeal—sometimes paralysed for lack of men and resources, sometimes goaded into activity by greed. We can do no more than highlight its most important aspects.

First of all, how were the two opposing sides composed? It is difficult to answer this question because the situation was constantly changing; here we are on shifting ground. On one side was the emperor, but he did not have an army which owed its sole obedience to him; he only had at his disposal a few regiments which had been recruited, according to the usual practice in those times, by the colonels who commanded them, Dampierre and Bucquoy. He had obtained the alliance of the elector of Saxony, but since the prersecution of the Lutherans in Bohemia, John George was no longer a sure ally. After the occupation of the two Lusatias, his role in the war became increasingly more hesitant and unreliable. Another alliance by which the emperor had greatly benefited was the one he had concluded with Maximilian of Bavaria. Like Ferdinand, Maximilian was very obedient to the Church and a fervent disciple of the Jesuits; like him, he longed with all his heart and soul for the triumph of Catholicism; but once he held the upper Palatinate and even a part of the Rhenish Palatinate which his troops had penetrated in 1622, and once he had been invested with the electoral powers, all his ambitions were satisfied. It might be feared that the old jealousy of the Wittelsbachs towards the Habsburgs would be awakened and would bring him to begrudge the services which he could still render to the imperial house. In any case, he had to think firstly of consolidating his gains, of persuading the other electors to accept his new title and the conditions under which he had acquired it, and to calm the anxiety which surrounded him. Besides, he was himself worried by the growing influence which the Spanish ambassador exercised at Vienna. He looked askance at the way in which the court of Madrid sought to extend the war, because any extension seemed to him to favour the Spanish monarchy. Ferdinand could not always be sure of being able to rely on Maximilian in the future. Only Spain remained. In her, the emperor had a faithful ally, precisely because she was fighting as much for herself as for him. But this could be a danger as well as an advantage. In 1621 the twelve year truce, which Philip III had concluded with the Republic of the United Provinces in 1609, expired. War had flared up again on the frontiers of the Low Countries. Thereafter, Spain was chiefly concerned with assuring the passage of her troops along the Rhine, from the duchy of Milan to Luxemburg. That was why the king of Spain had willingly authorised Spinola to occupy the fortified towns of the Rhenish Palatinate; but, under these conditions, all he was offering Vienna was a diversion on the easter frontier of the Empire and not co-operation in the conduct of the war. No alliance was concluded between Madrid and Vienna, and yet, because he felt that he was the stronger, the king of Spain wanted to direct operations. We shall see the consequences of this.

The other side did not even have a leader. Since Frederick V had taken refuge at the Court of Brandenburg, with his wife, the haughty Elizabeth Stuart, he no longer counted. He kept up an active diplomatic correspondence and, in particular, he did his best to interest his father-in-law, James I of England, in his fate. But although the king did not completely abandon him, he was very careful not to compromise English policy for the sake of a lost cause. In 1622, Frederick had gathered together a few troops and entered the Palatinate, but it was a hopeless and shortlived attempt. One after another his allies deserted. In January 1622, Bethlen returned to Transylvania. The Evangelical Union's attitude was even more deplorable. Though it had troops in the Rhenish Palatinate, Spinola had occupied most if it, taking town after town in his own good time, and the help which the princes sought from Louis XIII never materialised. Consequently they felt abandoned, and it was then that the Republic of Strassburg started negotiations with Spinola, offering to withdraw from the Union if the integrity of its territory was guaranteed. An agreement was reached without difficulty. Strassburg's defection was followed by that of the landgrave of Hesse-Cassel, who recalled his troops, and subsequently the margrave of Ansbach and the duke of Wurtemberg followed suit. The Union expired in May 1621 and an assembly which met at Heilbronn concluded that it was impossible to renew it. The result was that there was no longer an Evangelical Union. The Spanish troops remained masters of the Lower Palatinate and Spinola was able to leave the banks of the Rhine at the very moment when war broke out again between Spain and the United Provinces. After Bohemia's submission to the king-emperor, Germany submitted, in her turn, almost without a struggle.

Only a few minor princes remained under arms, such as the margrave of Baden who had been stripped of his estates and sought to reconquer them, the Count von Mansfeld and Duke Christian of Brunswick, prince-bishop of Halberstadt—and these in fact were truly soldiers of fortune, thriving only by warfare. Mansfeld had taken the Palatine's side from the beginning of the rebellion. Christian of Brunswick (or as he was more commonly called, Halberstadt, because despite being a Protestant he had had himself elected by the chapter of that diocese and had become its administrator) acted in concert with Mansfeld from 1622. They have usually been treated as adventurers, greedy only for the spoils of war, but attempts have been made to rehabilitate them, especially Halberstadt.[1] Perhaps they did have noble motives, but they did not have the means to execute them. Unable to seize victory, they could only prolong the horrors of the war. From 1622 to 1626 it was they who gave it its shape and its rhythm. They recruited when and where they were able. They campaigned whenever they had a few thousand men and wherever the opportunity arose. If they had some successes, their army swelled as they progressed but, as

[1] Cf. Wertheim: *Der tolle Halberstädter Herzog Christian von Braunschweig*, Berlin, 1929.

4

it had to live off the countryside, wherever it went it left a trail of plundered or destroyed crops, gutted villages, and peasants hiding in the forests. When winter came the mercenaries dispersed unless their chief could provide them with good quarters where they could live an easy life at the expense of the inhabitants and line their purses. If they could do this, hostilities began again the following spring. For the peasant, billeted troops are as terrible as troops on campaign. Callot's famous prints bring this war to life for us, for although they date from 1633, they would not have been different if they had been inspired by the German War ten years earlier.

In such a war, there could be no question of strategy. The leaders' only concern was to fill their depleted ranks, to nourish them and to find good winter quarters for them without regard to friends or enemies. And it was precisely this perpetual search for quarters along with the ill-ordered undertakings of men such as Mansfeld or Halberstadt that caused the war to spread by degrees. By the end of 1622 it had spread from the south-west of Germany, where the Bavarians and the Spanish had completed the occupation of the Lower Palatinate, to the Rhineland, where another theatre of war had just opened on the borders of the Spanish Netherlands and the United Provinces. Mansfeld, who had devastated Alsace and had recouped his losses there, wanted to move towards the Netherlands. Tilly immediately feared for Cologne, and his troops went down the Rhine valley to protect the town. Then at the approach of winter, Mansfeld went to take up his winter quarters in Frisia, but Halberstadt, who had recruited troops in Brunswick, wished to join him. Consequently Tilly moved to cover Münster which he thought was threatened, and it was on the fertile Wetterau Plain to the north of the Main that he installed his troops at the onset of winter.

In the following year, 1623, hostilities spread from the west to the east and, in north Germany, from the circle of Westphalia to the circle of Lower Saxony. In February, as they saw the war closing in upon them, the princes of Lower Saxony came together and decided to raise the circle's army both to defend themselves and to refuse free passage and quarters. At the same time the margrave of Hesse-Cassel called Halberstadt to his aid. Once more there were confused military operations. Halberstadt was finally beaten by Tilly, who then called on the princes of Lower Saxony to disband their troops. They obeyed and Tilly was able to quarter his own troops across the territory of Hesse-Cassel and the neighbouring lands. The only result of the campaign was to spread the war and its ravages even further and to arouse disquiet in the courts of Saxony and Brandenburg.

However, at the beginning of 1624, the triumph of the emperor and the League seemed complete. After Bohemia's submission, the occupation of the two Palatinates and the dissolution of the Evangelical Union, the enemies of Ferdinand II and Spain, from the Rhine to the Elbe, even as far afield as the circles of Westphalia and Lower Saxony, were reduced to impotence. It seemed that the end of the German war was at hand. But it was exactly at that moment that new factors came into play which not only extended the war, but gradually changed its character. These new factors were the intervention of Christian IV of Denmark and the policy of the count of Olivares, Philip IV's chief minister.

It might be said that the war lost its exclusively German character with the intervention of Christian IV, but we must remember that he was also duke of Holstein and, as such, a German prince. He sat and voted in the diet. He was a member and not the least important, of the circle of Lower Saxony. Moreover his younger son, Frederick, was also a prince of the Empire for he had had himself elected as bishopadministrator of Verden which lay between the lower courses of the Weser and the Elbe, and he succeeded Duke Christian of Brunswick as administrator of Halberstadt when he abandoned the office. Finally, he was named as coadjutor of the bishoprics of Bremen and Osnabrück, with the eventual right of succession. He thus disposed of four dioceses, of which two at least were considerable, in the circles of Lower Saxony and Westphalia. It was principally to defend their position as German princes in the Empire that Christian and his son sought to oppose the progress of the League's army in the direction of the North Sea and the Elbe.

Thus the war did not cease to be specifically German because of the nature of the belligerents or of the interests involved, but it assumed the new character of a struggle to control the bishoprics, and it is this which we must try to understand. To do so, we must also understand the role of the diocesan administrator, and the great attraction of these bishoprics for the princes of the Empire. These princes often had large families and it was the head of the family's responsibility to establish his children in good positions. Some of them seized the chance to infiltrate their sons into cathedral chapters since neither zeal nor learning was required of them at that time. The canons, who were primarily concerned with the value of their prebends, had no hesitation in admitting very lukewarm Catholics and sometimes Protestants, and the fact that their freedom of choice was not limited by any clause of the Peace of Augsburg made them all the less scrupulous. This invasion of the chapters very rapidly became a device for Protestants to circumvent the Ecclesiastical Reservation which they had never recognised anyway. Once they had secured a majority in the chapter they could by mutual agreement elect one of their own number to be bishop. He could not receive canonical investiture of course, nor did he have spiritual powers, but he administered the diocese and disposed of the revenues. The installation of a Protestant administrator in a diocese was almost the same as secularisation, with the one important difference that a diocese which had been secularised by the bishop was completely lost to the church and became a hereditary lay principality, whereas an administrator could only maintain the diocese in his family if he persuaded the chapter to appoint one of his sons as coadjutor. As might be expected, the Church protested against the election of administrators, seeing it as a violation of the spirit, if not the letter, of the Peace of Augsburg. The emperor refused them the right to sit in or be represented at the diet, but he did not dare to act against them. So it was that at the beginning of the seventeenth century Saxon princes were administrators at Merseburg, Meissen and Naumburg, three dioceses bordering the duchy of Saxony; princes from Brandenburg were installed at Havelberg and Lebus; administrators controlled the archdioceses or dioceses of Magdeburg, Bremen, Lübeck, Halberstadt and Schwerin in the Lower Saxon circle, and Osnabrück, Minden and Verden in the Westphalian circle; and we could name many others.

The Protestant princes were all the more encouraged to invade the dioceses by the fact that they were unwittingly aided by the example of the most Catholic princely houses. The Wittelsbachs and Habsburgs acted just like the Wettins of Saxony or the Hohenzollerns of Brandenburg when they endeavoured to set up their younger sons without worrying overmuch about their vocation. When Tilly's troops made their way into Westphalia, Maximilian of Bavaria passed over the Danish coadjutor and had, not one of his sons, but the Cardinal of Hohenzollern, brother of the president of his Privy Council, elected bishop of Osnabrück. As for the emperor, he had already obtained the dioceses of Passau and Strassburg for his second son, Leopold William, for whom he also coveted Halberstadt and Madgeburg. In this way the Protestant princes of Germany, who were endeavouring to maintain and increase their gains, were rivalled in this struggle for the dioceses by the emperor and his Catholic allies, who thus found a convenient means to serve the interests of both the Church and their own dynasties at the same time.

It should be added that Danish policy in the northern circles of the Holy Roman Empire was not only a religious policy but also, perhaps even to the same extent, a commercial policy. Denmark's wealth at this time was founded on the fact that she held the straits, in particular the Sound, which no boat could pass without paying a heavy toll to the Elsinore customs. She thus controlled all the Baltic trade, which meant not only the wood and grain leaving Poland and Prussia but also the foodstuffs and manufactured goods which northern and eastern Germany imported from western Europe. In the same way, through Bremen and Verden, the king of Denmark reckoned to control trade along the Weser and the Elbe, and thereby almost the entire food supply of the greater part of the German plain, since at that time the seaways and rivers were the only available trading routes. But there is little information about Danish economic policy because the defeat of Denmark did not allow it time to develop.

Furthermore the boundaries between religious policy and commercial policy are not very well defined. When the princes sought to take over the dioceses, it was not with any religious object in view but with the purely temporal goal of increasing their power. When the king of Denmark extended his control of the North Sea and Baltic trade, it was not because he hoped to develop Denmark's trading activity, which in any event could be no more than mediocre, but because, by exploiting the trade of others, he increased his revenues and hence his power. If the part played by economic interests continued to grow in this many-sided war, the same cannot be said for religious interests. On the contrary, they were increasingly subordinated to political interests. As the great German historian Brandi noted, the Counter Reformation itself no longer worked for the restoration of the Roman faith, but rather for the profit of the great Catholic families of the Empire, the Habsburgs or the Wittelsbachs, who dreamed of dispossessing the great Protestant families of their secularised properties and of the dioceses which their younger sons administered.

The other new element which gradually developed at this time and which was soon to change the German war into a European war was the policy of Philip IV's great minister, Olivares.

In Philip III's time a long financial crisis had imposed a policy of retrenchment in foreign affairs, which, at least for the time being, ran counter to the imperial policy which had ruined Philip II's Spain. Moreover, this policy of retrenchment was well-suited to the peace-loving character of Philip III's favourite, the duke of Lerma, but it only lasted as long as he was in favour. The return to an active foreign policy—which included, as in the past, a close understanding with the Habsburgs of Austria—was indeed being prepared for some years before Lerma's disgrace, not at the wishes of the Spanish government which the favourite directed as he pleased, but through the personal initiative of some of its representatives abroad who did not wish to break with the tradition of the preceeding reign. As we have seen, the first initiative had been taken back in 1617 by Oñate, the Spanish ambassador to the court of Austria, who concluded the secret agreement of Graz with Matthias's probable successor, Ferdinand of Styria. This had thus paved the way for renewing the Spanish policy of a close alignment of the two branches of the Habsburgs once Ferdinand had inherited the thrones of Bohemia and Hungary and attained the Empire. In 1619 Spanish influence worked for Ferdinand at Frankfurt. In 1620, after the Palatine's election at Prague, Spanish money helped to make possible the Bohemian campaign and the victory of the White Mountain. Again, it had been Oñate who pressed Ferdinand to take decisions which prolonged and extended the scope of the war, namely the banishment from the Empire of the elector Palatine and the transfer of the title of elector to Maximilian of Bavaria. In that very same year, 1620, a new move by the governor of Milan committed Spanish policy to a possible conflict with France: he took advantage of a rising of the Catholics of the Valtelline, who were subjects of the Grisons, to occupy the valley and the Alpine passes, while a Habsburg, the archduke of Innsbruck, seized the Engadine on the other slope of the Alps. Henceforward, if war broke out, the Spanish troops of the duchy of Milan and the Austrian troops of the Tyrol could combine operations by making use of the Maloïa, the Engadine and the Stelvio. Finally, after Philip IV's accession, the government in Madrid revived its imperial policy and committed Spain's fortunes to the triumph of the emperor and Catholicism in the Empire.

In 1621 Philip IV succeeded his father Philip III. He was fairly intelligent, a patron of arts and a lover of pleasure, but he suffered from poor health, as we can see from the fine, pitilessly honest, portraits of him that Velasquez has left us. He did not change his predecessor's system of government in any way. He attended the Council, took an interest in most of its business and made decisions, but in accordance with established custom he really left everything in the hands of a 'privado', a favourite who enjoyed his full confidence and who met with no resistance in the Councils. From the beginning of the new reign, the favourite was Don Gaspar de Guzmán, Count of Olivares and Duke of Sanlúcar, whom we usually call the Count-Duke. He was a minister of a quite different stamp from Lerma. By nature strong, energetic and untiring, he was also sustained by pride and limitless ambition. He might lose his way momentarily, through vanity or some fanciful notion, but his diplomatic skill rarely failed. He adopted Philip II's policy, namely to encourage the Catholic cause without letting religious zeal override the interests of state, and to maintain Spain's power at the level to which Philip II had raised it. It was a policy which soon led him into violent opposition to his successful rival, Cardinal de Richelieu, when the latter tried to free Europe of Spanish domination and to replace it with that of his master, the king of France. Neither in 1621, nor even in 1624, which was the year that Richelieu entered the Council, had this point yet been reached, but almost from the moment of Philip IV's accession, Olivares's policy involved Spain in a succession of wars which were interrupted only to be resumed on an even larger scale. The Spanish monarchy could not disentangle itself from these until, ruined and defeated, it made peace in the Treaty of the Pyrenees. For the time being, however, we need only consider Olivares's policy in relation to the evolution of the German war.

His principal concern during his first years of office was neither to assist the emperor to establish his authority within the Empire nor to eradicate heresy there. The most important event which concerned Spain at that time was the end of the twelve-year truce made with the Dutch Republic on 9th April 1609, and the resumption of hostilities in Flanders and Brabant. A few months later, in July 1621, Archduke Albert died. With his death the Netherlands became once more a group of Spanish provinces: the Infanta Isabella Clara Eugenia was merely the regent for the king of Spain with strict orders to remain on good terms with the commander-in-chief of the Spanish troops, Spinola, who had complete control over the conduct of the war. Religious motives were not involved, not even superficially. Olivares intended to renew Spain's prestige in Europe, and to do that he had first to break the resistance of the insurgent United Provinces. He did not however cease to take an interest in the German war; quite the reverse, in fact. He wanted to make it last and to sustain it, especially in the region of the Rhineland. It had already allowed his king to install Spanish garrisons along the left bank of the Rhine, to the north of Alsace, and in the Palatinate which was only separated from Luxemburg by the electorate of Trier. It might also perhaps allow him to occupy further south a few fortified towns in Alsace and to ensure free passage for his troops between Franche-Comté and the Low Countries.

This was almost entirely a Spanish matter, but its success was bound up with that of Austria. The emperor and the king of Spain had equal need of each other. If the emperor's successes within the Empire could not fail to alarm first the Calvinists and then the Lutherans, and then to unite against him all the forces of the Reformation, equally the victories of Spain against the Dutch and her penetration of Germany would necessarily provoke active intervention by the Empire's neighbours—first by Denmark and Sweden and then, soon after, by France. From this point, the German crisis became part of a European crisis from which the political and religious constitution of modern Europe was gradually to emerge.

CHAPTER IV

WALLENSTEIN

In all the confused complexity of the Thirty Years War the period from 1623 to about 1626 is if anything the most confusing, and it would be a waste of time to describe it in detail. It is enough to reveal something of its utter complexity by a brief indication of the national interests and diplomatic intrigues which became enmeshed in the German war at this time.

What was the German situation in fact, what had been achieved by the events of the previous years, and how did it appear in 1623 to the two main protagonists, on the one hand the emperor and on the other the imperial princes, in particular the Protestants?

The emperor had enjoyed a triumphant success far greater than anyone could have expected before the Battle of the White Mountain, though no more than Ferdinand, with his simple unquestioning faith in divine assistance still intact, had anticipated. He had expelled the usurper from Prague, recalled the Jesuits, revoked the Letter of Majesty, and re-established Catholicism throughout the whole of Bohemia and Moravia. Elsewhere, he had driven the sole Calvinist elector from the electoral college, thereby reducing the Protestant vote to two against five; he had sequestered both the upper Palatinate, which had become Bavarian, and the lower Palatinate, which was occupied by Bavarian and Spanish troops; he had forced the Evangelical Union into virtual dissolution, and had pursued and defeated as far afield as the Westphalian and Lower Saxon circles all those who had defended the Palatine's cause or shown it sympathy. By this victory on two fronts he had raised imperial authority to a degree of power and prestige which it had not known since Charles V's abdication.

None the less there was no escape for Ferdinand, either from the consequences of his triumph, or from those of the alliances which alone had made it possible for him. Victory had its obligations. He had to complete the restoration of Catholicism in Bohemia by following up the expulsion of the Brethren by that of the Lutherans themselves, despite the fact that this would certainly alienate the elector of Saxony and that he risked uniting the entire Evangelical Body, both Lutherans and Calvinists, against him. Throughout the Empire too, he had to serve the Counter Reformation, the Jesuits who had moulded his mind and who surrounded him, and a new confessor—a Jesuit, of course— Father Lamormain, who wasted no time in making himself the absolute master of Ferdinand's will and conscience. The point was that in central and northern Germany the Catholic Restoration had hardly begun. The monasteries, charitable institutions, and all manner of Catholic foundations which had been secularised by the Protestant princes within the territorial framework of their states—on the authority of an interpretation of the Peace of Augsburg which the Catholics and the Church did not recognise—had yet to be recovered piecemeal by the emperor. He had to exclude the canons suspected of Protestantism from the cathedral chapters and put bishops in the place of the Protest-ant administrators in those dioceses which had admitted them. In this, his dynastic interests often coincided with those of the Roman Church. We can see the enormity of the task which he had to accomplish, and its dangers.

Then again, Ferdinand, an emperor without an army, could not forget that he would not have been able to win his double victory had he not had at his disposal the League's army, thanks to the alliance with Maximilian, and Spanish money and troops, thanks to the tacit under-standing which had assured him of the help of his cousin, the king of Spain. This was where his difficulties and the clash of interests began. He had kept his word to Maximilian by conferring on him the title of elector, without the authorisation of a diet nor even a unanimous vote in the electoral college, but the transfer had made him many enemies. Neither Brandenburg nor Saxony, the two Protestant electors, had attended Maximilian's investiture, nor did they recognize his new title. The emperor had to stand by him, although he knew that the presence of both Spanish and Bavarian garrisons on either side of the Rhine in the Lower Palatinate, where the Bavarians held Heidelberg and Mannheim, created conflicting claims between Spain and Bavaria which it would not be easy to settle. He was equally aware that Maxi-milian's entry to the electoral college had if anything strengthened the age-old ambitions of the house of Wittelsbach, which was one of the oldest of the German princely houses and which thought that it had more claim to the Empire than the young house of Habsburg. The Bavarian alliance, which was indispensable to the emperor if he was to win the day against the Protestants, remained an uneasy alliance. Even more indispensable was the Spanish alliance. Since neither Lamormain nor the other Jesuits who surrounded him had bothered to warn him, he perhaps did not realise that Spain had intervened in the German war solely for her own ends and that, far from being a useful ally, Olivares was in fact making use of him. It was therefore inevitable that Spain's machinations and her influence at the court of Vienna should arouse suspicion among the German princes, even the Catholics, which would prolong and extend the war.

If the imperial victory was so heavily mortgaged, the opposition's defeat was perhaps not so complete or final as those at Vienna seemed to believe. After a stay in Brandenburg, the king and queen of Bohemia (for they had not given up their title), had settled at the Hague, the centre of resistance to the ambitions of the Habsburgs of Spain and Austria. They held a brilliant and frivolous court there and at times forgot the bitter disappointment of their winter monarchy, but they did not neglect their interests. Elizabeth, charming and well-read, was surrounded by a circle of admirers whose ardour she kept alive. One of them was Christian of Brunswick, who was to fight on her behalf right to the end. Her unshakable resolution forced itself upon her husband, who was as frivolous as ever. At the same time Maurice of Nassau, the Statholder of Holland, tried to arouse his enthusiasm for war, while by contrast Carleton, the English ambassador, constantly exhorted him to make peace. At all events, Frederick continued to correspond with Bethlen and Mansfeld. He took a hand in all the negotiations and all the plots and hoped that the prolongation of the war would one day offer him the chance of revenge. The question of the Palatinate was not settled: it remained a source of diplomatic concern, not only at Vienna and Madrid, but also at London, the Hague, Rome and the court of France.

Most of the German princes were either worried or dissatisfied, especially, of course, those who had suffered directly from the emperor's victories—such men as the Landgrave Maurice of Hesse-Cassel and the Margrave Frederick of Baden, who had been deprived of part of their estates for the benefit of catholic cousins. But there were many others, even the elector of Saxony, Ferdinand's ally, who felt their independence threatened or feared that the progress of the Counter Reformation might call into question the whole of Germany's religious constitution. They wondered what might happen if the emperor felt strong enough to summon a diet, as the Pope and the Jesuits urged him to do, and if he obtained a renewal of the Peace of Augsburg, amended in accordance with Catholic opinion. What would become of the secularised lands which for more than half a century had formed the foundations of the princes' territorial power? In a few days they risked losing all they had gained by the success of the Reformation. Moreover, what would become of the liberties by which they set such store? The medieval notion of a united Christendom, subject to the dual authorities of both pope and emperor, was now being challenged within Germany itself, within the very framework of the Holy Roman Empire, by the modern concept of national independence which allowed the prince to control the church and direct its policy as he wished. It was feared that a counter-offensive in the name of the old dream of unity might once again succeed, even though the Empire was surrounded by states in which the modern concept of national sovereignty had finally prevailed. And so it was that the German war gradually assumed a wider meaning, and neighbouring kingdoms could no longer stand aloof.

In fact hardly any had ever remained completely aloof, but domestic affairs or commitments abroad had not yet allowed many of them to commit themselves too fully. This was the case with England. James I was the Palatine's father-in-law and had known his plans right from the start. Though he had not approved them, he had let fate take its own course. However, it was natural that he should sympathise with his daughter and son-in-law in their difficulties and that he should not recognise the transfer of the hereditary possessions of the Palatine house to Bavaria or to Spain. He demanded their restitution, but he hoped to gain it by negotiation and on this point he seemed to be in agreement with Philip IV who, for a time, appeared to think that the Palatine could be re-instated in the lower Palatinate as long as he consented to serve Spanish policy. This absurd notion was quickly dashed by Frederick V's refusal, but yet another idle fancy forced James I to deal tactfully with Madrid. His favourite, the duke of Buckingham, had got it into his head that Charles, the Prince of Wales, should marry the Infanta. He even had no hesitation in undertaking a romantic voyage to Madrid with his young master, but the Spanish court avoided the planned engagement and the question of the Palatinate remained in abeyance. On 1st May 1623, without consulting his son-in-law, James went so far as to sign in his name a fifteen month truce with the Infanta Isabella, who had been authorised by the emperor to act on his behalf; during this period the Palatine was forbidden to levy troops or ally with those who might re-open hostilities. A disheartened Frederick V finally ratified the armistice in August.

James I's own character, the frivolity and inconsistency of his favourite Buckingham (who was also the favourite of his son, Charles) and the internal difficulties which Charles, like James, immediately encountered in his relations with the House of Commons, all combined to prevent any effective action in the Empire, and were to do so increasingly. By contrast, Sweden's intervention could have been predicted from 1623 onwards, although it did not happen until some years later.

In 1623, Sweden had a twenty-nine-year-old king who had taken over the government of the realm in 1611, at the age of seventeen, and had been forced, almost immediately, to conduct three wars at once, against Denmark, Poland and Russia. In these circumstances he had shown his gift for leadership and, even more, his personal courage. He had conquered Ingria at the head of the Gulf of Finland, from the Russians. Then from the Poles he had conquered Livonia with the port of Riga, whose possession allowed him at will to open or close the Russian market to trade with the Hanse. This triple war, punctuated by truces, had not prevented him from firmly establishing his authority in his realm. He was very popular, particularly among the peasants who were the country's backbone. He had organised an army and created a fleet, and these later enabled him to transform Sweden, a small and impoverished country, into a great and formidable power. From 1623 he could put twelve regiments into the field, each of twelve hundred men. It was a little army of 14,000 men recruited from the Swedish peasantry and therefore exceptionally loyal. The financial condition of the realm allowed him to add to it about four regiments of mercenaries and a few thousand horse. His war fleet too, with its 32 ships, was a force to be reckoned with. Furthermore, his successes in Russia and Poland had given him a self-confidence which ensured both clarity and speed of decision. Early on he realised that the great threat to Sweden was the triumph of Catholicism in northern Germany. If the emperor managed to reduce the Lower Saxon circle to obedience, it would not be long before he sent the troops of the Catholic League right to the Baltic shores, and from there he could dispose of the Hanseatic towns. No doubt the threat seemed remote to the young power of Sweden, but Gustavus Adolphus was determined not to wait until it was imminent before he countered it. He fully intended, he said, to oppose it in time, even if it was ten or twenty years before it became urgent.

So while he fought Poland, Gustavus Adolphus kept a close eye on the development of the German war. He considered that the two wars were in fact one and that his Polish conquest would provide him with a base for operations against the house of Austria when the time was ripe. At Stockholm in 1624 he received an English envoy representing both the king of England and the Palatine, Frederick V, and proposed to invade Silesia via Poland and then to march on Vienna. But such a plan would have led straight to general war. It could not please the king of England, nor the electors of Brandenburg and Saxony, whose states bordered Silesia to the west and whose friendly neutrality, at the very least, would have been necessary. Then Gustavus Adolphus learnt that his rival, the king of Denmark, was on the point of reaching an agreement with James I. He dropped the negotiations and reopened hostilities in Poland. His intervention in the German war was postponed.

France's intervention was delayed even longer. The results of the duc d'Angoulême's embassy and the treaty of Ulm differed so much from the ambassador's forecast that they left Puysieulx disappointed and worried. Then, in the years which followed, the internal state of the realm was aggravated by the Queen Mother's two insurrections. The situation remained difficult even after Marie de Médici's reconciliation with her son; it still was when Richelieu entered the Council in April 1624. Richelieu was determined that the intrigues of the *dévots* who sought a Catholic front should not distract him from his concern over Olivares's policies. The lampoonists in his pay continually warned the king of the urgency of the Spanish peril: the kingdom was surrounded to the south and the east by the king of Spain's possessions; at Dôle, Franche-Comté nearly reached the Saône; at Arras, Artois was only a few leagues from the valley and the peat bogs of the Somme, the only natural barrier that protected Paris on that side. In addition they showed armies on the march along the frontiers, from the duchy of Milan to Franche-Comté, from Franche-Comté to the Netherlands. The military highway which they followed from Milan to Brussels was interrupted only in the middle by Alsace and the Rhenish Palatinate, and Spinola had now occupied the Palatinate, and the close alliance between the two branches of the house of Habsburg allowed the Spaniards to cross Alsace on their way from Franche-Comté to the Palatinate. With every day Richelieu was gaining his master's confidence and encouraging his ambition; neither of them could have wanted a total victory by the Emperor in Germany. It would indeed have been a triumph for the Church, but it would also have represented such an increase in power for the two Habsburg families that they could well revive the imperial dream of Charles V. However, the most urgent task, and in any case the only one which Louis XIII could undertake at that time, was 'to halt the progress of Spain'. And to achieve this, Richelieu, who had to keep a wary eye at home on both the *dévots* and the Protestants, could only continue the work begun in Italy by his predecessors, Puysieulx, Luynes and La Vieuville. At first he limited himself to freeing the Valtelline from Spanish control, a task which he judged to be of the utmost importance since it linked the duchy of Milan to the Tyrol. For some time he succeeded.

He also tried (and in doing so, he was preparing the ground for some future intervention) to maintain good relations with the Protestant powers, England and the United Provinces, as well as with the protestant princes of Germany. When he entered the Ministry, he found that negotiations had already been started with the object of marrying the king's sister, Henrietta of France, to Charles of England, who shortly became King Charles I. He pursued them, refusing to be discouraged by obstacles, and the marriage was concluded. He could not foresee that, far from bringing the two courts closer together, this ill-assorted union—for the couple had different religions—would only alienate them. He was more fortunate with the States-General of the United Provinces to whom the French gave subsidies under the Treaty of Compiègne in order to help them continue the war against Spain.

Richelieu's relations with the protestant princes of Germany during those troubled years are more difficult to follow, but they are even more important to us because they help us to understand the Minister's intentions, which were still secret, and the way in which he understood the German question. They are not easy to follow because, more often than not, negotiations in Germany were conducted not by Richelieu, but by his intimate adviser, Father Joseph.

The 'grey eminence', who was well versed in German affairs, made ample use of his fellow Capuchin monks. Their names—Father Hyacinth, Father Alexander, and many others—crop up time and again in the diplomatic correspondence of the time which we find in all the minor German courts, as well as at Munich and Vienna, but their tireless activity has left very few traces in the official archives. Fortunately there were, here and there, other secret envoys about whom we are better informed. The canon Fancan was such a one: at this time he was completely devoted to Richelieu, though his career ended a little later as the result of a somewhat mysterious disgrace. In the autumn of 1624, he was sent secretly to the court of Bavaria and the instructions which he received on setting out have been preserved for us. Another was Marescot who, during the summer of the same year, travelled to Saxony and Brandenburg. Another, and the most important, was the Seigneur de Marcheville who, in September 1626, was entrusted with a most important mission to Munich and whose instructions are particularly significant.

As early as the autumn of 1624 we find in Fancan's instructions a clearly stated policy with regard to the Empire which was hardly to change at all and which it is therefore useful to define at the outset. The object was to ensure that the duke of Bavaria and the League 'should not give any assistance, direct or indirect, to Spanish enterprises in Germany.' The bait which Fancan was to use in Munich was the promise that the king of France would not only help Maximilian to 'come well out of the Palatinate affair', but would also strive 'to raise his person and his family to the highest honours of the Empire'. This was a clear allusion to the traditional ambitions of the Wittelsbachs. On the other hand, anticipating that Maximilian might not dare break with both the emperor and Spain, Richelieu already gave notice of France's future policy, although, as Maximilian well knew, Louis XIII was not yet in a position to carry it out. It was that 'if Bavaria helped Spain'—and these are the exact words of the instructions—the king of France 'would find himself obliged, for reasons of state, although against his will, to join forces with the English to recover the Palatinate; and should that happen, it was to be believed and feared that, under the shelter and protection of these two great kings, the Protestant princes, the free cities and the Hanseatic towns of Germany, would all take courage once more and would not fear to hurl themselves into the war to free themselves of the apprehensions caused by Spanish interference and Spanish arms within the Empire.'

These first advances were fairly coldly received at Munich and elsewhere. An anonymous memorandum preserved among Richelieu's papers and dated September 1625, gives the reasons. First, there was the distrust that the embassy of 1620 had left in Germany among the Protestant princes. Also, it was written in the Memorandum, 'our allies, seeing us discomfited by a civil war and very fully committed in the affairs of Italy, cannot imagine that we are so very ready to support them or that we can fulfil what we promise them.' But Richelieu was not discouraged. During the year 1626—the year of the intrigues when he was beset by so many serious preoccupations and when his very life was threatened—he did not neglect the affairs of Germany. Father Hyacinth went to Munich and drew up the articles of a treaty there. In June, the duke of Bavaria asked that Father Alexander should be sent to him secretly to put the finishing touches to the articles prepared by Father Hyacinth. In September, Richelieu dispatched to Munich not the Capuchin, but the Seigneur de Marcheville who was in Germany at the time, and negotiations were resumed. They only interest us in so far as they inform us of Louis XIII's intentions. At the time he was engaged in talks about the Palatinate, both with Charles I of England, and with Christian IV, to whom he granted a few subsidies. It was on the cards that a league might be formed between England, France, the United Provinces and Denmark to force the emperor and the king of Spain to restore the lower Palatinate to Frederick, but it seems that Louis XIII and Richelieu would have preferred to win over Maximilian and prepare an equitable peace through his intervention. Marcheville had to emphasize to the duke of Bavaria the dangers which the increased power of the house of Austria presented to the independence of the German princes. He was to try to convince him to 'consider deliberately and with all due speed how he may protect himself and the other princes of the Empire from the perils which beset them'. And, in case talks seemed in danger of breaking down, the king went so far as to allow Marcheville to propose the signing of a secret agreement to Maximilian, which was tantamount to a direct intervention in the Empire. 'Should it fall out', the article ran, 'that the king of England did not wish to agree to such conditions of peace as the King proposes, his Majesty will join with the Catholic League of Germany to help it preserve the Palatinate until such time as the Palatine and the English have accepted and executed the treaty. . . . But if the emperor and Spain refuse the aforementioned compromise the said League will promise to join with the king to execute it just as it has been agreed.' And the instruction bears at the bottom, in Louis XIII's hand: 'The above is my purpose. Louis.'

It is clear that, at the end of the year 1626, French diplomacy was neither inactive nor diffident. In order to restore peace in the Empire before the total victory of the emperor, Louis XIII himself proposed the conditions of an agreement and showed that he was ready to impose them. We can also see Richelieu's views towards the German war taking shape. He did not consider it a war of religion. It was a political war in which the main aim of the princes had to be to maintain the independence which they had gradually won, thanks to the Reformation. In Richelieu's opinion the Catholic princes of Germany had the same interests as the Protestants and, by siding with the emperor merely because they were Catholics, they were the victims of a deception. He also understood very clearly, that the maintenance of a strong Protestant party in the Empire, by presenting an obstacle to the emperor's ambitions, provided a surety for French interests, and that if he helped the Roman Church to triumph, he would be sacrificing the interests of the realm. That was the essence of his policy and he did not change it.

But Marcheville did not achieve the desired result, and Richelieu, since he could not find the support he needed in Germany, decided to become temporarily reconciled with the *dévots* in order to put an end to the perpetual threat of a Huguenot rising which was hampering foreign policy. France was therefore unable to take a more active part in Germany's affairs for more than two years, until La Rochelle had fallen.

While the kings of England, Sweden and France made do with more or less secret talks which came to nothing, the king of Spain on one side, and the king of Denmark on the other, found themselves more and more deeply involved in the German war. And it goes without saying that the great difference in size of their respective armies increased the considerable advantage which the emperor and the League already enjoyed.

This does not imply that Spain was completely committed. Olivares's prime intention was still to conquer the Dutch and reduce them to submission. The army of the States-General, however, was at that time the finest in Europe and its commander-in-chief, Maurice of Nassau, was one of the greatest military leaders. Consequently the capture of Breda on 5th June 1625, which followed closely on Maurice's death, was considered to be a tremendous Spanish success and was immortalised in the famous picture by Velásquez. It remains Spinola's chief claim to fame. But Maurice's successor as Statholder and commander-in-chief, his half brother Frederick Henry, was if anything his superior, and even the fall of Breda did not have any decisive result. Olivares then realised that the United Provinces' safeguard was the Dutch war fleet and its mastery of northern waters. It was there that he had to strike if he was to win. Philip IV's minister conceived a vast plan to establish Spanish command of the North Sea and the Baltic and to expel Dutch vessels. Success was possible, but only on the condition that the Spanish squadrons could find the naval bases, supply ports and shelter which they needed on the German shores of the two seas. These could be found if the emperor, with the help of the king of Spain, obtained possession of the Westphalian and Lower Saxon circles from the League and its leader Maximilian. As a result, Spain was compelled to extend its range of activities in the Empire.

The role played by Denmark was far more modest and remained entirely within the framework of the German war. Christian IV sought to preserve or to recover the bishoprics of lower Saxony and neighbouring Westphalia, and at times he thought that he had secured them for his son, but they always eluded him. For him the restoration of the Palatinate was merely an excuse. On the other hand, he was driven by a somewhat disordered ambition which was out of all proportion to his strength, and he was distracted by the antagonism between the two Scandanavian kingdoms, Denmark and Sweden, which was aggravated by their rival frontier claims, for at all costs he did not want Gustavus Adolphus to appear in Germany. Furthermore, he could not undertake a campaign without subsidies. In the end the king of England gave him a little money with which to levy a few troops, but the Lower Saxon circle hesitated to support him and was only willing to take up arms in its own defence. When Christian IV crossed the Elbe, he did so with only 10,000 men. As Tilly's forces barely exceeded this, the two adversaries took care not to march against each other. Tilly claimed that his only aim was to prevent the Lower Saxon circle from levying troops, which he declared to be illegal because it had not been authorised by the emperor. Christian affirmed that his only object was to prevent Tilly's army taking up its winter quarters in the territory of the circle, which had not given its consent. The only result of these two abortive undertakings was that the north German plain, as far as the Elbe, was pitilessly ravaged by each side in turn.

One event of the utmost importance occurred during these dark and barren years of the German war. This was the creation of an Imperial Army by Wallenstein.

Albert of Valdštejn, or Wallenstein (the German form of his name is normally used), was born in Bohemia in 1583 of a noble family of modest means. His father was a Lutheran and he was brought up in that faith, but then became a Catholic convert. On his return to Vienna after travelling in Italy, he attached himself to Ferdinand who, at the time, was duke of Styria. He was ambitious. A rich widow, whom he married and who soon died, left him extensive landed property which he managed well, and for some time he led the life of a great landowner. Then he entered Ferdinand's service during the duke of Styria's war against Venice. In 1618, at the beginning of the war in Bohemia, at the age of thirty-five, he had raised and was commanding a regiment in Moravia, and, as we have seen, he took the king's side when Moravia fell in with the rebels. He tried to carry his soldiers with him, but he had to go to Vienna almost alone. From that moment his fortune prospered.

Wallenstein distinguished himself above all as a recruiter and leader of men, but he was not without other talents. During the years which followed Bohemia's surrender he acquired by successful speculation an immense fortune, both in property and in funds, and he knew how to put this to good use to further his insatiable ambition. First he speculated in money. For some time a monetary crisis had been rife in the Empire; the causes are fairly complicated and are not of great importance here.[1] In any event, well before the Bohemian revolt, agricultural and industrial activity in Bohemia and its neighbouring regions had been paralysed by a shortage of money; the circulation of provisions had become almost impossible because the producers insisted on being paid in good currency which the merchants could not obtain, and the cost of living rose to such an extent that it caused great suffering among the populations both of the towns and of the country-side. The emperor tried to increase the flow of coin by minting currency of a much lower value than that which was no longer in circulation, and a number of mints were set up. In January 1622, the Governor Liechtenstein granted a monopoly for the purchase of fine silver and the manufacture of coins for Bohemia to a company of fourteen merchants, and among those who had an interest in the business, though this was well concealed, were Liechtenstein himself and Colonel Wallenstein. We cannot know of the company's activities in detail, but what is certain is that those who were in it or who had an interest in its operations made considerable profits; but its administration gave rise to so many complaints that in January 1623 the emperor refused to renew its privilege, halted the minting of devalued coins, and even had to repurchase some at their real value.

During the same period Wallenstein indulged in other, more fruit-ful, speculations in confiscated land. He purchased at a low price—and with the devalued currency which the company of fourteen

[1] A brief but exact summary of the monetary crisis in 1621 and 1622 may be found in Wertheim: *Christian von Braunschweig*, vol. I, p. 57 et seq.

merchants had minted—the estates of fugitive Bohemian nobles. Some
he resold at enormous profit; others he retained for himself. He col-
lected sixty-six in all, most of them situated in the same province in
north-eastern Bohemia, including the town of Gitschin where he built
himself a palace. He made them as productive as possible, extending
and improving the land under cultivation, setting up new industries
in the lands, and attracting specialised workmen to them. His fortune
grew with every passing year. Back in 1619 he had been able to lend
the emperor 40,000 florins; in 1620 he lent him 160,000; in 1621,
195,000; in 1622, 527,000; in 1623, 700,000.[1] He was then as rich in
land as Liechtenstein and had greater funds at his disposal. As he also
had a hold on the emperor, being one of his largest creditors, he had
little difficulty in obtaining leave to create a duchy out of most of
his properties and to bear the title of duke of Friedland. Then in 1623
he was made a prince of the Empire. In June of the same year, he
married the daughter of the Count von Harrach, one of the highest
officials at the Viennese court and one of Ferdinand's favourites.

It was also in 1623 that, for the first time, Wallenstein proposed to
raise troops at his own expense and to put them at the emperor's
disposal, on the condition that he should command them. At first
Ferdinand refused, doubtless fearing that Wallenstein would become
too powerful. During the years which followed, however, he increasingly felt the need for his own army in order to make himself
independent of the Catholic League whose first loyalty was to its
leader, Maximilian of Bavaria. In 1625, at the time when there was fear
that England, the United Provinces and Denmark might form a coalition against the house of Austria, Wallenstein renewed his offer, which
was accepted. The emperor merely reduced the number of men who
were to form the new army from 50,000 to 20,000. The duke of Friedland was to command them and they were to be concentrated as quickly
as possible about Eger (Cheb), in the north-west corner of Bohemia.

The army which Wallenstein recruited and which fought under
his orders during the years which followed was essentially no different
from the other German armies of the time, or at least it only differed in
the exceptional powers which Wallenstein exercised and in the highly
personal way in which he applied conventional methods of recruitment
and command. At that period the formation of an army always went

[1] These figures are taken from M. Ritter: *Deutsche Geschichte im Zeitalter der
Gegenreformation und des dreissigjährigen Krieges*, vol. III. I have been unable to
verify them, but on the whole Ritter is reliable.

hand in hand with financial speculation which, according to the circumstances, could be either ruinous or rewarding. The recruiting agent and the sovereign who commissioned him signed a contract known as a capitulation. The one drawn up between the emperor and Wallenstein gave him command of the twenty thousand men whom he was to recruit (this was usual), together with the exceptional right to direct operations as he judged best. He had to bear the costs of recruitment and the emperor the cost of the pay, but if the emperor could not meet this (and this was the case from the very beginning), Wallenstein would have to make do as best he could. Once the capitulation was signed, the commander-in-chief received a *patent* which listed the conditions imposed upon him, and a copy, known as the *counterpart*, was retained by the sovereign. This was the case with Wallenstein as with all the colonels who signed a capitulation. Immediately afterwards recruitment began with the commander making payments in advance. The commander, however, and Wallenstein was no exception, transferred much of the burden of these payments to the colonels responsible for recruiting their regiments, and the colonels in their turn—for Wallenstein demanded payment in advance—made the captains who were responsible for recruiting and equipping a company, share the expenses with them. Thus all the officers, from the captains up to the commander, formed a sort of syndicate in which every member shared the profits or losses and, in the conduct of their military operations, necessarily took into account the financial risks they were running. Their solidarity was assured, up to a certain point, by this community of risks, and their loyalty by the fact that Wallenstein paid them well. But the soldiers were treated quite differently. Their wages were reduced to the minimum and paid irregularly, which led to considerable discontent among the troops, who frequently deserted.

As for Wallenstein, he had recourse to numerous means of increasing his profits or reducing the risk of his making a loss. It is worth noting one of them, which reveals that, once he had become the head of the army, the duke of Friedland did not neglect his duchy nor forget how he had managed it. He was at pains to take from it (and it is hardly necessary to mention that he did not do it free of charge) some of the provisions, such as grain and fodder, that his troops needed. Weaving was among the industries which prospered on his estates, and this produced cloth for his uniforms. As duke of Friedland, therefore, Wallenstein also became a commissary.

We can quite easily envisage some of the consequences of all these practices. First, Wallenstein had to meet the large number of desertions by a process of almost continual recruitment, and this was made all the more necessary by the fact that the mercenaries were of poor quality (the good soldiers were put off by the low pay), and quantity had to substitute for quality. In fact Wallenstein hardly ever ceased recruiting and the disorders which accompanied recruitment are well known. Moreover, since Vienna always delayed the money needed for paying the troops, Wallenstein had to make do, either by allowing his soldiers to feed themselves at the inhabitants' expense, shutting his eyes to the abuses, or by levying contributions from the countryside. Both on the march and in quarters, the conduct of Wallenstein's troops spread terror wherever they went.

The conditions under which the army lived also influenced the conduct of military operations. For some time Wallenstein was too unsure of his troops to run the risk of committing them to battle. The disappointment which followed his first campaign was a direct result of this. Even a little later, when he had made his personal authority felt and had revealed himself to be every bit as good a leader as he was a recruiter, he still had to take into account the continual variations in his troop strength and the changing material conditions which by turns diminished or increased his army's effectiveness and the confidence which he could place in it. Doubtless this was the reason for a characteristic of Wallenstein's campaigns which it is hard to overlook: namely, the way in which long periods when military operations almost ceased, making Wallenstein appear as a hesitant leader, prudent to the point of fear, alternated with short periods of feverish activity and utter boldness during which he had his great successes.

For historians, Wallenstein's army has become the archetype of German armies during the Thirty Years War. Its advent not only provided Ferdinand with an instrument of power which he had hitherto lacked and which allowed him for some time to follow an independent policy; it also changed the character and the very rhythm of the war and, in so doing, it was a factor of considerable importance in transforming the German war into a European conflict.

When Wallenstein had finished concentrating his troops around Eger, the future of his undertaking still depended on the emperor's whim, and the capitulation which he had signed did not give him all the powers which he had been determined to obtain. But his power continued to grow during the years which followed.

It grew almost immediately because of the very cavalier way in which he treated his master. He was well aware that Ferdinand was the less able to do without him because he did not have the means to repay the large sums which had been lent to the imperial purse, though Wallenstein still had to justify his favour by indisputable military success. The year 1625 finished without his leaving his headquarters. Then, when at the end of the winter there were simultaneous offensives by the king of Denmark in the Weser valley, by Mansfeld in the diocese of Magdeburg, and by Christian of Brunswick in Hesse-Cassel, he prevented Mansfeld from carrying the bridgehead at Dessau (25th April 1626), but not from crossing the river and quartering his troops on the elector of Brandenburg's lands. It was Tilly who seized Minden on the Weser, and who forced the landgrave of Hesse-Cassel to make a complete surrender in July. In the meantime Christian of Brunswick-Halberstadt had died. Finally, the only big success of the campaign was a victory, once again by Tilly, over Christian IV at Lutter on 27th August.

All Wallenstein's enemies at the Viennese court, including the Spanish ambassador, united to persuade Ferdinand to take away his supreme command. They said that, without winning any decisive victories, Wallenstein's army had ruined the Empire and that its leader had ruined the army by his incompetence. To the jealousies and hatred which the duke of Friedland's rapid rise to fortune had necessarily aroused were added other more specific personal grievances, when it was learned in Vienna that he had quartered his troops in Bohemia and Moravia in regions where there were many imperial estates as well as others belonging to the most important Viennese nobles. Wallenstein would doubtless have succumbed to such a vigorous attack if he had not forestalled it by asking the emperor to discharge him. He was well aware that Ferdinand could not do so. The troops were waiting for considerable arrears of pay which the court was in no position to meet so that Wallenstein's dismissal would have been followed by the immediate disbandment of the imperial army. Ferdinand negotiated through one of Wallenstein's principal supporters and at a meeting held in November 1626 Wallenstein, far from being disgraced, obtained a new and more advantageous capitulation: he remained free to choose his winter quarters; he was allowed to carry out new levies and considerably increase his fighting force; and, finally, the 'contribution' or direct tax payed by Bohemia was to be allocated entirely for the maintenance of his army. This enabled him to plan his next campaign without any misgivings.

He was to conduct it with a larger fighting force and in conjunction with the League's army and the court of Spain, which had won him over to the idea of making a big effort to establish imperial garrisons in the Hanseatic ports and to create a war-fleet in the Baltic. In 1627, Wallenstein and Tilly marched separately towards the lower course of the Elbe where they joined forces. The Danish army, which could not resist the combined forces of the emperor and the League, dispersed into fortified towns. Without wasting time on a series of sieges, Wallenstein imposed heavy contributions on the two duchies of Mecklenburg, on the duchy of Holstein, on Schleswig, and on Jutland, where his troops deployed meeting little or no resistance. At the end of this rapid and victorious campaign there was no doubt that the king of Denmark would soon be forced to sue for peace. Thereafter, the emperor could not fail to acknowledge the debt he owed Wallenstein. During the course of the year he made him a gift of the duchy of Sagan in Silesia, and in view of the next campaign which was to realise the common ambition of both Spain and Austria along the north German coastline, he named him 'General of the Oceanic and Baltic Seas'. Finally, Wallenstein persuaded Ferdinand that, in order to carry out their plans successfully, he needed a solid base in the coastal regions which he had just conquered. As the dukes of Mecklenburg had taken the king of Denmark's side, Ferdinand dispossessed them, just as he had once dispossessed the Palatine, and, on his authority as emperor, independently of the diet and without consulting the electoral union, he gave Wallenstein the two duchies as securities for his debt. Then, by a secret pact which he quickly made public, he appointed him permanently duke of Mecklenburg. 1628 marked the height of the career of this great soldier of fortune. Wallenstein's arrogance, however, his complete lack of scruple, and his tactlessness towards the princes of the Empire, whether friend or foe, increased the number of those working for his downfall. More and more, the princes felt that he, and not the emperor, was the true master of the Empire. They had good reason to believe that Wallenstein's private plans would make peace impossible for a long time to come. Furthermore they felt that although his conduct of the war would lead to total victory, the restoration of the Catholic faith in the Empire and the ruin of the Protestant Churches, it would also mean the end of their liberties. It was not only the elector of Saxony who, in spite of his limited intelligence, began to think like this; a Catholic prince like Maximilian of Bavaria, who in truth was much more perspicacious than his Saxon colleague, John George, had reached the same conclusion. Maximilian soon became convinced that Wallenstein's prime aim was not to complete the Counter Reformation (he was not driven by any religious passion or Catholic zeal, and in fact placed more trust in his astrologers than in the Church) but to create, in the centre of Europe, a great Empire which would obey an absolute authority. And it was not yet clear what role he envisaged for himself in this Empire. It was only later that his intelligence foundered in his ailing body, but it seems certain that in 1628 he was already prey as much to fantasy as to conscious ambition.

It appears that his ambitions became increasingly clear as he was won over to Olivares's Spanish policy. In 1627 he still considered it impracticable, but the great success he had that year against the Danes, particularly the occupation of Mecklenburg and Holstein, doubtless made him change his mind. In actual fact the Hanseatic towns, especially Lübeck, the most important, were not prepared to compromise themselves on Spain's behalf to the extent of drawing upon themselves the active hostility of the States-General of the United Provinces and Denmark. They would not accept imperial garrisons and Wallenstein refrained from attacking them. The emperor also held back from the extreme policies urged on him by the Spanish court. Philip IV offered to subsidise the imperial treasury by contributing 200,000 thalers over two years to commission 24 ships, and 200,000 to maintain the League's troops, on condition that the League and the emperor should undertake to declare war on the States-General, and should only make peace when Spain did. This would have meant the emperor's policy taking second place to that of his cousin in Madrid. He refused. Besides he knew that if he accepted the League would not follow him. He agreed, however, to give Wallenstein the task of building a fleet, just as he had created an army, and, in place of Lübeck, to provide it with a base at Stralsund. Stralsund was in Pomerania, opposite the island of Rügen, and it had entered into talks with the king of Sweden to seek his aid in case of danger. For Wallenstein, the siege of Stralsund was the all-important military operation of 1628, but the town, which had received a Danish garrison, put up a stiff resistance. When a contingent of Swedish troops arrived, Wallenstein relinquished the command to one of his lieutenants, Arnim, who soon had to raise the siege (at the end of July 1628). For Wallenstein at any rate the Stralsund campaign had at least proved useful in winning the emperor's consent to his establishing himself in neighbouring Mecklenburg.

There can be no doubt that from this time onwards Wallenstein had private plans which escaped the notice of the Viennese court, but because of his successes and the strength of his army, which remained in the emperor's service, the latter was able to conduct a more independent policy towards the League than hitherto. On the other hand, since the new duke of Mecklenburg had become one of the princes of the Holy Roman Empire, Maximilian of Bavaria judged it necessary to take some precautions against him by not rejecting the French approaches, and even went so far as to encourage them. The victorious Catholic party therefore represented three policies: Wallenstein's, the emperor's, and the duke of Bavaria's. In waging war they all seemed to have the same end in view, and indeed this was true in part, yet their aims were not identical. I will leave aside the first—it remains a mystery and events were soon to prevent it becoming plain—but we must dwell for a moment on the other two.

Religion continued to play a leading part in imperial policy. Father Lamormain was still the director of Ferdinand II's conscience. The emperor remained the instrument of the Jesuits and the Counter Reformation, and in the next year, 1629, he tried to gain a victory, which at first seemed decisive, for the Roman Catholic Church. But it is more or less impossible to separate the religious and the political motives which then dictated his decisions, and it is likely that they were equally inseparable in his own mind. His dream of establishing absolute authority for his own advantage throughout the Empire could only be achieved by the triumph of Catholicism, and it seemed to him that Wallenstein's victories were making the early realisation of that dream possible. It is no less certain that as Ferdinand matured and grew bolder with success, political ambitions gradually took first place and this gave him a closer understanding with the king of Spain. He continued to ignore the susceptibilities of the princes and, despite the setback at Stralsund, did not abandon the attempt to establish the Habsburgs as a naval power in the Baltic. He had no hesitation in supporting Spanish operations in north Italy and he ignored the warnings of Wallenstein who was appalled at his forces being scattered in such a fashion. The emperor was no longer content with reconquering and reorganising Bohemia and breaking the Evangelical Union, nor with having become more powerful in Germany than Charles V had been. It seems that Ferdinand II was working for the hegemony of the house of Habsburg, and that not only the liberties of the German princes, but also the balance of power in Europe, was threatened by his imperial ambitions.

It was precisely this hegemony and the transformation of the Holy

Roman Empire into a unified monarchical state which Maximilian feared, as indeed did the king of France, although for quite different reasons. Maximilian was all the more attached to the old constitution of the Empire because he saw in it a guarantee of his own private interests, that is of his own influence in Germany and of his new title and the territorial acquisitions gained in the war against the Palatine. In fact, it was only in 1628 that his entry to the electoral college and the full possession of a part of the conquered lands were assured by a properly constituted act. On 22nd February, the emperor gave a written undertaking that the title, which at first had only been allowed to Maximilian as a personal title without prejudice to the future, should be handed on to his heirs. Moreover, the upper Palatinate, which Maximilian had been holding in the meantime merely as a security, was handed over to Bavaria. Only the question of the lower Palatinate remained unsolved because it involved a conflict of interests between Spain, who had garrisoned all the fortified towns on the left bank of the Rhine, and Bavaria, whose troops were installed on the right bank around Mannheim and Heidelberg. For that reason Maximilian, who already had little affection for the Spaniards, grew to hate them more and more. No doubt Spain was the protector of Catholicism, but it was also a model of a state in which the sovereign had absolute authority and it inspired the emperor to create a state of the same type in Germany for the Austrian branch of the house of Habsburg. And to a large extent, it was for the same sort of reasons that Maximilian feared and hated Wallenstein whose fortune was still in the ascendant and whose authoritarian ways seem to justify all his fears. 'Today,' Maximilian wrote to his brother, the elector of Cologne, 'it is not only the prosperity and the liberty of the whole Empire, and of all the estates of the Empire, which is at stake, but also the dignity and pre-rogatives of the electors.' He could not forgive Wallenstein for having robbed him of the political and military leadership of the Catholic party in Germany by creating the imperial army. He had little doubt that Wallenstein wanted to go much further. Had not the duke of Friedland said that the electors and princes were outdated, that an absolute sovereign was sufficient, and that the imperial title should be hereditary without any intervention from the electoral college? That at least was what they were saying throughout the Empire, and Maximilian believed that Wallenstein was plotting with the king of Spain to make the house of Habsburg into what was currently described as a 'universal monarchy'.

While he did not for a moment consider a rift with the emperor, we can easily understand how, in such a state of mind, Maximilian was nevertheless anxious to maintain good relations, or, as they said in those days, 'a good correspondence' with the king of France. In any case, there was no harm in sending the tireless Capuchin Fathers, Valerio Magni, Father Hyacinth and Father Alexander, backwards and forwards between Munich and Paris, sometimes at the bidding of Father Joseph, sometimes at that of the duke of Bavaria. They were on familiar ground and even drew up 'articles' which they carried from one court to another. And all this was done amid the utmost secrecy, without anyone being compromised. At the same time the new Pope, Urban VIII, who earnestly desired the restoration of peace in the Empire, was given some satisfaction by both sides. Until 1629 these secret talks did not lead to any concrete agreement. Nevertheless they constituted an element in the evolution of Bavarian policy and, as we shall soon see, of French policy too, and this cannot be overlooked. At the very least they showed that the policy of the duke of Bavaria, although he was the emperor's ally, was not identifiable with imperial policy, and this was a fact of the greatest importance.

Towards the end of 1628 the situation can be broadly defined in the following terms: the Catholic powers, whose field of action had spread to include the whole Empire, were everywhere victorious as they had been in 1623 in Bohemia and in upper Germany; but once again, their ever-growing ambitions prolonged the war, and their power, which was more formidable in appearance than in reality, was undermined by their disagreements.

Soon after the raising of the siege of Stralsund, the king of Denmark, Christian IV, had to admit defeat. Towards the end of the summer he had tried to take up the offensive again by concentrating his troops in the island of Usedom at the mouth of the Oder, and by moving them over to the neighbouring coast of Pomerania. However, he failed to establish them there, and his army, attacked near Wolgast by Wallenstein, had to re-embark in disorder. The only course open to Christian was to sue for peace. Negotiations were slow to start. It was only in January 1629 that a meeting took place at Lübeck, but the talks were carried on in the main either at Munich through the mediation of the duke of Bavaria in the presence of Louis XIII's envoy, Charnacé, or in Wallenstein's camp at Mecklenburg. At Munich, Charnacé did his best to delay the Danish peace, but he only succeeded in making the emperor, who wanted peace to be concluded, abandon some of the unacceptable conditions which he had originally drawn up. Thus, without wishing to do so, the French envoy supported Wallenstein's private representations, for the latter had alarmed the emperor by suggesting that if peace were delayed a League might be formed by Denmark, France, England, the United Provinces and Sweden, and he advised him to moderate his demands. Peace between the king of Denmark and the emperor was finally signed at Lübeck on 7th June 1629. Christian recovered his territories and, in return, abandoned on behalf of his sons all claims to the bishoprics of Lower Saxony and Westphalia, and undertook to play no further part in Germany's affairs. From that time he was no longer a force to be reckoned with.

Even before the Peace of Lübeck was signed—three months before, in fact—an imperial act had reduced its significance and made the prolongation of the German war inevitable. This was the Edict of Restitution of 6th March 1629, and its impact on the Thirty Years War was very similar to that caused by the transfer of the electoral title and Maximilian of Bavaria's investiture in 1623.

The way had been paved for the Edict of Restitution as much by Ferdinand's agreement with Maximilian as by the general pressure of events. It would seem that Maximilian had been the first to declare, back in 1627, that the time had come to restore the Catholic religion throughout the Empire and to return to the Church the possessions which the Protestant princes had usurped. He joined the ecclesiastical electors in asking the emperor to support the bishop of Augsburg in his demand that the duke of Wurtemberg and the margrave of Ansbach should return to him seven monasteries which had been secularised after 1552. During the course of 1628 extensive confiscations were made in aid of the war effort and for the benefit of Wallenstein, Tilly, and many others. The duke of Brunswick-Wolfenbüttel, for example, lost a large part of his estates in this way. Privately, the emperor had taken advantage of the situation to provide for one of his own sons, the little Archduke Leopold William. Back in 1626 he had acquired the bishoprics of Passau and Strassburg for him; in December 1627, when Leopold William was not yet fourteen, he had had him elected by the Halberstadt Chapter. He had then tried to procure the archbishopric of Magdeburg for him, but the chapter had elected one of the elector of Saxony's sons. Despite the fact that it would have been in his interest to handle the elector with tact, Ferdinand had had the election annulled by the Pope who, in addition, gave Leopold William the right of succession to the archbishopric of Bremen, whose administrator had not had the wit to make peace with the emperor quickly enough. Finally, the Jesuits were making ready to take over a fair number of monasteries, including some which had been secularised in accordance with the protestant interpretation of the Peace of Augsburg. After so many enforced restitutions it only remained for the operation to be made general and legalised, and Ferdinand was determined to do so.

He signed the Edict of Restitution on 6th March 1629, and we must weigh the consequences both of the actual clauses of the edict and of the legal form which the emperor's resolve then took.

The contents of the edict can be easily summarised. The emperor intended to restore within the Empire the actual religious and territorial situation which had existed immediately after the Peace of Augsburg. The clause in the peace known as the 'Ecclesiastical Reservation' which the Protestants had never accepted, was now given the force of an imperial law, and he turned the clock back seventy years by refusing to allow the guarantees established by the peace to apply to the Calvinists. The edict nullified and made illegal the assumption of dioceses by protestant administrators and the admission of protestants to chapters. It also made illegal the action of any protestant prince in secularising within his own territories any monasteries or religious foundations of any kind. These had to continue to belong to the Catholic Church, or be returned to it. The question of administering the dioceses which had been one of the main causes of conflict between Protestant and Catholic princes, and which for some years had given the German civil war the character of a war for the conquest of the dioceses of Westphalia and Lower Saxony, was settled once and for all. The dynastic ambitions of the Protestant princely houses were doomed, and with them went their best chance of increasing the size of their lands. Moreover, the advantages which they lost were seized by the Catholic princely families—as the career of the young Archduke Leopold William immediately demonstrated. The result of the edict was thus to be an enormous transfer of property and power from Protestant Germany, which lost almost everything it had gained from the Reformation to the triumphant German Catholics.

No less serious were the consequences of the legal manner by which the secularised territories were restored to their former condition as church property. In ancient Germany and until the beginning of the civil war, no act had the force of an imperial law until it had been passed by a diet and ratified by the emperor. It was an unbroken custom that the emperor did not take any decision affecting the whole of the Empire except by previous agreement, at the very least with the electoral college. In 1621 the emperor had already pronounced the banishment and deposition of the Palatine without consulting the electors. Nor had he waited for the opinion of the electoral college about whose unanimity he had no illusions, before sending Maximilian of Bavaria the secret act transferring his new title to him. This double abuse of power, which was how many princes regarded the emperor's actions, aroused lasting resentment in the Empire, but by its very form, the edict of March 1629 was even more serious. By the emperor's personal decree the territorial situation in the Empire was fundamentally transformed, and the Ecclesiastical Reservation, which had always aroused opposition from the Protestant princes, was given force of law. The emperor, who for so long had not dared to summon an imperial diet in the traditional manner, seemed determined to by-pass it as well as the electoral union, which in fact was losing the authority which had always been its acknowledged right. The entire constitution of the Holy Roman Empire had been altered to the advantage of the emperor's power which from then on scarcely differed from the power of an absolute monarch.

Finally, the way in which the emperor intended to put the edict into effect must equally have aroused doubts. The confiscation of former secularised possessions and the nomination of the beneficiaries could not be done without provoking many protests, if not armed resistance. The diet was powerless to deal with this. Any disputes which might arise in law had to be dealt with before an imperial commission which, after a rapid enquiry, would make a ruling and order the immediate execution of its sentence. The sentence would then have to be carried out with the help of troops. That meant that the emperor was entrusting to Wallenstein and his army the task of executing the edict. As a result, all the bitterness which Wallenstein's arbitrary and brutal conduct had aroused, all the fears which had long since been aroused by his almost limitless personal power, were augmented by the anger which the edict could not fail to provoke.

Coming three months after the Edict of Restitution, the Peace of Lübeck could not provide a basis for the general restoration of peace. The whole of Germany was mistrustful and up in arms. Until then the war had not spread beyond the Elbe in north Germany because the Lutheran elector of Saxony, John George, and the Calvinist elector of

Brandenburg, George William, both hesitated to break with the emperor. John George had been involved in the conquest of Bohemia and had gained the Lusatias out of it; but he occupied them only as a security until such time as the emperor should be able to repay him for what he had spent on the war, and he wanted them to become completely his own. Moreover, he sought a lasting peace and he was not clever enough to perceive the emperor's secret intentions amid all the soothing assurances which imperial diplomacy showered upon him. As for George William (the father of the future Great Elector) his weak character kept him in a perpetual state of suspense between the two sides, between his respect for the emperor's title and his grievances as a Calvinist prince. But the position of his territories did not allow him to maintain his neutrality unharmed. The march of Brandenburg lay between Silesia and Pomerania, and the duchy of Prussia between Poland and the Baltic Sea. As George William was known to be weak-willed, nobody bothered to spare him. In his march towards the Baltic, Wallenstein had no scruples about crossing Brandenburg, nor, once the campaign was over, about quartering his troops there as if the country belonged to him. Similarly, when Gustavus Adolphus was fighting in Poland, he occupied part of Prussia and, to obtain better communications between his army and his fleet, he seized the little port of Pillau which suited his purposes. He also thought that the duchy could serve as a base should he decide to take his army into Germany. George William hated and feared Wallenstein, admired and feared Gustavus Adolphus, but did not know which side to take. He waited passively for events to take the decision for him. All the same we must bear in mind that this wavering attitude of the two Protestant electors was a source of hope to the enemies of the house of Austria, and implied certain possible lines of action in the future which at least encouraged them not to be too hasty to conclude a general peace.

Gustavus Adolphus's victories in Poland which might at any moment leave him free to act, and the development of French policy, encouraged them even more.

From Prussia, Gustavus Adolphus was ready to intervene as soon as the time seemed ripe. We know (and this is a point which Swedish historians have brought to light) that he considered his campaign in Poland as the necessary preparation for his entry into Germany, so sure was he that the progress of Austria and Spain towards the Baltic imperilled by its recent conquests the essential interests of Sweden in the northern seas and the maintenance of the Protestant Churches. By

5

tossing a few Swedish battalions into beleaguered Stralsund at the right time, he had already helped to frustrate Wallenstein's overweening ambition. At the end of 1629 he seemed ready to go even further. Only the question of the cost of a war, for Sweden was a poor country, stayed his hand.

In France Richelieu's position was daily growing stronger. From 1626 he had been assured of royal favour. Louis XIII had given him a written promise never to abandon him and to defend him against all his enemies, even against his brother Gaston. The services which he had continued to render to the king since then, during the course of the year of intrigues, after the landing of the English on the Ile de Ré, and during the siege of La Rochelle, attached Louis XIII more firmly to the minister who had raised his prestige both inside and outside the kingdom. By the end of October 1628, La Rochelle had capitulated. Huguenot resistance had been kept up for some time by the duc de Rohan in Languedoc, but the peace of Alais on 27th June of the following year finally reduced them to obedience. In Italy, Louis XIII had been able to come to the aid of a new duke of Mantua, Charles de Gonzague-Nevers, against the duke of Savoy and the king of Spain who were unwilling to recognize his rights of inheritance. He had forced the Pass of Susa and freed Casale which was besieged by the Spanish army. France once again appeared as a force to be reckoned with, and Richelieu's policy, whose prime objective was to halt the progress of Spanish domination in north Italy, at the same time kept a closer watch on events in Germany. A mission entrusted to Baron Hercule de Charnacé and his parting instructions from Father Joseph are sufficient to prove the point. Charnacé was to go to Munich, then to the king of Denmark, and lastly to the camp of Gustavus Adolphus, to try to arrange a peace between Christian IV and the League through the king of France's mediation, and then to reconcile Denmark and Sweden. The mission failed because Maximilian of Bavaria did not want to break with the emperor and because Wallenstein offered more advantageous terms to Christian which were accepted and which became the terms of the peace signed at Lübeck on 7th June 1629. But Charnacé's embassy had none the less shown the German princes and the kings of the north that France had an interest in what was going on in the Empire. Richelieu knew the close ties which bound the courts of Vienna and Madrid; he knew that the restoration of peace in north Italy depended as much on the emperor as on the king of Spain. So, at the very moment when the Edict of Restitution was stirring the fears,

or the ambitions, of the princes and making the restoration of an
honest peace more or less impossible, the policies of the kings of France
and Sweden demonstrated that the war was to flare up once again and,
as it spread, become the European conflict which it remained until the
very end.

CHAPTER V

RICHELIEU AND GUSTAVUS ADOLPHUS

For many years French historians have oversimplified the relationship between Richelieu and Gustavus Adolphus. Indeed, they have explained Sweden's intervention in the Thirty Years War almost entirely in terms of French policy. Just as they believed that it was only by French subsidies that the king of Denmark had survived the victories of Wallenstein, so, when Christian had ceased to be a force, it was Richelieu who found another leader for the Protestant cause. By this view it was he who persuaded Gustavus Adolphus to conclude the Polish war and, by the subsidies promised in the treaty of Bärwalde, brought about the Swedish invasion of Germany. It all seemed to be part of a hidden struggle between the king of France and the house of Habsburg, in which France, as yet unable to act openly, awaited her opportunity and, in the meantime, allowed the sovereigns of the north to act on her behalf and in her pay.

The truth was quite different. We have seen that Christian IV, by virtue of his being duke of Holstein, was a German prince, who wished to increase his influence in the Lower Saxon circle to which the duchy of Holstein belonged. He could hardly have failed to take a hand in German affairs while Tilly's ravaging army quartered itself across the northern plains. We also know that Gustavus Adolphus, at a very early stage, considered that the advance of the armies of the League and the emperor towards the Baltic and the victories of the Counter Reformation in central Germany created a mortal danger for the young Swedish monarchy, and that he was determined to avert it before it was too late. We know that while he fought the Poles he had no thoughts of giving up his intervention in Germany but rather was preparing for it and that he did not need Richelieu's invitation to send troops into Stralsund. Richelieu very quickly realised that Gustavus Adolphus was not in the least disposed to allow his policies to be directed by France. The king of Sweden went to fight in Germany not for France (there was even a time when he was on the point of fighting against France), but for the Protestant cause and to defend Swedish interests.

On the other hand there can be no question that Gustavus Adolphus's constant need for money—for he had been campaigning outside Sweden almost since his accession—forced him to regard a foreign subsidy as a prerequisite for any new undertaking. If he had not concluded the treaty of Bärwalde, he might perhaps have had to postpone his effective intervention again. It is equally clear that in the spring of 1630, Richelieu was negotiating simultaneously in Germany with the king of Sweden and the elector of Bavaria and that he attached equal importance to both. So, with due reservations about Gustavus Adolphus's personal intentions, we may consider the situation from the French point of view in order to clarify it and to see how it changed at that moment.

The fall of La Rochelle was a landmark in the development of French foreign policy, and no historian has failed to recognise this. In this connection we always quote—and we should continue to quote—the advice given to the king in January 1629, which begins with something of a shout of triumph: 'Now that La Rochelle has fallen, if the king wishes to become the most powerful monarch in the world. . . .' Richelieu's aim at that time was not to prevent the emperor strengthening his authority in the Empire, nor to check his attempt to re-establish Catholicism there. It was not Vienna's policy in Germany which caused him the most concern, but Olivares's policy in Italy. Another sentence of his memorandum of January 1629 is no less important than the first: 'Outside our realm', wrote Richelieu, 'it must be our constant purpose to arrest the course of Spain's progress.' At that time, there was no doubt that the Spaniards had slipped into the Empire by occupying the strongholds of the Rhenish Palatinate on a temporary basis, but it was above all in Italy that 'Spain's progress' was most obvious. Louis XIII had had to use armed force to defend his protégé, the new duke of Mantua, Charles de Gonzague-Nevers. Since his brilliant action in the pass of Susa where Louis XIII had fought for the first time at the head of his troops, his own prestige was at stake and he was honour bound not to abandon the duke of Mantua. Unable to leave France in December 1629 because of the suspected intrigues of his brother Gaston, he put Cardinal Richelieu in command of the Italian campaign. Richelieu crossed the Alps in the depths of winter and took the fortress of Pinerolo by surprise. Had it been well fortified and manned, it would have been impregnable. The capture of Pinerolo was another landmark. As I have shown elsewhere, it forced Louis to choose between a policy of internal reform which the Chancellor Marillac urged upon him, and the decisive struggle against Spanish domination which might perhaps make him, as Richelieu promised, 'the most powerful monarch in the world'. We know that Louis XIII chose Richelieu's policy in preference to Marillac's and that the whole reign, and the very future of the realm, ultimately depended on this; but it was in Italy that the first consequences of the new French policy became clear. For several months the prime concern of Louis XIII and Richelieu was to prevent the capitulation of Casale which was once again cut off by the Spaniards. They also wished to preserve for Charles de Nevers, a prince who was more than half French, the two territories which had passed into his hands as the result of an unexpected inheritance, namely Montferrat between Savoy and the duchy of Milan, and Mantua between the duchy of Milan and the republic of Venice.

Events in Italy, however, did not absolve Louis XIII from having a German policy too; in fact we might almost say that they forced him to have one. Richelieu understood this quite clearly, since he wrote in that same memorandum of January 1629: 'France's only thought must be to strengthen herself and to open doors so that she may enter the states of all her neighbours to protect them from Spain's oppression when the opportunities to do so arise. . . . We must look to the fortification of Metz and advance as far as Strassburg if this be possible, to acquire an entry to Germany. . . .' But he added: 'this must be done in the fullness of time, with great discretion and by unobtrusive secret negotiation'. It could only be a question of planning for the perhaps distant future. At all events, Richelieu's advice to his master from January 1629 revealed his opinion that French foreign policy, committed though it was in Italy, ought also to be vigilant and active in Germany—and this in fact is what happened.

Circumstances there were favourable. The emperor was preparing for a meeting of the electoral college at Regensburg where he wanted the electors to nominate as King of the Romans his eldest son, the archduke Ferdinand, who had already been proclaimed king of Hungary, so that the young Ferdinand might succeed him without a further meeting of the electoral college. Such a manœuvre, however, could only arouse a great deal of distrust around him and bring into the open the dissensions which were rife among the Catholics. Ferdinand and Wallenstein, for example, were at loggerheads because the emperor blamed Wallenstein for abandoning too readily the siege of Stralsund and for virtually ignoring the instructions of the Viennese court when negotiating the Danish peace by offering the king of Denmark much easier terms than the emperor had wished. Moreover, had not Wallenstein shown a marked lack of enthusiasm for the Edict of Restitution which he considered to be singularly ill-advised? There was an even sharper disagreement between Wallenstein and the Archduke Ferdinand who thought he had some talent for war and was deeply aggrieved that the great soldier of fortune had robbed him of the command which he considered his by right. Finally, there were disagreements between the electors, particularly the elector of Bavaria, and the emperor, for they bitterly reproached him for having introduced the Spaniards into the Empire and for allowing himself to be so easily led by the Spanish ambassador and by Father Lamormain, who, in their eyes, was simply an instrument of Olivares's policy. As the electors saw Wallenstein become more powerful and more independent, as they saw him extend his quarters, levy contributions in all the regions of Germany without bothering about the princes' interests, and appropriate the absolute authority which the emperor had not managed to keep for himself, they feared even more that one day they would be reduced to the condition of subjects—not to an emperor elected by themselves, but to a soldier of fortune who owed his power only to his boldness and to the ever increasing number of mercenaries of all nations and creeds (there were many Protestants in Wallenstein's armies) whom he had managed to recruit and attach to his star. So they demanded Wallenstein's recall and the disbandment of a large part of his army which, in their opinion, no longer seemed necessary after the Danish peace had been signed. The rest—or so Maximilian of Bavaria at least suggested—were to be combined with the troops of the League and placed under Tilly's command. This, then, was the situation in Germany a few months before the electoral college met at Regensburg and when Richelieu, free at last of the Huguenot war, could turn his attention to the affairs of the Empire.

At the very beginning of 1630, Marcheville was once again sent to Germany. His instructions were dated 15th January, only two days from the date which Avenel, the editor of Richelieu's papers, assigns to the memorandum to the king which I have already quoted several times. We need not follow Marcheville on his mission which had no important results, but his instructions give a fairly clear outline of French policy in Germany when Louis XIII's envoys were making contact once again with the princes of the Empire after the internal

crisis of the three previous years. Moreover, and we should take note
of this, it was the electors, and first of all the Catholic electors, whom
Marcheville was to inform of the king's intentions. He had to contact
the elector of Trier, for there was no doubt that he was favourably
disposed towards French policy and he served as a friendly intermediary
between the king of France and the other electors. Marcheville was to
tell him that Louis XIII, 'being moved by a very sincere wish to deliver
Italy and Germany from the oppression to which they had been
reduced by the manifest violence and ambition of the house of Austria',
would not refuse to help the princes 'to re-establish the liberty of
Germany, and in particular of the electors, good neighbours and ancient
allies of his crown'. The king considered that the electors would not
be able to find a more favourable opportunity 'to put an end to the ills
beneath which the Empire has groaned for so long'. He thought that
they should, with one accord—and this meant Protestants and Catholics
together—demand the following conditions from the emperor: that
Wallenstein should be recalled; that he should restore peace to Italy or
at least withdraw his troops from it; that he should disarm and thus
make possible the summoning of a general diet. If the emperor refused
to meet these conditions, 'the king will be obliged to assist their purpose, either by sending a powerful army, maintained at his expense,
into some part of Germany where their intentions will not be suspected
... or by creating a diversion elsewhere'. The purpose was clear.
Louis XIII and Richelieu made no distinction between the two faiths.
They had no intention of intervening in a war of religion. They merely
wished to maintain the traditional liberties of the electors and princes
and, to do this in the face of imperial ambition, they wished to convince
the Catholic electors that their interests were the same as those of the
Protestant electors and that they could only safeguard them by breaking
with the emperor. The instructions given to Marcheville also show why
Richelieu could not isolate the Italian question from the German
question, since one of the objects which he wished to achieve was to
force the emperor to recall the army which he had sent to join the
Spanish troops in Italy, and to force the king of Spain to abandon the
strongholds of the Palatinate which Spinola had seized to help the emperor dispossess the Palatine. France's German policy was therefore
given precise definition at the very moment when the electoral college
was about to meet at Regensburg.

Naturally it was at Regensburg that all diplomatic activity was
centred during the summer of 1630. The emperor went there. The

three ecclesiastical electors of Mainz, Cologne and Trier were there in person, as was the elector of Bavaria; Saxony and Brandenburg, the two Protestant electors, sent plenipotentiaries to represent them. Louis XIII sent Brûlart de Léon and Father Joseph. Of the two, only Brûlart de Léon, a state counsellor and ambassador to Switzerland, had the powers of a special envoy; Father Joseph was merely the bearer of credentials to the emperor and to all appearances he was no more than an unofficial adviser attached to the ambassador—today we would call him an expert. None the less, his personal prestige, and the entire confidence which Richelieu placed in him, made him the real leader of the embassy, despite any ambiguity there may have been about his position in relation to the titular ambassador. Moreover, his role, at least so far as German affairs were concerned—and by this we mean the grievances of the electors and the emperor's desire to have the archduke Ferdinand elected as King of the Romans—could only be unofficial. Because of this we know little about it. It goes without saying that very few traces of his confidential talks with each of the electors were left in his correspondence. One is apt to summarise his work at Regensburg by quoting the words attributed to the emperor—which he probably never uttered—'that a lowly Capuchin had disarmed him with his rosary and that, however close-fitting his cowl, he had managed to slip six electoral hats underneath it.' The words are a good example of an 'historical saying', since it is quite impossible for us to know their origin and because the metaphor epitomises exactly the results achieved by Father Joseph. They reveal nothing, however, of the Capuchin's methods, nor the part which he must have played in the electoral college's decisions.

By and large, these decisions were in keeping with Richelieu's wishes, and yet it cannot be said that everything at Regensburg passed off as he would have wished. He had one overriding desire, and in this he was in full agreement with Father Joseph, as we know from the instructions that the latter carried and which he himself had dictated to Father Ange de Mortagne, another Capuchin who often served him as secretary. Above all he wanted to prevent the emperor from having his son elected as King of the Romans and from securing the electoral college's approval for the military aid he was giving to the king of Spain in north Italy and against the Dutch. In this way Richelieu hoped to separate the Catholic League and its leader, Maximilian of Bavaria, from the emperor, and to form a third party in Germany whose neutrality would have been guaranteed by the armed protection of the

king of France. But the electors had only one common goal which they
were determined to achieve: that was to obtain the dismissal of
Wallenstein and the disbanding of his army. Ferdinand now did something which nobody could have foreseen: he had the wit, or weakness,
to dismiss Wallenstein and to disband his army, thus throwing himself
on the League's mercy in the hope of ensuring the election of the King
of the Romans. However, the electors refused him that. As a result of
the electoral diet the emperor's power was weakened for the time
being, which could not fail to please Richelieu, but Ferdinand's prompt
capitulation had forestalled any breach with the Catholic electors. The
creation of a third party centred on the elector of Bavaria had to be
postponed.

From another point of view (which we need not emphasise here)
the embassy of Brûlart de Léon and Father Joseph did not have the
success for which Richelieu had hoped. When the two ambassadors
arrived in Regensburg they were denied permission to discuss Italian
affairs with the imperial ministers—yet it was in Italy that negotiations
were under way between Spinola, representing the king of Spain,
Collalto, commander of the imperial troops, and the Abbé Mazarini,
later Cardinal Mazarin, the unofficial envoy of the Pope. A French
garrison continued to defend Casale against a Spanish army. Spinola
would not hear of peace before taking Casale; nor would Collalto who
had seized Mantua during the night of 17th July. Mazarin's endless
journeys from one headquarters to another merely resulted in a series
of peace plans which were constantly subjected to revision, and the
garrison in Casale might any day be forced to capitulate through lack
of food or ammunition. Richelieu then had the idea of transferring the
negotiations to Regensburg in the hope that the emperor would lend
himself to an honourable solution of the conflict and would prevail
upon the king of Spain to accept it. In fact, it was the negotiation of an
Italian settlement which became the principal task of the two negotiators at Regensburg. Unfortunately, this provided the emperor, who
was well advised, with a golden opportunity to deal at once with both
the Italian and the German issues. He made a peaceful settlement in
Italy conditional upon Louis XIII's promising not to give direct or
indirect aid to the emperor's adversaries in Germany. That would have
obliged the king of France to renounce his Protestant alliances and to
break off the talks which were then in progress with the king of
Sweden. Brûlart and Father Joseph tried by every means within their
power to introduce loopholes into the article which the emperor

demanded so that Louis XIII would not have to abandon his allies, but they were not altogether successful and the king of France never ratified the treaty which they signed at Regensburg in October. It was not until June 1631 that the Italian war came to an end after supplies had got through to Casale and, through Mazarin's actions, a treaty had been negotiated at Cherasco. By the terms of the treaty Charles de Gonzague's possession of the duchy of Mantua was recognised by the emperor while a secret agreement with the duke of Savoy allowed Louis XIII to maintain a French garrison in Pinerolo. In the meantime much had happened in Germany, and we can now pursue the story without being distracted by events in Italy.

Richelieu's German policy, in which he was still being advised by Father Joseph, needed very careful handling indeed, but this suited his temperament. It entailed, throughout 1630, the pursuit of two distinct objectives, apparently incompatible yet of equal importance to him. On the one hand he wanted to arrange a defensive alliance between Louis XIII and Maximilian of Bavaria in order to deprive the emperor of Bavarian support. On the other, he wanted to conclude a treaty with the king of Sweden by which, in return for French subsidies, he would invade Germany and attack the hereditary territories of the Habsburgs. In addition to his policy set out in Marcheville's instructions at the beginning of the year—designed to establish a group of German princes to withstand the emperor's ambitions—Richelieu was now trying to provide in Gustavus Adolphus a king who was violently anti-Catholic, someone to lead the Protestants against the emperor without, however, endangering the Catholic Church itself.

As we already know, the idea of persuading Maximilian of Bavaria to oppose the emperor, or at least as head of the League to follow a policy of neutrality, was of long standing. It is not surprising that Richelieu should have revived it and, in so doing, tried to arrange a peace which provided for the essential interests of both parties but which allowed neither the establishment of an absolute authority in the Empire nor the triumph of the Protestants—whom Louis XIII, like Ferdinand, condemned as heretics. Certainly Maximilian and the king of France shared many interests and prejudices. They were both genuinely pious and ready to serve the Roman Church, but on condition that it preserved its independence and did not make common cause with Spain which, under cover of religious zeal, was seeking to establish a political ascendancy for its own ends. Maximilian was just as attached as any other prince in Germany to those 'German liberties' of which Louis XIII so loftily declared himself to be the protector. Nevertheless, even a defensive alliance between Bavaria and France could only rest on a fundamental misunderstanding. The two sovereigns did not have the same aim; the king of France's main object was to cause a rift between the emperor and the elector of Bavaria and to form around the latter a third party which would, in the face of the Protestant peril, become a pliable instrument of French policy; the elector, on the other hand, wished to separate the king from his Protestant allies and to use French support to free Germany from Habsburg domination without compromising the success of the Counter Reformation.

Bavaria's interests in the face of the French proposals are clearly indicated in a memorandum from the elector's advisors which has been brought to light for the first time by a Bavarian historian, Döberl. It is true that it dates from 1629, but in that year, just as in 1630, there was already a question of a defensive alliance with France. The only difference was that at that moment Wallenstein still commanded the imperial armies. In 1629, Maximilian's advisers considered (and they were certainly still of the same opinion in 1630) that in view of Spain's influence at Vienna and the 'golden shackles' by which she held the emperor's chief ministers, one could not 'blame Bavaria for thinking about her security'. They recognised that the emperor was personally 'well-disposed towards the elector'; but they added that 'his minister of war and his other ministers had allowed it to be understood clearly enough that they were not kindly disposed towards him'. On the other hand, France was offering to guarantee the elector's acquisitions[1] and his electoral title; and her intentions, which had never varied, were to be trusted. If she were rebuffed and subsequently made an agreement with England and Holland to reinstate the Palatine, his restoration would become certain, given Spain's suspect attitude. Consequently, Bavaria would no doubt lose the part of the Rhenish Palatinate which she had occupied and possibly both the Upper Palatinate and the electoral title.

Those feelings were very probably still prevalent among the Bavarian ministers at Regensburg when Father Joseph, in great secrecy and unbeknown even to Brûlart, was instructed to resume negotiations for an alliance with the elector Maximilian. The talks, about which we have no detailed account, made little headway since Father Joseph was extremely busy and had to keep breaking off negotiations. It was not Wallenstein's disgrace, when it happened, which changed the elector's

[1] The Upper Palatinate and a part of the Rhenish Palatinate.

mind. He simply did not wish to renounce his obligations to the emperor, whereas Father Joseph tried every means to include an article in the treaty which would, in certain circumstances, have compelled him to do so. The negotiators exercised all their skill—in opposite directions—over the drawing up of the article, for every one of its words had to be carefully weighed. In fact Father Joseph did not manage to conclude a formal alliance, but only to draw up a new project rather more satisfactory than the Bavarian counter-project which had served as a basis for negotiations, and which he had brought back from Regensburg. What decided Maximilian to approve it was not his grievance against the emperor—for he had been disarmed by Wallenstein's dismissal and the disbanding of his troops—but alarm over Spanish policy in the Rhenish Palatinate. Six months later, after Swedish troops had landed on the German coast of the Baltic, he then concluded a definite treaty in the hope that the king of France would protect him against Gustavus Adolphus. The Franco-Bavarian defensive alliance, signed at Munich on 8th May 1631 and at Fontainebleau on the 30th, was to run for eight years. In it the king of France promised not to give direct or indirect assistance to anyone who might attack the territories of the elector of Bavaria and for his part the elector under- took not to assist, in any way, anyone who might attack the king's. The king also promised 'to defend and maintain the electoral title for the elector and for the house of Bavaria against all who might wish to take it from them'. The two contracting parties mutually guaranteed their possessions, both old and new,[1] which, as far as the elector was con- cerned, meant the parts of the Palatinate which he had occupied; but Maximilian of Bavaria reserved the right, in all circumstances, to fulfil all his obligations as an elector and as a prince of the Empire with regard to the emperor.[2] Such was the treaty upon which the relations between Bavaria and France were based until the end of the war, but these were not without their vicissitudes and we will have cause to mention them.

Despite several interruptions, negotiations with Gustavus Adolphus had been concluded four months before Louis XIII signed the defensive alliance with the elector of Bavaria. To a certain extent their success was due to the perseverance and skill of the Baron de Charnacé and to the confidence which he had managed to inspire in the king of Sweden.

[1] Hereditarias et acquisitas.
[2] Reservat ideo ac excipit hic Elector juramentum suum imperatori et im- perio praestitum.

However, the overriding factor had probably been Gustavus Adolphus's urgent need for money. As soon as the Edict of Restitution had been made, back in the spring of 1629, Gustavus Adolphus had made up his mind to intervene in Germany to defend the Protestants and to prevent the Habsburgs from dominating the southern shores of the Baltic. After landing in the island of Rügen, at the beginning of summer in 1630, an advance unit of the army had established itself in Pomerania, whose duke had placed himself under Swedish protection. Then, in July, Gustavus Adolphus had taken Stettin, at the mouth of the Oder. It was a solid base for military operations, but it had to be broadened, and to this end he needed the benevolent neutrality or, better still, the active support, of the two protestant electors, the margrave of Brandenburg and the duke of Saxony, neither of whom had so far shown his hand. Equally, he was in need of a subsidy to increase the size of his army and to cover the expenses of a long campaign. It was at this moment that negotiations with France were finally resumed and an understanding reached. By the treaty of Bärwalde, on 23rd January 1631, a five-year agreement was concluded between the king of France and the king of Sweden. In return for subsidies, Gustavus Adolphus undertook to march 36,000 men into Germany. Further, he promised to allow Catholicism to be practised wherever he found it established in such areas as he might occupy. He was also to respect the neutrality of Bavaria and of the League too, provided, of course, that its members declared themselves neutral. Properly speaking, it was not an offensive alliance because there was no question of France taking part in the war; nor could it be termed a defensive alliance because Louis XIII did not guarantee the king of Sweden's conquests, nor his territories. It was simply a financial arrangement. Furthermore, it had only been possible to sign it because neither of the contracting parties had any desire to clear up the misunderstanding on which the treaty was based. Richelieu hoped to use Gustavus Adolphus against the emperor while protecting Bavaria and the League against him. Gustavus Adolphus, however, was determined to pursue his own policy in Germany if he was victorious. This was to establish Swedish domination on the German shores of the Baltic and to assure the victory of Protestantism by gathering all the Protestant princes of Germany under his command. He hoped—and events soon proved him right—that if Maximilian of Bavaria and the League refused to stay neutral he would then be quit of his obligation towards them. On the other hand, Richelieu gave aid to Gustavus Adolphus only in the secret hope of containing and channelling his thirst for conquest. His views on the Swedish alliance are well conveyed by the colourful terms of one of Father Joseph's notes to the Cardinal: 'we have to use these things like poison—a little serves as an antidote but too much kills.' At the time, however, the treaty of Bärwalde seemed to be a great success for French policy. Its inherent dangers were only to appear later. If it did not turn out as Richelieu had intended when he had secured his master's signature to it, the consequences, as we shall soon see, proved to be more momentous than he could have foreseen.

In the spring of 1631, France's German policy was based upon two treaties which had been independently negotiated and concluded, the one with a Catholic prince, head of the German Catholic League, and the other with a Protestant king who considered himself first and foremost as the protector of Protestantism. The problem was to reconcile them. Clearly this could only be done if Maximilian and Gustavus Adolphus themselves were prepared to be reconciled, but as neither of them was willing it was not long before the pressure of events upset all Richelieu's plans.

From January to September 1631, the situation in Germany was so confused and changeable that the intentions of the princes and diplomats counted for very little. The emperor no longer had an army. The rump of Wallenstein's army was added to Tilly's—that is to the troops of Bavaria and the League—but Tilly's troops were short of everything. Wallenstein, who had not forgiven either Ferdinand or Maximilian for his disgrace, refused to open the granaries of his duchy of Friedland or those of Mecklenburg, except for ready money. Tilly, who did not want to enter Saxony for fear of forcing the elector into the Swedish camp, nor to attack the Swedes because Maximilian was still doing his best to avoid a breach of the treaty, did not know what to do with an army in which hunger and poverty took their toll with every day. In March, after an assembly of the Protestant princes had met at Leipzig, John George of Saxony, with the full agreement of George William of Brandenburg, offered the emperor the full support of Protestant Germany against the Swedish invader if the emperor agreed to revoke the Edict of Restitution. For Ferdinand, however, the maintenance of the edict was a moral duty which he could not abandon, even though Gustavus Adolphus continued to advance his army. On 13th April he seized Frankfurt-am-Oder. Already he had allied with the dukes of Mecklenburg who had been dispossessed for Wallenstein's benefit and who counted on recovering the two duchies with Swedish aid. He also had as an ally the Protestant administrator of Magdeburg who had been expelled from the archdiocese the year before by the troops of the League and who had just re-entered it. Soon, the Swedish troops who had occupied the New March surrounded and overflowed into the electorate of Brandenburg so that poor George William could hardly remain neutral any longer, however much he may have wished to. When Gustavus Adolphus marched on Berlin and seized the fortress of Spandau, the elector of Brandenburg had to accept a provisional alliance which could not fail to become permanent in very short time. It was then that Germany learned of the fall of Magdeburg.

It was to get out of the almost hopeless situation in which he found himself that Tilly, egged on by one of his lieutenants, Pappenheim, decided to try to take Magdeburg which held the middle course of the Elbe and which was believed to contain a considerable stock of provisions. From the borders of Mecklenburg, Tilly crossed the Middle March and reached the Elbe valley. On his way, he took and sacked Neu-Brandenburg, and then joined forces with Pappenheim before Magdeburg. The town was strong, but the townspeople, who were quite ready to surrender, hindered the garrison's efforts. Magdeburg was taken by storm on 20th May. Neither Pappenheim, who had decided on the assault without his leader's orders, nor Tilly himself, could restrain their troops[1] who were determined to take revenge for the long months of misery which they had suffered. There was a terrible massacre, and the fire which broke out simultaneously in all districts consumed almost the entire town, including the provisions which Tilly had counted on finding there. In no time the news of the sack of Magdeburg had spread, and the reaction of horror which it caused now rendered impossible the elector of Saxony's attempts to mediate between the Catholics and Protestants. On 22nd June, George William ratified his alliance with Gustavus Adolphus; he placed his resources, which included the two fortresses of Spandau and Custrin, at the king's disposal for the duration of the war. Then when Tilly, who was still anxious to feed his starving troops, decided that there was no other way open for him but to invade Saxony, John George, in his turn, came to terms with the king of Sweden on 11th September. He promised to attach his army to the Swedish army when it reached the Elbe, and agreed that they should both be under the king's command

---

[1] This at least is the interpretation suggested by contemporary documents; and Tilly's desire to provision his troops at Magdeburg would hardly be compatible with orders to fire the town.

'for the duration of the critical circumstances' which the policy of the emperor and the League had created in the Empire. He did not commit himself irrevocably, because it was always open to him to decide that the 'critical circumstances' on which he justified the alliance no longer existed. But at the end of the summer of 1631, Gustavus Adolphus, now sure of the electors of Brandenburg and Saxony, could advance without fear of his army being cut off from its bases. Furthermore, he considered that he was no longer bound by the clauses of the treaty of Bärwalde which obliged him to respect the neutrality of Bavaria and the League, since it was they themselves who had broken it first.

The consequences of this new situation were almost immediately apparent and ran quite contrary to Richelieu's hopes. At the end of the summer, Gustavus Adolphus had completed the pattern of his alliances: he had won over the margrave of Hesse-Cassel and also Bernard of Saxe-Weimar, a prince of the house of Saxony who only possessed small estates but who quickly revealed that he had considerable military talents; he became Gustavus Adolphus's best lieutenant. Then, immediately after his alliance with John George of Saxony, the king of Sweden followed Tilly into electoral Saxony. He marched straight at Leipzig and the two armies met near the town. At Breitenfeld on 17th September, the Swedes won a decisive victory and the dream of Richelieu and Father Joseph was shattered. No longer could the French king hope to mediate between the Catholics and Protestants, two rival groups who were united against the house of Austria only through the ambitions of their leaders. Faced with the Swedish threat, the Catholic princes would certainly close their ranks around their natural leader, the emperor. As for the king of Sweden, it was he, and not the king of France, who had gathered the Protestant princes of Germany about him under the protection of his arms. Henceforward, it was he, and not the king of France who was going to call the tune, and Richelieu had good cause to wonder whether he could persuade the victor to spare the princes of the League, and whether he could ever check his victorious career without recourse to arms.

However, he did not lose heart. He could secure what he wanted, and the French king could benefit from his alliances with the elector of Bavaria and the king of Sweden, if Gustavus Adolphus, after his great victory, would either quarter his troops and give the diplomats a chance to take over, or set about Ferdinand's dynastic territories, beginning with Bavaria. For reasons which cannot be elucidated, Wallenstein, who had retired to his palace at Prague, was actually inviting Gustavus Adolphus to invade, and throughout central and southern Germany the great numbers of Czech émigrés who had fled their country after the battle of the White Mountain hoped to find in him an avenger. They formed armed bands and were already crossing the frontier and inciting the peasants to revolt. But Gustavus Adolphus did not trust John George. He, who had for so long refused to join him, might desert at any time, and Gustavus Adolphus had no wish to leave him with a free hand in electoral Saxony while he himself penetrated southwards into the very heart of Habsburg territory. He preferred to give the elector and Arnim, the commander-in-chief of the Saxon troops, the task of liberating Bohemia while he himself pushed forward towards the valley of the Main. The elector's army, therefore, accompanied or followed by bands of Czech émigrés, marched on Prague and entered it without meeting much resistance, for Wallenstein had been careful to leave a few days earlier; but the expedition was short lived. The liberating army soon degenerated into a band of looters, which permanently damaged the Protestant cause. As for Gustavus Adolphus, he took Erfurt on 2nd October, reached the Main at Würzburg, and captured the town after a four-day siege. Aschaffenburg fell on 11th November, Frankfurt-am-Main, the imperial capital, on the 27th, and finally Mainz on 20th December. By this time he was already across the Rhine.

While the triumphal march of the Swedish king continued right on into winter, the king of France could only send Charnacé yet again to Munich with instructions which Father Joseph had drawn up himself. In them, the Capuchin reminded the ambassador of the aims of French policy: 'to put an end to Austria's violent course whose formidable power constituted a threat to every prince'. He contrasted the ambitious behaviour of the Habsburgs with the moderation of the king who sought only to preserve for each and every one what he owned, and to contain the house of Austria within limits which it should not attempt to exceed. He emphasised that France had not abandoned hope of establishing neutrality between the elector of Bavaria and the king of Sweden which in accordance with the treaties of Bärwalde and Fontainebleau they should both undertake to respect in the future. 'Thus,' he concluded, 'the good faith of these two treaties may be guaranteed, maintaining the balance between Catholics and Protestants for their mutual preservation, and by these salutary means we may put an end to the over-mighty power of the house of Austria and the king of Sweden.'

Most certainly they were excellent instructions, but they smacked a little too much of the optimism that Father Joseph's unruffled confidence in divine providence inspired. However, he was well aware that neither the king of Sweden, nor the emperor, nor even Maximilian, were concerned with 'maintaining the balance between Catholics and Protestants', and that in wishing to contain both 'the over-mighty power of the house of Austria and of the king of Sweden' at the same time, there was a grave risk that France would be left in isolation between the two sides, mistrusted by both. Both Maximilian and Gustavus Adolphus were striving for quite different ends. Maximilian wanted to drive the Swedes out of Germany without in any way either encouraging the Habsburg ambitions or bringing about any breach with the emperor. Gustavus Adolphus wanted to establish Swedish domination along the German coasts of the Baltic, and perhaps beyond, and to create a solid bloc of Protestant states in north Germany whose natural protector would be the king of Sweden. In the midst of these passions loosed by war, this rivalry of the German Catholics and Protestants, there was no room for Father Joseph whose policy comprised nothing but half-measures, reflecting both the interests of the statesman and the preoccupations of a man of the Church.

To distinguish between the policies of Father Joseph and Richelieu is clearly hypothetical. The two men were never very far from one another and we have no proof that at that moment there was any difference of opinion between them. Father Joseph nearly always drew up the instructions of the king's envoys to Germany, and obviously he did so after agreement with the minister. At the very most he may have allowed himself some latitude to develop his own thoughts in the instructions, and this is what he seems to have done in those given to Baron de Charnacé. It is at least certain that between the end of October 1631 and the beginning of the following year, French policy hesitated somewhat between two courses of action, of which one would perhaps have provoked open warfare with Spain and the other tended above all to avoid it. What were the feelings of Richelieu and Father Joseph during those weeks of uncertainty? There is no direct evidence which allows us to say. It is interesting to study this brief crisis of French policy a little more closely and to take stock of the consequences of the resolutions which put an end to it.

After Gustavus Adolphus's victory at Breitenfeld the situation in the Empire was completely altered in the space of a few weeks. Tilly retreated to the south and established himself in the Upper Palatinate where he could shield Bavaria, which the king of Sweden had no intention of attacking at that time. On the other hand, a few troops under Pappenheim fell back to the north, in the direction of the Weser, in an attempt to bar the way to any reinforcements which might be sent to the Swedish army from Pomerania. The ecclesiastical princes of Franconia and the middle valley of the Rhine—the bishops of Bamberg and Würzburg and the elector of Mainz—fled before the invasion. Even the electors of Trier and Cologne no longer felt secure and begged the King of France to protect them. Further to the south, the few Spanish garrisons which still held the Rhenish Palatinate were in great danger of losing control since Bernard of Saxe-Weimar had seized Heidelberg and Mannheim. The weary Swedish troops were able to recuperate in the Franconian countryside which had so far suffered very little from quartered troops and requisitions. When, rather than attack Ferdinand II's hereditary possessions, he advanced on the valleys of the Main and the Rhine, no-one knew Gustavus's plan, but it was quite clear that he was consolidating his position there. Without making any territorial changes in the 'priests' alley' he was expelling the bishops and abbots, and he summoned his chancellor, Oxenstierna, from Sweden to organise a provisional administration there. He did not seem concerned either about the League or about the king of France. He allowed it to be rumoured that a Grand Duchy of Franconia might perhaps be created and given to Bernard of Saxe-Weimar, and it was commonly thought that he wanted to transform the Empire, giving the Protestants the upper hand and having himself elected emperor. The Protestants welcomed him as a messenger from heaven. In the Catholic camp, some were goaded into action by hatred, but the majority were paralysed by fear. With so many unexpected events taking place with ever-increasing speed, what should the king of France do—indeed, what could he do?

Richelieu was not disposed, either by temperament or by the logic of the situation, to await events. As far as he was concerned, action demanded action. It was not a question of modifying the principles of French policy, but of adapting the means by which it was carried out to suit the circumstances. In his eyes the essential fact was that France ought to be just as apprehensive of the establishment of the Swedes in the valley of the middle Rhine as she had been of the Spanish. Now that detachments of Swedish troops from Mainz or Mannheim were beginning to infiltrate Alsace, they had to be stopped if possible by installing French garrisons at a few well-chosen points. In this way,

Richelieu was only resuming the programme which, as we have seen, he had proposed to Louis XIII after the fall of La Rochelle, 'to open the gates . . . and . . . acquire an entry to Germany', in order, he had written in January 1629, to guarantee its neighbours 'from Spanish oppression'; in the autumn of 1631 he could have written 'from Swedish oppression', without changing the principles of his policy.

Historians who still think that French kings were always trying to expand eastward to the limits of ancient Gaul—and happily their number decreases—never fail to invoke the so-called 'policy of natural frontiers' to explain the action during the period when Gustavus Adolphus's ambitions were rampant in the Empire. In fact the instructions given to the royal envoys in Germany, and Richelieu's correspondence itself, are enough to explain what happened without any need to refer to theoretical claims which, in any case, are nowhere mentioned in the documents. The king of France had to provide for the very real possibility that, after bringing the Swedish king into Germany, he might be forced to fight him. The treaty of Bärwalde, which, apart from the promise of subsidies, was nothing more than a political agreement with no precise obligations, could not prevent the two allies drifting very gradually from mistrust into hostility. And that was exactly what nearly happened.

In order to take the necessary precautions on the Rhine, a road across Lorraine had to be opened to French troops, thus linking Champagne with Alsace. Lorraine's position between the kingdom of France and the Empire was confused because it comprised three separate regions, the term Lorraine being nothing more than a geographical expression. To the west were the lands of Bar-le-Duc, known as the Barrois fief, which owed allegiance to the king of France so that the duke was the king's vassal. Further to the east, beyond the Meuse, the duchy of Lorraine itself had been declared independent of the Empire in 1542. Nevertheless it continued to form part of the circle of the Upper Rhine and contained numerous imperial fiefs in which the duke of Lorraine continued to be invested by the emperor. Finally, three towns, Verdun, Toul and Metz, were free cities, as well as being the seats of three dioceses whose temporal possessions included estates scattered all over the lands of Lorraine. In 1552, with the consent of the princes of the Empire, the king of France had occupied these three towns as Imperial Vicar. He had then gradually gained recognition of his sovereignty and had extended it to the temporal possessions of the three dioceses. It is easy to imagine how such a confused complex of legal rights could give rise to frequent disputes, and some of these were still being contested in 1629. It was on account of such a dispute, involving the bishopric of Metz, that the emperor had sent garrisons into Vic and Moyenvic, two of its dependent towns. For his part, the king of France had strengthened his sovereignty over the three bishoprics by extending the powers of Moricq de Juzé, an administrator who had been sent to Champagne.

The fact that the Duke Charles IV had adopted an attitude of open hostility towards Louis XIII made it all the easier for Richelieu to find a pretext to intervene in Lorraine. After the Day of Dupes and Marie de Médicis's flight to Brussels, Gaston in his turn had left the kingdom to join the duke of Lorraine at Nancy. Soon afterwards there was a rumour that the duke favoured an engagement between Monsieur and his sister, Marguerite of Lorraine. In January 1632 Marguerite and Gaston were secretly married, a fact which the court only learned a little later. In addition, the king of France could hardly allow imperial troops to be garrisoned permanently at Vic and Moyenvic, only a little way from Metz. In December 1631, a French army besieged Moyenvic and took the town. As a result, Charles IV had to accept an agreement which became the treaty of Vic, signed on 6th January 1632. He handed over the fortified town of Marsal, to the north east of Nancy, to the king of France; he granted French troops right of passage through his duchy; and he undertook from that time onwards to avoid 'all understandings, leagues, associations and dealings whatsoever with any prince or state which might be to the detriment of the king, his states and lands, his fealty or protection'. In spite of the very explicit nature of this clause, Richelieu was well aware that Charles IV's word was not to be trusted; but at least, until he broke it, the treaty of Vic allowed Louis XIII to move troops into Alsace when necessary without having to force a passage for them. An active policy in the Rhineland was becoming feasible and it was not before time. At the very beginning of January 1632 immediate action became imperative.

Richelieu had not ceased negotiations after the battle of Breitenfeld. He continued to urge the members of the League to declare themselves neutral and asked Gustavus Adolphus under what conditions he would agree to recognise their neutrality. But this only led to shilly-shallying, wrangling, and ill-will on all sides. The fruitless negotiations dragged on and all the while sporadic warfare, whose only object seemed to be pillage, gradually spread along the left bank of the Rhine. Richelieu became convinced that it would be pointless to wait until the Spaniards or the Swedes were established in sufficient strength to deny the French access to Germany.

In the Swedish section of the archives at the Ministère des Affaires Étrangères there is a moving document which is well worth reading.[1] It is undated but contains the reference: 'On the affairs of Germany. Moyenvic, January 1632.' It was doubtless written during the first days of January, before the Council of the 6th at which Richelieu's course of action was decided. It is in the hand of Father Ange de Mortagne, and it was dictated. So hasty was the dictation that he hardly had time to form the words. Who was the author? We know that Father Ange often acted as secretary to Father Joseph, but nothing in the text is in keeping with the Capuchin's cool temperament. On the contrary, the clarity of thought, the intense introspection, the strength of the feelings and the burning desire to justify a policy of action to the king all point to Richelieu. It may be that it is the first draft of one of the memoranda which Richelieu was in the habit of using to guide his master's decisions. On the other hand, perhaps he wished to commit his thoughts to paper as they emerged, to make them clearer and firmer and to justify himself in his own eyes. The half-formed words conjure up a compelling picture of the Cardinal, pacing about his study and dictating with no thought for Father Ange who can hardly manage to keep up with him. He states in a voice which brooks no doubt: 'It is quite clear to anyone with a grain of common sense that Christendom is torn by two powerful factions. On the one hand there are the Protestants who are fighting the Church; on the other, the house of Austria which oppresses liberty and attains its ends by the subversion of justice and other means contrary to the profession of Christianity, such as ambition, usurpation, dissimulation, and the art of sowing dissension among the great, revolution among the people, and slander among men of good will who do not take its side. By these means it overthrows the very foundations of public faith and justice which are inseparably linked. The proof of this double truth is the history of the recent and present disorders.' Richelieu gives a broad outline of this, and then goes on to contrast the French king's policy with that of the house of Austria: 'In the same way it can be openly said of France, who throughout the ages has opposed all excesses of impiety and injustice and who has been God's chosen instrument for maintaining the Church and the common weal in the face of the greatest onslaughts of these two monsters, that only she continues the struggle at great cost to herself.' And finally he

[1] Arch. Min. des Aff. Étr., pol. corr., Sweden, vol. II, Fol. 233. Unpubl.

shows how, while Louis XIII 'was actively engaged in establishing both religious and domestic peace within the state by the capture of La Rochelle, acting from motives which were generally agreed to be the most just of our time', the house of Austria had taken advantage of the situation to kindle once more the flames of war in Italy. How then can his very Christian Majesty ever be accused of coming to terms with heresy if he is compelled to engage in a struggle with sovereigns for whom religion is only a pretence and whose policy, against all justice, has as its sole aim the oppression of freedom and the encouragement of divisions among peoples?

We may easily judge from this the trend of Richelieu's thought at the beginning of January 1632. He was still pondering over which course of action to adopt before presenting it to the king, but he could plainly envisage the consequences of an ever-widening conflict. The fate of the German princes was not his principal concern and the defence of German liberties was only a means to an end for him, much as the Catholic cause was for the king of Spain. What worried him most was the division of Christendom where two 'powerful factions' were vying for supremacy. Of the two he feared the Habsburg alliance more, because he considered that it was still the stronger, and so at times he encouraged his master to intervene and even make war against it. But he saw little to choose between it and the Protestant 'faction', and although he supported the latter he was apprehensive of being the instrument of its triumph. He was torn between the temptation to take advantage of Gustavus Adolphus's victories to overthrow the house of Austria's hegemony and the desire to let the two factions fight until they were exhausted. The dilemma was all the more acute because he doubted whether France, even with the king of Sweden's alliance, was in a position to resist the united forces of the emperor and the king of Spain.

Apart from the memorandum dictated to Father Ange de Mortagne we have no direct evidence of his personal feelings during the few days which preceded the Council of 6th January 1632. Nevertheless, we can hardly doubt that at times he leant towards a policy of belligerence. He continued to work towards the conclusion of a treaty of neutrality between the League and the king of Sweden, but when the League's envoys brought to Metz a somewhat belated promise not to attack the Swedes again, they attached to it the unacceptable condition that all the lands which had been conquered or occupied at their expense should be restored. Richelieu sent more envoys into Germany. The

Comte de Bruslon was despatched to the elector of Trier who was seeking the protection of the king of France. In exchange for this, de Bruslon demanded the right to put a French garrison into one of the elector's strongholds in the Rhineland, preferably Koblenz. Melchior de Lisle, France's resident at Strassburg did his best to foster confidence in the king and to prevent the town being won over by the emperor. At the beginning of January he visited Gustavus Adolphus and vainly tried to persuade him to evacuate Mainz and to stop sending troops over to the left bank of the Rhine. Finally, on 8th January 1632, Louis XIII sent an extraordinary embassy from Vic to Gustavus Adolphus, led by the Marquis de Brézé, the captain of his guards, and one of Richelieu's brothers-in-law. It would appear that the clearest idea of the cardinal's intentions, uncertain though they still were on the very eve of the Council of the 6th, may be gained from de Brézé's instructions of 5th January.[1] They were dictated by Father Joseph, but certainly reflect Richelieu's views.

The Marquis de Brézé was instructed to announce the capture of Moyenvic to Gustavus Adolphus. He was to add that now that the town was in Louis's hands he 'was free to employ his forces as befitted the common good' and he begged the king of Sweden 'to tell him what he judged to be for the best' since the latter 'had better intelligence of German affairs, possessing as he did that portion of the country which his valour and skilful command had acquired'. As it was unlikely that Gustavus Adolphus would want to be the first to show his hand, in this event the marquis might also remind Gustavus Adolphus 'of the great enterprises which he was pursuing' and let it be understood that the German princes and towns which supported him were weary of war and 'without the French king's help, peace would have to be made'. Perhaps he might also insinuate 'if he judged it opportune, that Gustavus Adolphus should not lose so fine an opportunity to enter Italy and the Archduke Leopold's lands,[2] whilst Louis would attack the hereditary lands of the emperor in upper Germany'. If this last line of argument were used, de Brézé was to 'treat the idea as if it had come from Gustavus Adolphus and say that it seemed likely (without giving any definite undertaking) that Louis would willingly accept the proposal'.

[1] In general the dating of the group of documents to which this belongs (Min. des Aff. Étr., Sweden, vol. II, fol. 192) is unreliable. However, the contents of de Brézé's instructions leaves no doubt that they are prior to the Council of the 6th. It would thus appear that the 5th is the most probable dating.

[2] In Alsace.

What this amounted to was a suggestion by Richelieu, in Louis XIII's name, for an alliance between France and Sweden, but one whose objectives were to be revised in such a way as to remove the Swedish troops from the region of the Rhine, leaving the king of France complete freedom of action. He did not actually propose this to Gustavus Adolphus: on the contrary, Louis wanted Gustavus Adolphus to take the initiative and offer him an offensive alliance against the house of Austria in place of the financial arrangement embodied in the treaty of Bärwalde. In another passage of the instructions he laid further stress on the limits of the fields of action within which the two allies should work. The ambassador was to ascertain 'whether the king of Sweden wishes to take it upon himself to seize the emperor's lands and hereditary provinces and wishes the king (i.e. Louis XIII) to take possession of the Archduke Leopold's, notably Alsace (the remainder is not detailed here). A permanent arrangement can be reached at a later date in consultation with the Princes and Estates of Germany.'[1] At the same time Richelieu makes it quite clear that Louis XIII will not leave the king of Sweden to deal with the Catholic princes as he pleases. He 'firmly believes that the king of Sweden has no more intention than he himself has of oppressing others, particularly the electors and princes of the Catholic League, for this would be quite contrary to the object of their treaty and to its articles regarding neutrality with the members of the League and the preservation of the Catholic religion.'

We can see that Richelieu was taking infinite care to keep open all his lines of retreat so that he could withdraw if he considered it necessary, but if we read the Marquis de Brézé's instructions, and take them in conjunction with the memorandum dictated to Father Ange de Mortagne, it is difficult to believe that Richelieu was not tempted, provided that he could get the king of Sweden to co-operate, to suggest a more vigorous policy to Louis XIII, and that he did not completely rule out the idea of armed intervention in Germany. The only record we have of the discussions held on 6th January comes from Father Joseph's biographer, Lepré-Balain. According to him, most of the ministers were in favour of sending the king's troops into Alsace, and Richelieu was on the verge of adopting this view while Father Joseph roundly opposed it. Louis XIII, however, put off the decision

---

[1] It seems that in this case Richelieu has in mind the occupation of a part of Alsace using a procedure similar to the one which had enabled Henry II to occupy the Three Dioceses. However, there is clearly no question of his having made any firm decision at this stage.

until the next day. After a sleepless night, the cardinal went at dawn to Father Joseph's room to reassure him that he would advise the king not to send troops into Alsace and to continue to maintain the Catholic electors who had put themselves under his protection against the king of Sweden. This single piece of evidence is not sufficient proof,[1] and we cannot be sure that Father Joseph's and Richelieu's attitudes were the ones attributed to them by Lepré-Balain, but there is no doubt about the Council's wavering between two policies nor about the decisions which were made the next day.

French policy therefore remained unchanged, but it could not fail to encounter the same obstacles and run the same risks as before. Its ends were clearly defined but there were no obvious means of attaining them. Fortunately the winter still left a breathing space before the next campaign. While the Marquis de Brézé, with modified instructions, went off to negotiate with Gustavus Adolphus, Richelieu and Father Joseph were left to work out the best way to reconcile the need to maintain relations with Sweden with their decision to protect the Catholic princes and electors against her. Several 'memoranda on the affairs of Germany' dictated to Father Ange de Mortagne by Father Joseph or Richelieu during this critical period are still in existence. It is impossible to analyse all of them but we cannot entirely overlook them for they are direct evidence of the intentions and manoeuvrings of a policy which from that time onwards played a considerable part in determining the course of the German war. The ones dated 21st January and 1st February 1632 are the most informative.

The memorandum[2] of 21st January, in which the Cardinal's contribution seems to me to be greater than Father Joseph's, shows quite clearly what Richelieu thought of the king of Sweden and how he envisaged the difficulties of his task. He thought that the king of Sweden wanted to consolidate his positions on both banks of the Rhine in order to prevent the French king helping the Catholics. Gustavus Adolphus no doubt felt sure that he could rely on the loyalty of the Protestant princes and use his command of the rivers, towns and roads to prevent the Spanish and imperial armies joining forces. Then, when he had beaten the emperor, it would be easy for him to 'extend his conquests at will'. This would substitute Swedish domination for that

---

[1] This has been pointed out, and rightly so, by a German historian, W. Mommsen in his book *Kardinal Richelieu; seine Politik in Elsass*. Unlike Lepré-Balain he believes that it was Father Joseph who inclined towards the more vigorous policy but this is not my own impression.

[2] Min. des Aff. Étr., Sweden, vol. II, fol. 253. Unpubl.

of the house of Austria. Richelieu went on in characteristically metaphorical style: 'It is more difficult to recognise the illness than to cure it, all the more so because of the very violence of the illness. Moreover, in this case the old maxim of meeting force with force cannot apply, since to do so would put France and Christendom in extreme danger, for reasons which are well known to men of sound judgement and who can apply in matters of statesmanship the same care as doctors who avoid drastic purges during prolonged fevers. The chief difficulty lies in the contradiction presented by the disease, for we are torn between fear of the house of Austria and fear of the Protestants. The perfect answer would be to reduce both to such a point that they are no longer to be feared, and it is to this end that efforts must be directed. But at the same time care must be taken to ensure that if the means used do not attain this end, the perfect answer, they should at least serve to ward off the worst effects and provide breathing space in which to muster one's forces and turn events to account without danger.'

But what was to be done in the present straits? 'As to the Spaniard and the Swede,' dictated Richelieu, 'we must above all take care that in bringing down one we do not raise the other to such a point that he is more to be feared than the former. We must also act with such caution that instead of setting one against the other, we do not become involved in war with one of them. Such a step would allow the other to increase in such strength that even if the king were victorious he would lose more from the easy manner in which the other became more powerful than he would gain from his own victory.'

Finally, Richelieu drew the following conclusions from his reflections: France should not 'at the present time' engage in war against the house of Austria or against Sweden. However, it was necessary 'from this moment in time . . . to think of limiting Sweden's progress' as much as Spain's, 'who retreats instead of advancing', without however providing Spain with any opportunity to recover her strength. He added: 'to carry out this difficult operation, in which the issues are so delicate, we must combine industry with force, and diplomacy with arms'.

The French king's intentions did not change between the memoranda of 21st January and of 1st February, but in the latter the means which Richelieu intended to use are discussed in greater detail.[1] Richelieu examines four possible approaches: a united front with

---

[1] Min. des Aff. Étr., Germany, vol. VIII, fol. 149. Fagniez (*Le Père Joseph et Richelieu*, vol. I, p. 587) sees Father Joseph's influence and ideas at work here.

Sweden against the house of Austria; an agreement with the emperor and the king of Spain to oppose the king of Sweden; an attempt to obtain under the best possible conditions a treaty of neutrality between the League and the king of Sweden, leaving the latter to 'continue the war in Germany without becoming involved'; or, finally, if such neutrality were achieved, 'to occupy Alsace, Breisach and the Rhine crossings which the Catholic electors hold, and maintain an army there which may be used when the opportunity arises'. The memorandum goes on to list the arguments in favour of each one of the four policies, but in the margin he expresses doubts about their value—for example, 'this argument does not seem good', or 'these arguments are not sound', or 'this argument is worthless'. The memorandum concludes by recommending a policy which is not entirely any one of the four which I have just outlined. There is to be no break either with the king of Sweden or with the house of Austria. 'No means of saving the Catholic League and Catholicism in Germany is to be overlooked.' As far as possible the king of Sweden is to be diverted from his intention to occupy the Rhine and Alsace: negotiations must be held with the Rhineland electors to ensure a free passage to the Rhine, without which they cannot be helped, and an army of 30,000 foot and 6,000 horse is to be held in readiness on the frontier. 'By this means we would break with no one. We would be on a war-footing and in sufficient strength to take advantage of whatever opportunities presented themselves. The electors and the Catholic League could have no complaint against the king.'

By the end of the winter, therefore, Louis was still waiting on events, but with a wary eye so that, as Richelieu hoped, his policy could be adapted to suit the circumstances without committing him to any future line of action. We can now resume our narrative and it will be enough to outline the events of greatest consequence.

The first of these was Wallenstein's recall. The emperor had sacrificed him only in the hope of obtaining from the electoral college his son's election as King of the Romans, and he regretted his weakness immediately after the election was rejected. Wallenstein had accepted his dismissal without complaint, if not without bitterness; since then he had lived in royal style in his immense estates in Bohemia, sometimes at his palace at Gitschin, but more usually in a vastly more sumptuous palace in Prague which he had had built by an Italian architect when he was at the height of his power. The emperor had not completely broken off relations with the duke of Friedland, and though he was perplexed by his arrogant and whimsical character along with his general unpredictability, he knew well that he could not do without him. In the autumn of 1631 he asked him to resume his command. At first Wallenstein seemed in no hurry to accept. It was only in December, after Gustavus Adolphus's victories, that he agreed to raise 40,000 men for the emperor, but it was on the condition that a new treaty gave him the same powers as before. When the levies had been completed he imposed further conditions before agreeing to accept command of the troops. One of them was rather questionable since he was to be authorised by the emperor to make peace with the elector of Saxony and to conduct the negotiations as he saw fit. Furthermore, Ferdinand promised to reinstate him as duke of Mecklenburg, and in the meantime gave him the principality of Gross-Glockau in Silesia. In May 1632, Wallenstein's batallions entered Bohemia from which the elector of Saxony had fled some months earlier, in the process carrying off to Dresden some of the finest paintings from the Prague collections. John George's marauding expedition finished as it had begun: the whole of Bohemia was reconquered and the Czech émigrés who had so foolishly entrusted themselves to him went once more into exile.

Wallenstein's recall—the most important event of the period—partly explains the confusion of the next few years and we must return to the subject later and at more length.

If a treaty of neutrality had been negotiated between the king of Sweden and the League, events would doubtless have taken another course, but the intransigence of both parties made this impossible despite Richelieu's patience and his prolonged efforts. Gustavus Adolphus's aggressive mood had not been sweetened by the arrival of so lofty a person as the cardinal-minister's brother-in-law. Soon Baron de Charnacé, who had given ample proof of his skill, had to be sent to join the marquis de Brézé. Brézé and Charnacé went together to the king of Sweden in his camp. He received them at once, but their welcome was brusque, as we can judge from de Brézé's despatch of 28th February 1632.[1] They presented the proposals which Maximilian had made them accept, with one or two modifications, but the king of Sweden, who regarded Louis as an ally, refused to accept him in the role of a mediator. From the very first, wrote Brézé, 'we found him so bitter that if we had wanted to break with him and declare war, we could have done so quite easily'. Gustavus Adolphus began by asking Charnacé 'whether he brought him peace or war and whether the

[1] Min. des Aff. Étr., Germany, vol. VIII, fol. 169.

king's troops were marching against him'. When the two ambassadors announced the impending arrival of the electors' delegates, 'he told us', wrote Brézé, 'that they were rogues and traitors who wanted to use us to fool him and that if they came he would have them hanged'. Charnacé tried to calm him, but failed. Gustavus Adolphus 'angrily asked him what the king would do if the treaty were not made and what he was to expect'. Fortunately, Charnacé was not a man who took fright easily. He calmly replied that the king had not thought that the treaty of neutrality which was so useful to both sides could be refused by either and, thus, 'his majesty had made no plans for this contingency, or at least none that he had mentioned'. The ambassadors were able to leave without breaking off relations, but it was becoming extremely difficult to conclude the negotiations. Moreover, as it turned out, the elector of Bavaria himself took matters out of Louis's hands. He put his troops into the field again and Tilly recaptured Bamberg from the Swedes. The bridges between the League and the king of Sweden were now burned.

Although Richelieu had not abandoned any of the negotiations which he had set in motion, he was principally occupied with home affairs during the spring and summer of 1632. Once again he was not short of worries. The Queen-Mother was plotting with the Spaniards from her retreat in Brussels. Gaston, who had fled to Lorraine, had secretly married Charles IV's sister Marguerite—a marriage which Louis XIII could not accept. Then, at the beginning of summer, the duc de Montmorency, governor of Languedoc, had rebelled and the duke of Orléans had re-entered the country accompanied by armed bands and had joined up with Montmorency in the lower Rhône valley. Montmorency was beaten, wounded and taken prisoner at Castelnaudary on 1st September. As in 1626, after the Chalais conspiracy, Gaston had feebly surrendered, but Montmorency was not beheaded until 30th October, and the indignation which his execution caused among the upper ranks of the nobility made Richelieu's position rather difficult for some time. We cannot help admiring the cardinal's coolness and clear thinking when we see him beset by all these difficulties, yet never relaxing his guard nor diminishing his activities in Germany. He spared no effort to create a network of garrisons around the frontier and beyond Lorraine. In case of open war and a Spanish attempt at invasion they could hold back the advance of enemy troops, and if events allowed, they would also help to ease the passage of French troops into the Empire. Richelieu's concern over this is shown quite clearly in an article from a memorandum sent to Charnacé who was then returning to Germany[1] before the interview which I have described. It says that 'the ambassadors must ascertain whether, if the king of Sweden attacks and takes Breisach, he would be willing to place the town at his majesty's disposal, providing the costs of taking it were reasonably defrayed.' It is true that Richelieu added 'to all intents he will not agree'. At the same time he exploited the inconstancy of the duke of Lorraine who had stupidly become involved with Gaston of Orléans, and violated the treaty of Vic. This allowed Louis XIII to send troops into Lorraine and to force the duke to accept the treaty of Liverdun (26th June), renewing the treaty of Vic but in harsher terms. The county of Clermont-en-Argonne was ceded along with Marsal, and Louis XIII could also put French garrisons into the two fortresses of Stenay and Jametz. Finally the duke promised to 'unite his forces with his majesty's to render all possible assistance in any war which his majesty might undertake'. As soon as the treaty of Liverdun was signed, Louis XIII used it to occupy a few Rhineland forts with the consent of the elector of Trier. An army of 20,000 foot and 3,000 horse crossed Lorraine under the command of Marshal d'Effiat. In a memorandum dated 7th July 1632[2] Louis XIII gave the news to Charnacé. 'This army,' he said, 'is on the way to Strassburg. From there it will follow the course of the Rhine and if possible take over Philippsburg and all the other fortresses which the archbishop of Trier wishes to put into our safekeeping.' In any case, Richelieu was determined that the king should not be caught unawares.

The year 1632, however, is important above all else for marking the final campaigns, the victories and the death of Gustavus Adolphus. He marched out of Mainz on 2nd March leaving Bernard of Saxe-Weimar to guard the Rhineland. First he went to Nuremberg where he received an enthusiastic welcome. From there he crossed the Danube at Donauwörth and marched on Augsburg. Before him there stood only the League's army which was drawn up around the fortress of Ingolstadt, since Wallenstein was engaged at the time in expelling the Saxons from Bohemia with the new troops which he had just raised. Tilly tried to stop the Swedes as they crossed the Lech but he was mortally wounded, and the Swedes crossed. Tilly died some time later

[1] Memoranda for Charnacé rejoining Brézé in Germany, 6th February 1632. Min. des Aff. Étr., Germany, vol. VIII, fol. 157.
[2] Memorandum drawn up on the King's orders to M. le Baron de Charnacé, ambassador to his Majesty in Germany. Min. des Aff. Étr., Germany, vol. VIII, fol. 263.

at Ingolstadt where he had been taken, and Maximilian, abandoning the idea of defending Munich, retreated to Salzburg. The spring campaign was over and practically the whole of Bavaria was occupied by the Swedish king.

At this point his position became difficult. Having encountered no difficulty in his reconquest of Bohemia, Wallenstein marched westwards to link up with the Bavarian army commanded by Maximilian. Gustavus Adolphus tried to stop them joining forces, but failed, and when the autumn campaign opened the Swedish army was practically face to face with the Bavarian and imperial forces in the region of Nuremberg. Wallenstein had Bohemia and his duchy of Friedland at his back. They were both stocked high with fodder and grain and the mills kept on turning. By contrast, the Swedish army was backed by devastated lands which could yield scarcely any food. Sickness, fostered by an exceptionally wet summer, combined with the lack of forage and bread to decimate the Swedish troops. Men and horses fell in their hundreds, and Gustavus Adolphus could not contemplate marching on Vienna with his reduced army. The very danger which he had avoided the previous year by not leaving the region of the Rhine now threatened him. What would happen to the Swedish army which had ventured so far south if the elector of Saxony, whom the king of Sweden had never trusted, came to an agreement with Wallenstein and cut off the route to the Baltic? Gustavus attacked Wallenstein's prepared positions, but the attack failed. He then proposed to make peace on the basis that the emperor was to revoke the Edict of Restitution, that the Swedes should occupy the German Baltic coast and that a duchy of Franconia be created for Wallenstein, but the negotiations were no sooner begun than they broke down. At the beginning of November, Gustavus Adolphus decided to break camp at Nuremberg and headed north towards Erfurt. Wallenstein shadowed on a more easterly route, heading for Leipzig, and it was near there at Lützen that the decisive battle was fought on 16th November 1632. It began in a thick mist which covered the valley. Careless as ever of his life, Gustavus Adolphus charged with his cavalry and was killed, but Wallenstein's troops began to falter and Bernard of Saxe-Weimar gained a complete victory.

When Gustavus Adolphus died at the age of thirty-seven he had undoubtedly reached the height of his success and the dangers born of this success were beginning to gather about him. The further he strayed from the Baltic, the more he was in danger. Not that he had much to fear from Wallenstein who from that time on seemed to place more faith in negotiation than in arms, but he was unsure of his allies. With his customary insight Richelieu had very accurately summarised the nature of the relationship between the king of Sweden and the Protestant princes of Germany in the memorandum of January 21st 1632: 'He believes that the protestants are so feeble and already so completely under his thumb that they cannot withdraw. He holds Saxony by the throat at Magdeburg. He has the main fortresses of Brandenburg. The dukes of Pomerania and Mecklenburg are completely in his control. The landgrave of Hesse has seriously offended the Catholics and as he can do nothing on his own will always do what the king wants. The imperial cities and the northern plains will follow him to maintain their religion and out of hatred for the house of Austria, which has treated them so badly that they can fear nothing worse.' In point of fact, Gustavus Adolphus could only rely completely on the free cities and the countryside which had welcomed him as a liberator and followed him 'to maintain their religion', but there was no great advantage in that. He had nothing but contempt for his allies the princes, who only supported him out of fear or necessity. An alliance based on fear and contempt cannot be sound and, even before Gustavus Adolphus's death, the seeds of dissolution were apparent at the very heart of the Protestant cause. Soon after his death they flourished.

CHAPTER VI

WALLENSTEIN'S TREASON AND
THE SWEDISH DEFEAT

The victories and conquests won by Gustavus Adolphus in the course of his campaigns of 1631 and 1632 had no lasting effect; they merely constituted a dazzling episode in the story of the Thirty Years War. None the less, on the morrow of the battle of Lützen, Germany was no longer what she had been before the Swedish invasion. Its violent shock had hastened the gradual transformations which were already taking place in the Empire. Before continuing the story, therefore, we must pause for a moment on the day of that battle, 16th November 1632. After this date the German civil war gradually petered out and gave way to a European conflict, characterised by a further clash between the houses of France and Austria, which laid the foundations of the territorial and political framework of modern Europe.

The civil war in Germany had already lasted for fourteen years. After beginning in Bohemia it had spread first to southern then to central, and finally to northern Germany. The fighting had moved from region to region but few areas had escaped the billeting, the requisitions and the violence of the soldiery. No one can number the villages put to the flame, the harvests destroyed, or the victims of disease—since typhoid and plague followed in the wake of the armies decimating not only the inhabitants of town and country but also the troops.

The original causes of the war had long since been forgotten, but new ones had sprung up in their place. The emperor's victory over the Bohemian rebels had created a new Catholic Bohemia obedient to the Habsburgs. Only a handful of exiles, whose flight had isolated them from their native land, still thought it possible to resurrect an independent Bohemia. The problem of the Palatinate had not yet been settled, but it had already undergone several changes both before and after Gustavus Adolphus's intervention. From 1623 to 1631 it was no longer a question of whether it would eventually be returned to its former master, but of whether the Spaniards who had invaded it with Spinola at their head could keep it, or whether the elector of Bavaria, who held a few fortresses, would manage to add it to his states. Subsequently the Swedes had expelled both Bavarians and Spaniards and had occupied it in their turn, but the Swedish occupation was on a very precarious footing and it became obvious that the fate of the Palatinate could only be settled in the terms of a general peace. At the outbreak of the Bohemian rebellion and during the years which followed, the Protestant princes of Germany had fought in defence of the Protestant faith and, above all, to safeguard their liberties. A little later they had been forced to follow Gustavus Adolphus, but in no ime at all the king of Sweden's scant respect for them had led them to fear a Swedish domination of the Empire as much as they feared Austria's, and many of them would have been glad to rid Germany of all foreigners, Swede and Spaniard alike.

The men who had taken part in the war from the beginning had either disappeared one after the other or else seemed weary of the long struggle, and their place was taken by a new generation. Thurn was content with a command in the Swedish army; Mansfeld was dead; Christian of Brunswick and Tilly had been killed; Frederick V, the winter king', broken by misfortune, had died at the age of thirty-six rom a mild fever, a few days after learning that Gustavus Adolphus had been killed at Lützen. Emperor Ferdinand II himself, although only fifty-four, was worn out by asceticism and mortification. In the old court his son, already proclaimed king of Hungary, was gaining power, and he was surrounded by a group of young men who were impatient of what they considered to be a weak policy and who wanted stronger ties between the governments of Vienna and Madrid.

In short, the spirit of the new generation was no longer that of its predecessors. We have already noted, along with the German historian Brandi, that the Counter Reformation had changed in character immediately after the house of Austria's early successes. No doubt it continued to seek the restoration of Catholicism wherever it had been ousted by Protestantism, but it seemed to be working much more for the great Catholic princely houses than for the Church. The struggle for the bishoprics at the time of the Danish invasion had not been a religious war. When, for example, the Catholic troops had done their best to occupy the dioceses of Halberstadt or Osnabrück they had certainly wanted to expel the Protestant administrators, but their main aim was to install one of the emperor's sons, Archduke Leopold

William, as bishop. Most of the princes gradually lost their religious fervour. They continued to fight no longer for their faith but to assert their territorial claims, to satisfy their greed, to reconquer or increase their states, or to consolidate their gains. There was still a struggle between Protestants and Catholics, but both sides now put interests of State before the interests of the Church. To quote only one example, it is significant that almost all the princes, with the exception of Ferdinand II, viewed the Edict of Restitution simply as a vast political operation in which someone's loss was another's gain; whether or not it was revoked was only a matter of force. The Empire's religious settlement was not yet established in 1632 and would not be so until 1648, but the princes were far more concerned with its territorial settlement.

It was these very territorial disputes which widened the rift between Sweden and her German allies after Gustavus Adolphus's death. Apart from the cities, which still saw the Swedes in the role of protectors of Protestantism, and the minor princes, whose only hope of restoration lay with Sweden, only the electors of Brandenburg and Saxony held the Protestant party together. They, however, had only joined it unwillingly, and at the last possible moment, and neither of them had very much to gain from the Swedish victories. Now that the elector of Saxony had the Lusatias—although this still had to be confirmed by treaty—he was only interested in ensuring that the Saxon princes stayed in the bishoprics where they had become administrators. Furthermore, he was hopeful of obtaining the emperor's backing which seemed to offer more security, and to this end he had continued to negotiate with the Viennese court, and with Wallenstein after his recall. Gustavus Adolphus had little faith in John George's loyalty and the hurried evacuation of Bohemia by the Saxon troops—before Wallenstein had even entered it—had increased his suspicions. On 9th March 1632, the marquis de Brézé, who was still with the king of Sweden, wrote to Paris: 'News has reached us today that the elector of Saxony has withdrawn his troops from Prague and four other fortresses in Bohemia, which is therefore a total loss to the king of Sweden. There is some doubt whether he acted from fear or cunning.' Doubtless it was a mixture of both, but one thing which was certain was that John George was carrying on secret talks with Wallenstein through Arnim, and suspicion about these grew daily.

As for the elector of Brandenburg, he had every reason to fear a permanent occupation of the Baltic shores by the Swedes. Though their military occupation of Prussia was supposed to be temporary, in fact they were masters of his duchy, but a more serious issue between the elector and the king of Sweden was the matter of Pomerania. By an agreement made in 1529 between the two families of Pomerania and Brandenburg the first of them to die out was to bequeath all its territories to the other. In 1632 Bogislav XIV, the duke of Pomerania, was the last of his line, since he had no children and his death seemed imminent. If the war ended without the Swedes being expelled from Germany and if Bogislav died in the meantime, George William wondered whether Sweden would voluntarily hand over the fertile lands of Pomerania with the mouths of the Oder and the well-sheltered port of Stettin, which seemed to him to be Brandenburg's natural maritime outlet. His preoccupation with securing this coveted inheritance dominated his policy as it was later to dominate his son's after 1640.

The position of the great warring powers was also confused and uncertain. Obviously the news of Gustavus Adolphus's death had been joyfully received at Vienna. Ferdinand II must have seen it as a dazzling sign of the will of God to save his Church and its defenders after they had been put to the test. It also gave him new heart to pursue un-relentingly the task he had undertaken. He might of course have taken the opposite view and seen it as the last chance to put an end to the warfare and suffering which had beset the German nation for so long. This, at any rate, seems to have been Wallenstein's view, and it was one reason among many which encouraged him to negotiate with the elector of Saxony. He even found an ally in Gudacker von Liechten-stein, an imperial minister—albeit temporarily in disgrace—who drew up a closely reasoned memorandum, first brought to light by Srbik,[1] in which peace was openly advocated. He emphasised the bankruptcy of the Austrian and Spanish governments and the unreliability of their troops who, because they were not paid, had to live off the land. He affirmed that even an imperial victory, apart from prolonging the war, would only bring about the armed intervention of the king of France who could not allow the house of Austria, with its close ties with Spain, to establish Habsburg domination in Europe. He listed the Catholic princes of the Empire, some hostile, some taking refuge in neutrality, others ruined. He referred to the growing hatred for the emperor in large areas of the Empire and showed that even the

---

[1] Srbik: *Wallensteins Ende*, p. 16. The original memorandum is among the Trautmansdorf family papers in the Vienna State Archives.

emperor's own subjects, overwhelmed by insupportable burdens, deprived of their trading outlets to the Baltic and resentful of the religious persecution, were only too ready to join the enemy if he invaded Austrian soil. He concluded that the only thing to be done was to forget about further conquests and to try to reach a reasonable peace settlement instead of prolonging a disastrous war. Liechtenstein's memorandum which he gave to Trautmansdorf, one of the ministers closest to Ferdinand, never reached the emperor. Ferdinand, in any case, would not for one moment have considered bringing peace to Germany after Gustavus Adolphus's providential disappearance, nor would he have been allowed to do so by the militants who had grouped themselves around his son Ferdinand III, king of Hungary. None the less the Viennese court was divided. The king of Hungary's supporters had to reckon with those of Wallenstein; and Lamormain, who was Ferdinand II's confessor, was secretly opposed by Quiroga, the Capuchin confessor to the empress. Where Lamormain opposed any concession to the Protestant princes, Quiroga wanted peace restored to the Empire, even at the price of religious concessions, so that the emperor could join forces with Spain against France. In those difficult days, amid such a maze of intrigues, it would have required a firmer hand and a more ready understanding than Ferdinand II's to guide imperial policy.

Under the feeble king Philip IV, who was more interested in hunting and dancing than in gloomy council meetings, Spanish policy was firmly directed by Count-Duke Olivares. Its aims had not changed, and Olivares still hoped to overcome the resistance of the United Provinces. Frederick Henry, the statholder and captain general who owed his prestige and power to the war, was roundly opposed to any compromise, but the republican bourgeoisie led by the city fathers of Amsterdam deplored the way in which the war disrupted trade, and wanted peace. One of the aims of Olivares's policy, therefore, was to break the alliance between France and the States General. He hated France and was resolved to weaken her as much as possible and no doubt this was one of the reasons for his personal vendetta against Richelieu. He was quite ready to invoke the interests of the Roman Catholic Church to conceal the ambitions of the Spanish government. He accused Richelieu, for all he was a cardinal, of giving aid to heretics and, less than two months after the death of Gustavus Adolphus, in a council meeting held on 9th January 1633, he spoke out violently against France, calling her the Roman Catholic Church's most dangerous enemy. He hoped that she would suffer 'every kind of misfortune, and shouted: 'the more she suffers the better it will be for Christendom and the well-being of the Catholic Church'. The particular interests of the house of Austria, or even those of the emperor, concerned him no more then than they had in the past, but it was in Spain's own interest to remain in close alliance with Vienna. If he was to threaten France and vanquish the United Provinces, he had to control the roads which led from Milan to Brussels and keep them open for his invincible *tercios* to march along the Rhine to the battlefields of the North. Because the Swedes had deprived Spain of her strongholds in the Rhenish Palatinate, it was all the more necessary for Olivares to have at his disposal either the forest towns of the upper Rhineland which controlled the passes from Switzerland into Swabia, or Breisach with its strong bridgehead on the right bank of the river downstream from Basel. Spanish troops, therefore, camped in the Sundgau to the south of Alsace and for the same reason the king of Spain became the protector of Charles IV, duke of Lorraine, whom Richelieu had twice tried in vain to reconcile with Louis XIII at Vic and again at Liverdun. Olivares's policy in the Rhineland was determined first and foremost by the requirements of the war; victory in the United Provinces had to be assured and, equally, Richelieu had to be prevented from breaking through the line of Spanish possessions and subject states which encircled the French frontiers. Consequently he had to give effective support to Ferdinand in the struggle which the emperor had been conducting in the Empire for the past fifteen years. Moreover, he had at his disposal powerful means of defending the court of Madrid's interests at Vienna; chief among these were the activities of the Spanish ambassador, the influence of Lamormain over Ferdinand II, and of the Infanta Maria over the king of Hungary whom she had married in February 1631. At the end of 1632 the alliance between the two families was closer than ever.

Naturally enough it was at the court of Sweden and in the Swedish camp that Gustavus Adolphus's death produced the greatest reaction. The king of Sweden had involved his chancellor, Axel Oxenstierna, very closely with his work and he was determined to follow it through. He had come to fear that the young queen, Christina, who succeeded Gustavus would fall under the influence of the nobles whom her father had removed from power, but there was little likelihood of this for the time being. Oxenstierna was still chancellor and the queen gave him complete control over Swedish policy in Germany. However, there was another more acute problem. Oxenstierna was a diplomat and an administrator but by no stretch of the imagination could he be called a military leader, and his relations with the generals were often strained. Until then they had all taken their orders directly from Gustavus Adolphus whose indisputable talents as a warrior had given him complete authority. After the king's death the high command had to be reorganised and the Swedish and German troops were henceforward commanded by four generals—two Swedes, Horn and Baner, and two Germans, William of Hesse-Cassel and Bernard of Saxe-Weimar. Oxenstierna was on quite good terms with the first three but not with Bernard, who thought that he was the only man capable of succeeding Gustavus Adolphus at the head of the army, and who often acted as though he were its sole commander. As for the army itself, it was clearly nothing like the little band of hardy, obedient peasants who had disembarked in a mood of religious enthusiasm on the isle of Rügen in 1630. With each campaign it had been augmented by mercenaries, recruited with no thought for nationality or faith, who fought only for their pay and what they could commandeer or loot. By now it was barely distinguishable from the armies of Wallenstein and the League. It also suffered from the same misfortunes—lack of money, the difficulty of finding quarters and supplies, typhoid, plague and insubordination, and it inspired in the country populations, for example in Alsace, the same terror as did the Catholic bands of the duke of Lorraine or those of the infamous Johann von Werth.

Oxenstierna's particular concern, however, after Gustavus Adolphus's death was the attitude of John George, the elector of Saxony. Oxenstierna knew that John George was carrying on some rather mysterious negotiations with Wallenstein and that he hated foreigners and would willingly have helped to expel the Swedes from Germany. He also knew that Gustavus Adolphus's death had encouraged John George to try to succeed the king of Sweden as leader of the Protestants. This would have strengthened his hand with the Emperor and made it easier to conclude the peace he sought. Oxenstierna, therefore, lost no time in summoning delegates from Swabia, Franconia, the upper and the lower Rhineland—the four circles dominated by Sweden—to a meeting at Heilbronn. He went personally to Saxony to invite John George to join the delegates, but the elector showed his resentment by boycotting the meeting. This was an error of judgement on his part for it left the way clear for Sweden to assert her influence, which she succeeded in doing without too much difficulty. The assembly of

Heilbronn recognised Oxenstierna as head of the four circles which combined in what became known as the Heilbronn League. In this way Oxenstierna retained the same authority over Sweden's German allies that Gustavus Adolphus had exercised before his death. Moreover, he made great efforts to retain the alliance of those who had not joined the League; he frightened the elector of Saxony by pointing out the dangerous consequences of a unilateral peace settlement, and dangled before the elector of Brandenburg the lure of marriage between the electoral prince and the young queen Christina. Thus, in the first instance, the disposition of the two sides in Germany remained more or less what it had been all along.

Among Sweden's allies, however, there was one who had so far managed to retain his freedom of action and from whom Sweden had as yet received only indirect and intermittent aid, apart from subsidies. This was the king of France. The news of the king of Sweden's death aroused mixed feelings of relief and anxiety in France, at least as far as Richelieu was concerned, and the same was probably true of Father Joseph. As we have seen, they had quickly come to look upon Gustavus Adolphus's genius and his grandiose plans as a danger scarcely less disturbing than that presented by Spain. His unexpected death heartened them. Queen Christina was a child of six and Oxenstierna would have to take account of the ambitions of his commanders. It was perhaps an opportunity for Richelieu to put his king at the head of the alliance with the help either of the Swedish chancellor or of the elector of Saxony, who was known to be obstinate but not very shrewd. On the other hand Richelieu could see a new threat. The princes who had declared themselves against the emperor might become totally discouraged by the king of Sweden's death, and there was a danger that they might be tempted to negotiate separately with the Viennese court, no matter how unsatisfactory the terms, in order to cut their losses. He feared that the elector of Saxony would lead the way, followed by the elector of Brandenburg and the other princes and towns of the League. There was no guarantee that France could prevent peace being concluded without her and, if so, it would be a German peace in which Sweden would be forced to abandon her German conquests, leaving France bereft of allies and open to a Spanish invasion which Richelieu did not think could be resisted. From the end of 1632 he had begun to ask himself an agonising question; if peace in Germany could be prevented only by a general war in which Louis XIII would be obliged to engage all his forces, what was to be done? The answer which began to grow in his mind was that an open offensive war conducted by the king in agreement with his allies—the States General, the queen of Sweden and the Protestant princes of Germany—was preferable to a defensive war in which France, abandoned by her allies, would find herself alone against the combined forces of the king of Spain and the emperor. Such a course, however, could only be taken in the last resort, and Richelieu had high hopes of avoiding it by redoubling his diplomatic efforts in Germany, seizing with both hands any opportunity offered him by the fates which had hitherto been so fickle.

One such opportunity was Wallenstein's betrayal but, since French diplomacy only had a passing interest in it, we must examine it on its own account along with all the repercussions it had on the general situation in Germany. We shall then return to Richelieu. His policies, driven by events which he could not foresee, were to lead France within a few years into open war—a war which he had dreaded for so long and which constituted the French phase of the Thirty Years War.

Wallenstein's betrayal is one of those psychological problems which historians find so attractive, and for which they can offer no definite solution because the mysteries of the individual mind always elude them. In Wallenstein's case, as in many others, it is not enough to assemble and compare all the indirect evidence preserved in the contemporary documents concerning this great soldier of fortune. To believe that the weight of evidence authorises us to draw conclusions with any assurance would be to accept the same arguments as the criminal judges of ancient France who thought that three pieces of circumstantial evidence constituted proof. If the historian, once he has completed his investigations, does no more than suggest a likely and vivid interpretation he is merely producing an historical novel, no matter how skilfully he presents his hypothesis, and it will be scarcely more likely and certainly less vivid than the work of a great artist like Schiller. The historian who sets out to solve a problem of this order also runs the risk of unconsciously arranging the historical evidence to fit his own a priori interpretation of the events. The result is that he fails to convince all his readers, and other historians come after him who offer alternative theories on the pretext that they have discovered some hitherto unnoticed evidence in the documents or because they claim to have pursued their researches with more care and impartiality than their predecessors. The result—and this is particularly true in Wallenstein's case—is an abundance of historical literature. If you consist every book and article that has been written about Wallenstein's treason, you will find enough to fill a library. Fortunately you can read one or two volumes which make the rest superfluous.[1] I make no claim to any novel solution to the problem in a book such as this. We are not interested in Wallenstein's treason for its own sake, but because it is the key to a better understanding of the state of confusion in Germany after Gustavus Adolphus's breathtakingly victorious campaign and his untimely death.

One indisputable fact which Pekař has brought to light is that Wallenstein was not, as was long thought, a *German* soldier of fortune. He was born in Bohemia of a Czech family and always remained attached to his native Bohemia even though he took the side of the king-emperor after his compatriots' rebellion. We must also be careful to bear it in mind that patriotism, as we know it today, did not yet exist. Wallenstein thought it only natural to be paid for his services to the emperor at the expense of the Bohemian nobles, and to acquire the confiscated lands cheaply in order to build up his Bohemian fief, the duchy of Friedland. Yet Wallenstein's attachment to Bohemia cannot be denied. When the war did not take him off to Germany he was happiest living in his duchy of Friedland or at Prague. He had turned the duchy into one of the best run and most productive estates in the Empire. This was done no doubt to increase the immense fortune in land and goods which had been and remained the basis of his power, but it was also because he loved it. He protected it jealously from quarters and requisitions. The little town of Gitschin, capital of the duchy, still preserves evidence of his desire to embellish his property, and his palace at Prague, which is still one of the city's most splendid monuments, is a triumph of Italian influence and it paved the way for the introduction of baroque into Bohemia. He had not been alienated from the Bohemian nobility to which he belonged by his first act of treachery, if we so regard his flight to Vienna in 1619 while still in the service of the estates of Moravia, nor by the way in which he had grown rich on confiscations. He remained on good terms with a large number

[1] The most original and penetrating study of Wallenstein's treason is by the great Czech historian Pekař. It was published in its original form in 1895 and the revised version, a second edition in two volumes (*Valdštejn*, Prague, 1933–34), appeared shortly before his death. It has been translated into German under the title *Wallenstein, Tragödie einer Verschwöru ng*. Most of Peka's theories were adopted by Ernest Denis in *La Bohême après la Montagne Blanche*. Account should also be taken of the pages on Wallenstein in Moritz Ritter's *Deutsche Geschichte im Zeitalter der Gegenreformation und des dreissigjährigen Krieges* (Stuttgart, 1889–1908); in Hallwich's great work, *Fünf Bücher Geschichte Wallensteins* (1910); and in Srbik's more recent *Wallensteins Ende* (1920).

of Czech exiles and they were with him again in 1633. The Trčzkas, one of the branches of the famous family of Lobkowitz, and the Kinskýs, particularly William Kinský, played an active part in the conspiracy, and William Kinský and Adam Trčzka had their throats cut a few hours before Wallenstein at the bloody banquet of Cheb on 25th February 1634. We must therefore agree with Pekař in emphasising the part played by the Czech nobility—in fact William Kinský perhaps acted more wholeheartedly and with more determination than Wallenstein himself. Nor should it surprise us (and it is of little importance whether he acted from motives of local patriotism or ambition) that Wallenstein dreamed of freeing Bohemia from Habsburg domination and of re-creating an independent kingdom to which all the exiles could eventually return and of which, no doubt, he would be king. It was not only to free Bohemia that Wallenstein betrayed the emperor, but the liberation of Bohemia formed part of the feverish plan which took shape in his disordered mind at least as early as 1632.

The fact that he was going mad is something else that Pekař uncovered, and it is now generally accepted by historians to be true. Although very intelligent, Wallenstein, like so many of his contemporaries, was very credulous, but in his case this credulity had become pathological. He consulted astrologers at every turn, believed in their horoscopes and acted accordingly. This mental weakness became worse of course as his health, which he had always neglected, began to give way. Though he was only forty-eight when the emperor recalled him in 1631, he was already an old man. His health was ruined and his faculties dimmed. He was always contradicting himself and throwing himself wholeheartedly into enterprises which were then suddenly dropped. Historians have always sought logical reasons for his conduct and these simply do not exist. 'One of the mistakes which has led to false conclusions in earlier works,' wrote Pekař, 'is the deep-rooted conviction of historians that the duke was a man of infinite cunning and great political acumen who was incapable of acting without reason or even contrary to reason.' As far as Pekař is concerned, all that remained of Wallenstein at the time of his treason was an 'invalid, racked with physical suffering, tormented by superstition, haunted by plans of vengeance and by his meglomania. He was a traitor who was losing his reason, a schemer who had gone mad.'[1] If the historians cannot fathom the mysteries of a normal, sane mind, how can he be

[1] Pekař's words are taken from an article by Tapié published in *Revue d'histoire moderne*, June–August 1935.

expected to understand a half-crazed invalid? He must resign himself to relating the facts and ignore motives and secret purposes.

At the root of Wallenstein's treason was the disillusion he felt when the emperor sacrificed him in 1630 at the insistence of the electors, especially of the elector of Bavaria. Though he resigned his command without a murmur, hoping perhaps that his disgrace would be short-lived, his thirst for revenge never slackened. Something which slipped out a little later during an interview with Arnim, which Arnim recorded, reveals that he regarded his dismissal as a personal affront which called for vengeance without mercy. 'The emperor and his whole house,' he shouted, 'will be made painfully aware of what it costs to insult a gentleman.' Although he had no doubt made up his mind quite early on to have revenge, and although his disordered mind had little trouble in dreaming up plans of vengeance, his state of nervous exhaustion made him incapable of carrying them through. During the years which followed, his behaviour was so erratic and at times so disconcerting that although the emperor was put on his guard by Wallenstein's conduct of the war and the negotiations he had entrusted to him, it was a long time before he was convinced that he was being betrayed. In the campaign of 1632 he failed to seize the opportunity to attack and destroy a Swedish army which was weakened by famine and decimated by disease and desertion in a devastated area where Gustavus Adolphus had the greatest difficulty preventing his troops dying of hunger. His hesitations, indeed his inertia on this occasion, calls for some explanation. Perhaps he felt resentful towards Maximilian and was in no hurry to come to Bavaria's rescue. It is also possible that he was suffering from one of the nervous depressions by which he was increasingly incapacitated. Why, in the following year, despite a posi-tive order, did he refuse to take the offensive against Bernard of Saxe-Weimar and thus allow him to seize Regensburg, the key to communi-cations between Bavaria and central Germany (26th November 1633)? It is true that he gave as his reasons the advance of winter, the lack of money to pay the troops, his lack of confidence in a discontented army and the unanimous opinion of the army commanders whose advice he took, but might he not have had the ulterior motive of weakening the emperor's position in order to negotiate peace on his own terms? Neither of these theories can be proved. We need only say Wallen-stein's behaviour during the last years of his life defies explanation and it is hardly surprising that he became increasingly enveloped in a shroud of suspicion.

In any case his mysterious intrigues would not have been possible but for the lack of trust revealed mutually by all the princes engaged in the war. Confusion was rife in Germany, particularly in the Protestant camp now that it was no longer directed by Gustavus Adolphus's firm hand. Because of this ambitions ran wild, though more often than not they were only to be frustrated. All this explains why Wallenstein had no hesitation in exceeding his powers to negotiate with the elector of Saxony by trying to secure a general peace. It explains why Oxenstierna and Richelieu sometimes seemed to welcome Wallenstein's secret overtures and sometimes to evade them. It explains why, within the Saxon court, for example, the policy of Arnim, John George's chief adviser, was not the same as his master's. But this tangle of intrigues is of little importance and it would be fruitless to try to unravel it, especially as we lack the documentary evidence to do so. I shall merely select a few important details.

In the first place, Wallenstein's approaches to the emperor's enemies were, in the case of France, made quite early. They are referred to as far back as February 1633 in the parting instructions given to a new ambassador to Germany, the marquis of Feuquières. These are dated 6th February and were soon followed, on the 18th, by a note regarding the proposals 'which have been put to him on behalf of Friedland 'by Count Quinsqui'.[1] In it there is mention of Wallenstein's declaring himself against the house of Austria and the terms which the king of France would grant in such an event. Secondly, Wallenstein's secret dealings were greatly eased by the great number of Czech refugees at all the German courts, for we must remember that many Czech nobles and bourgeois emigrated immediately after the battle of the White Mountain and were still to be found in most of the Protestant capitals. Kinský and Trčzka were in close touch with Wallenstein, but no doubt plenty of others furthered his ambition by spreading the idea that the rebirth of the old feudal, protestant, Bohemia was still possible. Lastly, the extensive powers which Ferdinand had given his great captain—the right to conduct the war as he saw fit and to conduct negotiations with the Saxon court without reference to Vienna—deprived the emperor of all contact with the army commanders, such as Gallas or Piccolomini, who held their commands from Wallenstein alone. This allowed Wallenstein to disobey imperial orders with impunity so long as the powers which he had managed to acquire were not revoked.

His secret negotiations with the elector of Saxony, the king of

[1] Min. des Aff. Étr., Germany, vol. IX, fol. 9.

Sweden and the king of France remain shrouded in mystery despite the many references to them which we find in the archives. We cannot be certain to what extent he was sincere nor how welcome his proposals were to the courts which received them. Negotiations between Wallenstein and the elector of Saxony were carried out only through Arnim, and it seems likely (Pekař is quite convinced of this), that Arnim merely used them in order to discover Wallenstein's plans and upset them. Indeed, Wallenstein's confidence in Arnim, which persisted to the very end in spite of everything, is quite incomprehensible, and Pekař, who finds no reason for it, goes so far as to wonder whether it might not have been due to some astrologer's prediction. As for Sweden, it seems that Oxenstierna remained deeply mistrustful of Wallenstein, and his only reason for not breaking off the talks immediately was his desire to overlook no opportunity, no matter how suspect. Finally, relations between Wallenstein and Richelieu are not clear. The editors of the Memoirs state that the cardinal never took the talks seriously. This is to be expected since they had no outcome, but the archives give a different, if somewhat confused, impression. In a note dated 3rd September 1633,[1] one of the French king's delegates to Germany, La Grange-aux-Ormes, recalls, as if it were commonly known, the fact that 'M. Du Hamel (another of the king's delegates to Germany) has been the first to court Wallenstein in his talks with Kinský'. We have already seen that back in February of the same year detailed proposals had been brought to Feuquières by the same Kinský and that in them Wallenstein was already talking of declaring himself against the house of Austria. A coded document, to which a key was attached, lists the 'six points proposed and given in writing in Italian to de Feuquières by Count Quinsky (Kinský) about the business with the duke of Friedland on the tenth of June 1633 and answered on the eleventh of the aforementioned month by de Feuquières[2]'. During the summer of 1633, Richelieu seems to have taken the proposals seriously enough to inform La Grange-aux-Ormes about them, and the latter discussed them at various times with Oxenstierna. Wallenstein's silence in September gave rise to further suspicions. At the time, knowing of his enemies' activities at the court of Vienna, he had set his troops on the road once more, beaten a Swedish army under Thurn, reconquered Silesia, and even entered Frankfort-am-Oder. But some months later, on the very eve of the murders at Eger, Richelieu

[1] Min. des Aff. Étr., Germany, vol. IX, fol. 73.
[2] Min. des Aff. Étr., Germany, vol. IX, fol. 44.

apparently had still not lost heart since, on 1st February, he sent Feuquières a memorandum 'to negotiate with the duke of Friedland'. It seems that in Richelieu's opinion the talks had a great deal more importance than the Memoirs would have us believe.

By contrast, it is fairly easy to follow Ferdinand II's feelings towards Wallenstein. They are explained by the events themselves and, apart from this, we have detailed information about the duke of Friedland's enemies at the court of Vienna and about the accusations they cast against him.[1] The story became increasingly serious. At the end of 1632 the emperor reproached Wallenstein for failing to take advantage of Gustavus Adolphus's death and the Protestants' confusion. Instead of pressing home an attack on the Saxons, who were incapable of prolonged resistance, Wallenstein had spared them. A little later, in June 1633, he negotiated an armistice with them and offered them peace terms which were not made properly known at Vienna, and his enemies presented them in such a way that they already looked like an act of treason. Did the emperor believe everything he was told? It seems unlikely since he went on dragging his feet for several months. Even so in August he sent Count Schlick, one of Wallenstein's personal enemies, to urge him to act more decisively and to avoid taking winter quarters in the hereditary estates of the Habsburgs. The only visible result of Schlick's mission was that Wallenstein was irritated. His brief was to conduct the war as he saw fit without being answerable to anyone, and that was exactly what he intended to do. However, Schlick also had secret instructions to sound out the commander-in-chief's senior lieutenants, Piccolomini and Gallas in particular, and to ensure that they would no longer obey Wallenstein 'in the event of any change in his position which might arise for reasons of health or any other reason'. It was a vague and disquieting phrase. We know that from that time Piccolomini kept an eye on his commander and reported to the emperor everything he observed at headquarters.

It was at about this time that Wallenstein resumed hostilities and reconquered Silesia, but the situation was soon aggravated by his failure to react to Bernard of Saxe-Weimar's offensive and the Swedish capture of Regensburg. Trautmansdorf, one of Ferdinand's closest advisers, who so far had not been openly hostile to Wallenstein, was then sent to Pilsen. The two men met on 26th November 1633, but the meeting was no more fruitful than Schlick's mission and, as a result,

---

[1] The activities of the anti-Wallenstein faction are closely examined in *Wallensteins Ende* by Srbik.

Wallenstein forfeited the good will of one of the most influential men at the imperial court. After that, Schlick, Slawata, the Bavarian delegate, and all those who were opposed to Wallenstein, including the king of Hungary himself, began to act openly together. Their efforts were supported by the Spanish ambassador, Oñate, who had run up against stubborn resistance from Friedland in his efforts to secure a free passage across the Empire for a Spanish army that one of Philip IV's brothers was marching to the Netherlands. By December 1633 Ferdinand had certainly made up his mind to revoke Wallenstein's powers and thought that he could depend on most of his lieutenants. Wallenstein, who sensed his enemies closing in, chose this moment to resume talks with the courts of Sweden and France and seemed resolved to break his oath and finally declare himself against the house of Austria. It could not be long before matters came to a head.

The final act of the drama began in January 1634. Wallenstein was preparing to make a decisive move and had called his chief officers to Pilsen for a council of war. The emperor heard of the meeting and was in no doubts about Wallenstein's plans. The commander-in-chief could only be preparing an officers' plot against the emperor, hoping to carry the whole army with him. The treason had to be nipped in the bud, either by arresting Wallenstein or, if all else failed to bring him down, by eliminating him. None the less Ferdinand, who was still subject to scruples of conscience, first wanted to sound out three advisers who had never been openly hostile towards Wallenstein and whom he chose precisely for that reason. They were Trautmansdorf, Eggenberg and the bishop of Vienna. They all decided against Wallenstein and thereafter Ferdinand could no longer shirk what he considered to be a duty of conscience. On 24th January 1634 he drew up an imperial order addressed to those of Wallenstein's lieutenants whom he knew he could trust. We still have the actual text of the order, which was 'to arrest the leader of the conspiracy and his chief accomplices and bring them to Vienna, but if this were not possible, to have them killed as convicted traitors.'[1]

Piccolomini and Gallas still needed some time to set the scene for the drama of 24th February 1634, but the story of their preparations belongs to a detailed study and has no place here. We need only

---

[1] The imperial order was later communicated to the General of the Jesuits by Lamormain which is how the authentic text has survived. It was published by Srbik who translated it into German from the original Italian and my translation is taken from the German, but the meaning is quite clear.

observe that during the last weeks of his life the great condottiere's physical health declined more than ever, as Pekař has very rightly pointed out. He was sick and worn out and had to be carried about on a litter. He remained credulous and right to the end he trusted Piccolomini, who had been in league with his enemies for several months. When, on the evening of 21st February, Trčzka informed him that the order for his dismissal had already been published in Prague and that the greater part of the army was abandoning him, he panicked. He realised at last that he was in mortal danger, and, as Pilsen was already virtually surrounded by troops, he decided on a hasty departure, accompanied by the little band of loyal supporters, in the hope of reaching the fortress of Cheb (Eger) close by the borders of Saxony. It was there, on the evening of 24th February, that the drama took place. It was divided into two distinct acts. The first was a banquet at which the guests were Wallenstein's closest accomplices—Trčzka, Kinský and two senior officers, Ilow and Niemann, who trusted their host because he had taken an oath of loyalty to Wallenstein. The banquet had only just finished when the three foreign officers who had elected to perform the execution, Butler, Leslie and Gordon, let some dragoons into the room. First of all they murdered Kinsky and Ilow. Trčzka, who was strong as an ox, managed to fight his way out of the room and was cut down by musket balls in the courtyard. Niemann went in the same way. The butchery was complete. Long live the emperor! The second act was even more tragic. Wallenstein knew nothing of what had happened; he was sick and had stayed in bed. After a quick debate, Butler, Leslie and Gordon decided to kill him too, although he was in no state to defend himself, and that was that.

There are only two points to be made. The first is that Piccolomini and Gallas, who planned the whole thing, did not take a hand in the execution. Nevertheless, in the communication which they sent to Vienna they managed to claim all the credit for the great service which they thought they had rendered to the emperor. The other point is that although Leslie, Butler and Gordon may have been convinced that Ferdinand would approve their action, they nonetheless exceeded their orders. It would have been just as easy for them to arrest Trčzka, Kinský, Niemann and Ilow as to kill them. It would have been even easier for them to seize Wallenstein and take him to Vienna; they did not have to kill him in his bed. But the historian merely records the facts; it is not his place to judge them.

It was not until he no longer had to reckon with Wallenstein's private intrigues, and until the great condottiere's forces had at last become an imperial army, that the emperor could regain his freedom of action. In the meantime Richelieu had enjoyed a breathing space which he had exploited in order to adapt French policy to the new situation created by Gustavus Adolphus's sudden death. We can now afford to dwell on the intricacies of his diplomatic and military manoeuverings during this brief spell since they help us to understand how the German war as it continued became more and more bound up in the renewed conflict between the houses of Austria and France.

At the end of 1632 and during the following years this conflict was primarily conducted through diplomacy. Louis XIII's military operations in Italy to help the new duke of Mantua to hold on to his inheritance had been interrupted by the peace of Cherasco in June 1631. Charles de Gonzague-Nevers had obtained the imperial investiture and the king of France continued to garrison the fortress of Pinerolo on the eastern slope of the Alps, thanks to a secret agreement with the duke of Savoy. The war might have broken out again at any time because the king of Spain had not resigned himself to accepting a French presence at Pinerolo and in 1626 the peace of Monçon, which was hardly favourable to French interests in its settlement of the thorny question of the Valtelline, had not been ratified by the Grisons. But at the end of 1632, in the face of the uncertainties and dangers of the German situation, Richelieu was very anxious to avoid the renewal of hostilities in Italy. On 14th December, Henri de Rohan, the former commander of the Huguenots who had since become a loyal servant to Louis XIII and who wanted a firm line to be taken with both the king of Spain and the emperor, presented a memorandum[1] to Richelieu. In it he recommended that one army should be sent to Lorraine and another to occupy the Valtelline 'and establish firm bases there in order to deny the king of Spain for ever the hope of receiving succour from the Germans whenever he takes it upon himself to stir up trouble in Italy'. But the duc de Rohan was ignored and received an order to leave immediately on a mission to Venice.

It was also by a diplomatic move that Richelieu did his best to dissuade the States-General of the United Provinces from negotiating with the king of Spain. Charnacé who was chosen for the task was only partially successful. On 15th April 1634, less than two months after Wallenstein's murder, the States-General agreed to a defensive alliance

[1] Min. des Aff. Étr., Germany, vol. VIII, fol. 263—see also Fagniez: *Le Père Joseph et Richelieu.*

with France and continued the war without compelling the king of France to break with Spain, but the agreement was only for one year. In this way, therefore, Richelieu confined himself to a policy of inactivity in Italy in order to avoid any premature breach with Spain, while seeking to assure himself in Holland of an alliance which in the not too distant future might allow him to wage war against Spain in the Netherlands. However, after Gustavus Adolphus's death, it was in Germany that the future seemed most unsettled, and it was there above all that Richelieu was most active.

His principal aim was to prevent the emperor from helping the king of Spain once open war between Spain and France could no longer be avoided, and we must bear this in mind if we are to understand his policy with regard to the left bank of the Rhine in the years 1632–1634. There was one single thread linking events in Germany with those in Italy and the Netherlands, and it all stemmed from Spanish policy both inside and outside the Empire. It was this which drove Richelieu to oppose 'the progress of Spain' wherever it was apparent, both in Germany and elsewhere. For this reason, whenever we deal with the German war from now onwards, it must be as an integral part of the general conflict between the houses of France and Austria.

The situation in the Rhineland at the time of Gustavus Adolphus's death at Lützen gives us some idea of the generally confused state throughout Germany. The Rhenish provinces constituted four of the ten imperial circles. To the north was Westphalia; then there was the electoral Rhineland which comprised the states of the three archbishop electors of Mainz, Trier and Cologne; the Upper Rhineland included the Lower Palatinate, the duchy of Lorraine and a considerable area of Alsace; and finally there was the Austrian circle to which belonged the Alsatian possessions of the Habsburgs administered by an archduke under the title of Grand Bailiff or Prefect. The most interesting feature of this divided and defenceless region was the continual ebb and flow of foreign troops. Imperial, Spanish, Swedish and French troops, not to mention the duke of Lorraine's bands of mercenaries, roamed across it, looting, making their winter quarters there and even occupying it piecemeal in a situation of indescribable chaos. Sometimes a few hundred or even a handful would garrison one town or castle while another town or castle close at hand would be occupied by a few dozen more who served some other prince. It is quite easy to understand both the anxiety of those townspeople who had so far managed to defend their walls and the terrible devastation that the continual passage of armed bands left in their wake.

Of course the situation changed from year to year and in some places from month to month. In the electoral Rhineland, for example, at the end of 1632, Philip of Sötern, the elector of Trier, had placed himself under the king of France's protection and had allowed him to occupy the bridgehead of Philippsburg and Ehrenbreitstein opposite Coblenz in order to ensure the defence of the electorate. The governor of Philippsburg, however, refused to open the gates of the town to the French, and a Spanish force garrisoned Coblenz so that Spaniards and French faced each other across the Rhine. The Spaniards had occupied Trier but the French managed to oust them and occupy it themselves without bloodshed. Since they were only there, as Richelieu put it, to guarantee freedom of worship for the Catholics, the Spaniards need have no cause for anxiety. In Alsace at the end of that same year (1632), those occupying towns were so mixed up with those in winter quarters that no-one can say with any certainty who controlled what. In December the count de Salm, who administered the diocese of Strassburg and the bailiwick of Haguenau on behalf of the archduke Leopold, entrusted both to the protection of the duke of Lorraine, allowing him to occupy the Haguenau and Saverne. Away to the south, an imperial garrison was defending Breisach against a Swedish army, Spanish troops were encamped in the Sundgau, and Swedish troops were everywhere.

These circumstances explain Richelieu's Alsatian policy. If French troops entered the region they were no more likely to be accused of wanting to conquer it than the Spaniards or the Swedes. It was never a question of conquest, only of protection. It was to protect the king's allies that Richelieu asked Oxenstierna to hand over the bridgehead of Philippsburg as soon as the Swedes had taken it. It was to strengthen the French frontier beyond Lorraine in the event of a breach with the king of Spain that Richelieu wanted the right to protect and garrison a certain number of Alsatian towns. He explained the reasons for his Alsatian policy over and over again in memoranda to the king and in despatches to the ambassadors. In those days, at least, it was a defensive policy, dominated at all times by his fear of a Spanish invasion of France's eastern provinces, which he had not yet had time to prepare against invasion. But there was more to Richelieu's policy than that, because it was also governed by his mistrust of the Swedes. He wanted to occupy the Rhine bridgeheads and the Alsatian forts not only to be in a better position to defend the realm against the Spaniards but also to prevent the Swedes occupying them themselves. A Swedish occupation of the left bank of the Rhine alarmed him no less than a Spanish one. On this point his policy had not changed since he dictated the memoranda to Father Ange de Mortagne in January, and we must always bear in mind this twofold anxiety when we study the entry of French troops into Alsace after Gustavus Adolphus's death.[1]

Because of the confused situation, Richelieu's main fear until the autumn of 1633 was that he might alarm the Protestant princes and anger Oxenstierna. He therefore played a waiting game, approving the action of his ambassador to Germany who did not even dare to mention the Alsatian towns in front of the Heilbronn allies. Moreover, in the same border regions of the Empire, another and more urgent question had arisen over Lorraine, where Charles IV, duke of Lorraine, had failed to carry out the terms of the treaty of Liverdun. Far from adding his troops to the king's, as he had promised, he was serving the imperial cause by protecting Haguenau and Saverne against the Swedes. The duke of Feria had assembled some Spanish troops in the Tyrol to march them into Upper Alsace and Richelieu feared that Charles might go ahead of them to force the Swedes to raise the siege of Breisach. Above all he was determined to obtain the annulment of the secret marriage between Gaston and Marguerite of Lorraine both at home and abroad. For a long time he had hoped that the king and the duke might be genuinely reconciled. Moreover, he wanted to avoid any military intervention which might seem to contradict the assurances, which he lavished on the German princes, that he was not pursuing any permanent territorial acquisition in the Rhineland. None the less he could not avoid sending an armed expedition in September 1633 which gave Louis XIII possession of the new town of Nancy and one of the gates of the old town which was all that Charles IV still held. The Lorraine question was not yet settled, nor was the matter of Gaston's marriage, which Charles continued to deny in the face of all the evidence. However, from then on Louis could send his troops across Lorraine without fear of opposition.

As for the question of the Alsatian towns, it was only on Feuquières's return to Germany at the end of the following winter that this cropped

[1] There is a detailed examination of Richelieu's Alsatian policy in W. Mommsen: *Kardinal Richelieu, seine Politik in Elsass und in Lothringen*. He explains it more or less as I have above. It is also worth consulting Louis Batiffol: *Les Anciennes Républiques alsaciennes*, although in places he has taken the theory so far that it has not met with the general approval of all historians.

up in any precise form. Feuquières's instructions left no room for any doubt. He was to reassure Oxenstierna 'by removing the idea that the king wishes to increase his power permanently in those quarters'. On the contrary, the king's sole object was to set up 'barriers against events the better to sustain his friends'. Feuquières was also to do his best to dispel the German princes' doubts. He was to declare that 'far from seeking further benefits from the continuation of the war, his majesty hopes to see his ventures reduced to such a point that, by returning the fortresses that his troops hold only for the defence and protection of those who require it, he may clearly demonstrate that he has no other interest but the common good.' In fact, as far as Alsace was concerned, the position of the allies, and of France herself, had already improved. By the autumn of 1633 the Swedes had expelled the imperialists, the Spaniards and the Lorrainers from nearly every region except the Sundgau, where the Spaniards still held out and from where they had managed to send supplies to Breisach. Furthermore, in October 1633, the duke of Wurtemberg, fearing the Spaniards and the Lorrainers, had put his duchy of Montbéliard, which partly covered the Burgundian Gate, under the king of France's protection. In December the Count of Hanau had admitted the French to his three towns of Bischwiller, Ingwiller and Neuwiller in Lower Alsace. In January 1634, when the Lorrainers had gone, the count of Salm, administrator of the Bailiwick of Haguenau, invited the French to protect Haguenau and Saverne and allowed them to garrison Hohbar whose castle commanded the entire plain. Finally, in January 1634, the diocese of Basel was also put under French protection and, together with Montbéliard, it helped to cover the gap between the Vosges and the Jura. Feuquières's chief objective, therefore, was to obtain from Oxenstierna and the Heilbronn League their recognition of the changed state of affairs and, beyond that, their permission to occupy Philippsburg, which the Swedes had taken and were still refusing to hand over to the French.

Needless to say, the maintenance of French garrisons in the towns of Alsace depended on events in Germany. When the marquis de Feuquières met Oxenstierna at Würzburg on his first embassy at the beginning of May 1633, things looked black for the Protestants and Sweden. Oxenstierna, who was on his way back from Dresden, had been unable to find out what the elector of Saxony intended to do. La Grange-aux-Ormes, who in March had also seen John George and George William, had found the elector of Brandenburg fairly well disposed but thought that the elector of Saxony was not to be trusted.

He wrote that he was 'still strongly attached to the emperor and Spain and cannot bear any foreign influence in the Empire'; moreover, he spent all his time drinking. He concluded that he was 'half-hearted and whimsical'. Feuquières soon came to the conclusion that he would be making a mistake if he stuck to his instructions and tried to win over the elector of Saxony by offering him the leadership of the Protestant party in the Empire. He thought it better to come to some understanding with Oxenstierna, despite his difficult mood; and consequently at Heilbronn he helped him to be recognised as leader by the four Confederate circles. As for the circles, he was content to secure a treaty of alliance drawn up on the same lines as their agreement with Sweden, and this was signed at Frankfurt in September.

During the whole of 1633, when events were leading up to Wallenstein's treason and the tragedy at Eger, the reorganised Protestant party was able to resist the imperial forces without too much difficulty. It was the period when Wallenstein's inactivity allowed Bernard of Saxe-Weimar to seize Regensburg. A year later, however, Wallenstein's old army, now commanded by Gallas and Piccolomini, went on the offensive again and it expelled the Swedes from Regensburg on 26th July 1634. Horn and Bernard of Saxe-Weimar lost the initiative and could only try to halt the imperial advance at the borders of Franconia. At the same time Feria had entered the Sundgau and another Spanish army was preparing to cross Germany under the command of one of Philip IV's brothers, the cardinal-infante, who had to go to Brussels to replace the Infanta Isobel in the government of the Netherlands. All these events explain the new attitude shown by the States-General of the United Provinces and by Oxenstierna at the end of that summer, and for a time the whole of Richelieu's policy in the Empire was called into question.

Richelieu's intentions remained unaltered until the end of the summer. He kept on trying to persuade Oxenstierna and the Heilbronn League to hand over Philippsburg, and as far as possible he completed the king of France's annexation of Lorraine. At the beginning of 1634 he had laid before the Parlement of Paris a suit for the annulment of Gaston and Marguerite's marriage and had added to it the somewhat extraordinary charge that the duke of Lorraine had abducted and illegally confined the king's brother. Faced with such a threat Charles IV chose to abdicate in favour of his brother Nicolas François on 19th January 1634 and to exchange the ducal authority, which he could no longer exercise freely, for a command in the imperial army.

Nicolas François, however, fared no better than his brother Charles, and he too had to flee. By August the French occupation of Lorraine was complete, though the situation remained rather precarious because Charles IV's subjects remained loyal and no foreign prince would recognise the annexation of Lorraine to France. This, however, did not alter the fact that France could now protect the open frontier of Champagne behind Alsace. At the same time, during the course of a long inspection, Sublet de Noyers, one of the principal members of the council of state, together with other inspectors, were putting the fortresses of Champagne, Burgundy and Picardy into a state of preparedness. The defensive nature of Richelieu's policy at this time was thus made quite clear.

Even before the annexation of Lorraine, however, events in Germany had given rise to two new initiatives, one by Frederick Henry, Statholder and commander-in-chief of the Dutch, the other by Oxenstierna, which put Richelieu's intention to the test and which established beyond doubt that Richelieu was as determined as ever to avoid, or at any rate to delay as long as possible, an open breach between France and the house of Austria. Frederick Henry made the first move, which arose from the defensive treaty of alliance made in April 1634 between the States-General and Louis XIII. Frederick Henry was alarmed because the city fathers of Amsterdam (i.e. the ruling oligarchy in the city) wanted to end the war. In order to compel them to fight on he hit upon the idea of involving the king of France more fully in the struggle. A Dutch embassy was sent to Paris on 30th May to complete the ratification of the treaty of April. It was then given other instructions. The delegates of the States-General were to propose a new alliance to Louis XIII, only this one was to be both defensive and offensive with the object of supporting Sweden and the confederated German princes against the emperor and of maintaining 'German liberties'. At the same time, and what was more important, it aimed at bringing about a breach between France and Spain. Once the breach had been made, the States-General and the king of France would join forces to overrun the Spanish Netherlands and would partition them. France was to have all the French-speaking area and the Flanders coast as far as Bruges, while the rest would be annexed to the United Provinces. It was an attractive offer, but Richelieu was not won over. His advice to the king was inserted in the Memoirs. In it he weighed up, in his usual fashion, the pros and cons of the proposed agreement. It would completely bind the States-General. If the Netherlands were conquered and shared, the northern frontier of the kingdom would be pushed well beyond Artois and the capital would be sheltered from invasion. But there was no certainty that the conquest would be achieved. There were terrible risks involved in waging war simultaneously in the Low Countries, in Germany and perhaps in Italy. And, even if it succeeded, Richelieu was apprehensive of the consequences of this joint conquest. 'It could happen soon afterwards,' he wrote, 'that, lacking any barrier between ourselves and the Dutch, we should find ourselves entering upon the same war with them as they are presently engaged in with the Spaniards.' And Richelieu concluded by advising his master against a long, costly and hazardous war at a time when he still had no heir and his health, like his minister's, was poor. He answered the Dutch proposal with a counter proposal to help the Belgians to win their independence and then to 'form separate cantons' under the joint protection of France and the United Provinces. All in all it was the solution which was finally to be achieved—namely Belgian independence. It appealed to Richelieu but not to Frederick Henry, who dropped the negotiations.

Although there seems to have been no collusion between Oxenstierna and Frederick Henry, the former's proposals would have had the same results. Oxenstierna had been cut to the quick by the Swedish troops' defeat in July and the return of the imperial troops to Regensburg. Since this might well hasten the elector of Saxony's defection and even that of the elector of Brandenburg, the alliance had to be given a new lease of life by arming the Protestant side with new instruments of victory. In August Oxenstierna made up his mind to hand over Philippsburg to the French and had the transfer approved by the members of the Heilbronn League. He then communicated to France through Feuquières some wholly unexpected proposals. Like Frederick Henry, he offered Louis XIII a firm alliance to wage war together on the Habsburgs. Sweden would direct her efforts against Bohemia and Silesia and would withdraw her troops from the entire region of the four circles, which would be left for France to defend. The Swedish offer was as attractive as the Dutch offer and was complementary to it. It would have left Louis XIII completely free to act along the Rhine. But in point of fact the chancellor of Sweden was proposing a totally novel policy to the king of France. Richelieu's policy so far had been to reconcile the aims of France and Sweden to the satisfaction of the German princes in defence of the 'German liberties'. In return, when peace—that is a general peace—was re-established, he expected to

obtain from the princes security for the French frontiers. If Oxenstierna's offer were accepted, the allied powers would hardly be able to
count any longer on the princes who would no doubt rally round the
head of the Empire against the foreign invaders. France and Sweden
would be left on their own to carry out a war of conquest against the
house of Austria and there was no means of foreseeing the outcome.
Richelieu advised Louis XIII to turn down Oxenstierna's offer just as
he had rejected Frederick Henry's.

The Richelieu whom we see here is not the Richelieu of the legends.
He is the good counsellor, too well acquainted with the weaknesses of
his king and of his kingdom to drag them both irresponsibly into an
enterprise which might be both glorious and profitable, but whose
risks it was impossible to calculate. Once again he put off a decision
which one day might be forced upon him, but which he was determined to avoid for as long as he could.

He did not know at the time that this day was soon to come, but
once the imperialists had recaptured Regensburg events moved swiftly.
To the north of the town the Swedish troops of Bernard of Saxe-
Weimar confronted the imperial troops of Piccolomini and Gallas. At
the end of August the latter were reinforced by the duke of Lorraine.
Then the Spanish army led by the cardinal-infante, Don Ferdinand,
interrupted its march to Brussels, crossed the Danube at Donauwörth,
and went to the support of the imperial army. The difference in the
relative strengths of the rival armies was by now enormous. Bernard
and Horn tried to avoid battle but failed. On 6th September at Nördlingen, to the west of Donauwörth, they were routed and their troops
fell back towards the Rhine in confusion. Suddenly the tide had turned
in favour of the Habsburgs. In the history of the Thirty Years War,
6th September 1634 is one of the decisive dates like those of the White
Mountain and the Edict of Restitution.

CHAPTER VII

RICHELIEU, OLIVARES AND OXENSTIERNA

Among the Swedish papers in the Ministère des Affaires Étrangères[1] there is a 'memorandum to the king' with the superscription 'IIth September 1634, regarding the Swedish defeat at Nordlingen, written on the same day, six hours after receiving the news'. So it was on IIth September that the French court learned of the defeat at Nordlingen, and only six hours after the messenger arrived with the news, Richelieu had drawn up the memorandum which he no doubt sent to Louis XIII straight away. This 'memorandum' is totally different from the ones we have quoted so far. As a general rule Richelieu considered several possible solutions, outlined all the pros and cons which occurred to him and suggested the one which seemed preferable, but always in such a way that the king was left with the impression that he was making the decision himself. This particular document has none of the usual circumspection. Richelieu saw quite clearly the full consequences of Sweden's defeat and expressed them with equal clarity. One expression, 'it is certain that', which was rare coming from him, occurs in nearly every sentence. 'It is certain that if the (Protestant) side is completely ruined, the brunt of the house of Austria's might will fall on France. It is also certain that after the recent defeat the Protestants cannot survive without considerable and immediate aid and that they need the name of a powerful ally to sustain their hopes, for without such aid it is certain that all the imperial towns will disband, Saxony will make his settlement, and all will act in such a way as to reduce this great alliance quite quickly to a shadow of its former self. . . . It is further certain that the worst advice that France can take is to act in such a way that she is left alone to maintain the struggle against the emperor and Spain.'

There was no question of formulating a new policy. For a long time Richelieu had been prepared for the day when France would have to move from covert to open war in order not to find herself alone against the Spanish and Austrian monarchies. After Nordlingen he

[1] Min. des Aff. Étr., Sweden, vol. III, fol. 265. Previously noted by Fagniez.

recognised that this moment had come. Nevertheless his natural caution still held him back. 'And consequently,' he went on, 'it seems that there can be no doubt that we must aid the Protestants. The only question is how this can be done.' And the word 'how' immediately leads him on to advise the king not to be too hasty. 'In order to make a good decision in a matter of such difficulty and of such importance we must find out all the facts, await news of the vanquished, sympathise with them and with the requests they may make to the king, and throughout it all we must put new heart into them and let them know that his majesty is in a strong position to help them so long as they show him that they can continue with his help. Nevertheless we must increase our forces and prepare ourselves to carry out the courses of action which prudence and necessity will impose upon us.'

This, in Richelieu's opinion was the decisive argument. The kingdom could not undertake the long war he envisaged without serious risks. The king had neither enough men nor the money to raise and pay them. So far as the cost was concerned, Richelieu had not only to face the problem of raising the necessary funds by means of various expedients; he had also to overcome Louis XIII's reluctance to spend money. 'If we count the cost on this occasion,' he concluded, 'and wish to reduce it to a scale modest enough to be borne for a long time, we must face the fact that there are no fixed rules for dealing with major contingencies. This is not a matter of spending money over the course of several years; if we entirely fail to meet the extraordinary costs of remedying the present urgent problem, we shall at some future date be engaged in endless and fruitless expense which will in no wise prevent our collapse.'

In the autumn of 1634, at the moment when the Swedish disaster seemed to compel the French to take a strong line, their position in Germany, though not unfavourable, was not yet as strong as Richelieu would have wished. France occupied both the diocese of Basel in the southern part of upper Alsace and the county of Montbéliard from which her troops could command the Burgundian Gate between the Vosges and the Jura. In lower Alsace, Haguenau, Bouxwiller, Bischwiller and Saverne had been taken under her protection. On the Rhine, France held Ehrenbreitsein and Coblenz and could now put a garrison into Philippsburg. Further to the south she also held the line of the Moselle through Trier and Sierck, and it was more or less certain that the Swedes would authorise the replacement of Swedish by French garrisons in all the Alsatian towns which the former had not yet abandoned. In fact there were only two serious gaps in the line of defence which protected the external frontier beyond the occupied area of Lorraine. These were Breisach, where the imperial forces were still holding on, and Strassburg, whose citizens might at any time allow an enemy force to cross the Rhine by the Kehl bridge. As for the allied assembly which was meeting at Frankfurt at the time, it declared that the only hope of salvation was an immediate breach between the king of France and the house of Habsburg. Richelieu, however, required at least a few months delay during which he could only offer hope rather than troops to the allies. Once these few months had elapsed, France found herself forced to enter the war even though the situation had changed to her disadvantage. We cannot say definitely either that the brief period of waiting was indispensable or that Richelieu should have taken his courage in both hands in September 1634 by advising his master to give the enemies of the emperor and the king of Spain all the help they expected. Whatever the answer, it is important that we should pause on the threshold of the French period of the Thirty Years War to examine the reasons which delayed French intervention, for the future of France herself, of Germany, and of a large part of Europe was going to depend on the conditions under which the struggle began. To discover these reasons we must examine the internal state of the kingdom.

The government of the country rested squarely on the shoulders of two sick men, Louis XIII and Richelieu. When we talk of Richelieu we think only of his indomitable energy, which compels our admiration. We rarely remember that a good deal of this energy was wasted in a struggle against the illnesses he suffered, and that all too often his activity was interrupted by bouts of fever. Using documents from the archives it is almost possible to compile a diary of his state of health. They show that he was often confined to his bed or his room at Rueil or at one of his other retreats. I will only give one example of this, taken from the very beginning of the war. Less than a month after its declaration, about the time of the deplorable consequences of the victory of Avein, Richelieu had to abandon temporarily the direction of affairs. As soon as he felt better, one of his most faithful servants, the surintendant Bouthillier, reported the news to the king on 15th June 1635, in the following terms. 'It is a miracle to see him in his present state after the great pain he has suffered. We are increasingly optimistic that he will soon be in a state to render his customary services to your majesty, but until now his doctors have forbidden us to tell him anything that might upset him.' Richelieu therefore had actually been unable to give the king his 'customary services' or to take notice of public affairs. As for Louis XIII, he was often the victim of attacks of melancholy, as those closest to him called them, which severely taxed his health. It was also in October 1635 that the same Bouthillier, who was with the king this time, wrote to Richelieu: 'I despair to see him in one of his attacks of melancholy since it seems that nothing can be done for them. As soon as they are upon him he is gripped by his stomach pains and his face changes quite suddenly. He wants the world to know that he is brave and that he wishes to go against his enemies, but the fact is that everyone knows the truth of the matter.'[1] From the notes that these two invalids sent to each other it is quite easy to deduce the part that doctors and medicine played in their lives. We can also understand Richelieu's great fear of involving the kingdom in an open-ended and unpredictable war so long as he, and his king too for that matter, could be put out of action by illness, and so long as he felt that he was surrounded by a host of enemies who were only waiting for his or his master's death in order to reverse his policy.

But the deplorable state of the finances and the army gave Richelieu even more cause for concern than his health. To a large extent the state of the army was dependent on that of the finances. Except for a short period under Sully when results were achieved by somewhat empirical means, the crown had never managed to acquire the resources to meet its needs. Even in peacetime only a fraction of the ordinary expenditure was met from taxation and it was necessary to depend very heavily on the sale of offices and every conceivable form of borrowing. The result of this was that the king was unable to maintain a permanent army. He had only a few regiments of regulars, of which foreign troops formed the backbone. In war time the situation quickly became critical. The budget estimates never took account of warfare and made no provision for it. Troops had to be raised hastily, and they were clothed, armed, paid and fed without any funds earmarked for the purpose. The result was that the surintendants were always having to dream up expedients in order to set aside a little ready money in a special fund known as the emergency war fund. Above all, they had to make special agreements with financiers which were more or less loans against future revenue by which the financiers reimbursed themselves at the expense of the people.

The minister could never depend upon having the money he needed

[1] Both Bouthillier's notes are unpublished.

to provision any fortress whose loss might have opened the frontier to the enemy, or to maintain an army in the field. Richelieu's correspondence with his surintendants is eloquent testimony to his anxieties. He reproaches them for their slowness and their negligence but never with any bitterness, because he was well aware of the extent of his dependence on them. 'In conclusion,' he wrote to them in February 1636, 'I beg the surintendants to be good enough in the future to expedite without delay matters which have been resolved; otherwise I can assure them that it is quite impossible for any venture to succeed. . . . I say this without wishing to carp, but with great feeling and grief.'[1] And he shows that it was quite impossible for the king to provision the Alsatian towns because wheat had not been stored at Basel as it should have been. These financial difficulties which could jeopardise everything without a moment's warning were not simply discovered by Richelieu during the course of the war. He had foreseen them before war was declared, and we should bear this in mind when trying to understand the mental torture he went through at the time of the irrevocable decision.

In reading through the *Testament Politique* or Richelieu's correspondence it comes as a surprise to us to find how little confidence he had in the army and its generals. However, there are plenty of explanations for this. The army which was formed in haste when war seemed imminent was organised, like armies in most other countries, on the contract system. The system was made even worse by the fact that the king was not free to choose the officers because the custom of venality had spread to the army as well as the exchequer and the judicature. When war threatened, the king drew up the captains' commissions and sold them. The captain recruited his company, either himself or through junior officers, equipped it, and presented it to one of the king's commissioners whose job it was to check the complement. The captain then received a pro rata bounty for the levy, and equipment in proportion to the number of men presented, after which the troops were promised pay in the form of a certain number of equal payments per year. These were called 'musters' because each instalment of pay had to be preceded by a further review or 'muster' of the strength of the regiment. For example, a regiment might be raised on the condition of four musters a year. The king also sold the commissions of colonels, or 'mestres de camp' as they were then called, and each 'mestre de camp' commanded a group of companies, a regiment, in the field. But

[1] Min. des Aff. Étr., Mem. and Doc., France, vol. DCCCXX. Unpublished.

7

he was also captain of the first company, called the 'colonel's company', which he personally had raised and equipped. The enormous weakness of the system was that because of the bounty and the pay it was in the captains' and colonels' interest to inflate their numbers artificially in order to obtain more money than they had to pay out. The result of this was not only the employment of false soldiers, the famous 'dummy soldiers' who only appeared at musters; it also made the captains very lax over checking desertion. As far as they were concerned deserters were merely soldiers who did not have to be paid any more, and desertion was all the more easy because the captains did not know their men. More often than not the latter had no civilian status. They joined up under a pseudonym such as La Fleur, La Violette, La Fortune, La Jeunesse, etc., which they changed when they moved from one company to another. How could they be traced if they had managed to escape? The French government never completely succeeded in remedying the scourge of desertion. The result of all this was that at the beginning of a war, and still less during the course of a campaign, the king never knew how many troops he could count on.

The leaders—whether regimental or field officers—were no more than mediocre. The captains were more concerned with recovering their outlay than with doing their duty. On the whole they were brave enough, but they rarely had any sense of discipline and they would leave their companies without asking anyone's permission. In 1636, Marshal de Schomberg, referring to a regiment recruited in Languedoc where he was governor, wrote to Richelieu: 'it's not that the colonel lacks courage, but he has the most bizarre officers I have ever set eyes on. Apart from one or two of his captains none of them is worthy of the name.' The position was even worse in the high command. In 1635 Richelieu was wondering who could be trusted to command the armies that were being formed. 'M. de La Force's age worries me,' he wrote to Bouthillier, 'and I do not know what to suggest. The king knows the officers better than anyone, but in my opinion he could scour the whole kingdom and not find any who are up to the mark.' In fact neither the aged La Force, nor the marquis de Brézé, nor Cardinal de La Valette, nor the duc d'Angoulême, prince of the blood though he was, had any real military talent. Quite often the king could not trust the loyalty of any of his commanders-in-chief. They were jealous of each other and frequently squabbled among themselves. In his Memoirs, Fontenay-Mareuil wrote that Richelieu, mistrusting his generals, 'thought that if there were several of them they would be less likely to fail or disobey their orders, so he always put several generals in each army. That is why he sent M. d'Angoulême along with M. de La Force.' But this practice, which was evidently only a last resort, irritated the high command and did not always make the generals more reliable.

Finally there were no organised medical or ordnance corps. There were no military hospitals, with the result that there were enormous losses among the sick and wounded. To provide the troops with bread and the horses with forage the king dealt with 'commissaries' who not only swindled him, but often did not even keep their bargains, with the result that stocks of flour or hay which the armies had been relying on were not available at the last moment. This was a greater danger than most of the others. 'In the course of history,' wrote Richelieu in his *Testament Politique*, 'more armies have perished for lack of bread and forage than by enemy action, and I can bear witness that all the enterprises which have been undertaken in my time have come to naught only through this failing.' He could only deal with the problem in a makeshift fashion. 'The task of provisioning,' he wrote, once again in his *Testament Politique*, 'must be entrusted to persons of quality whose vigilance, reliability and capacity are well known. . . . There is nobody so noble that he cannot be employed in such offices.' He usually gave the job to bishops, especially those who had been attached to his household and whom he knew he could trust, such as the bishops of Nantes or Mende. But they could not do without the services of the 'commissaries' and the provisioning of the troops remained very much a matter of luck.

At the time, France was the most populous country in Europe. Her resources were superior to those of the other powers and doubtless even to those of Spain, but she still lacked a good instrument of war.

For the sake of clarity we must try to separate three series of parallel but closely related facts which occurred during the few months between the battle of Nordlingen and French intervention in the Thirty Years War. These were Richelieu's hasty efforts to improve France's position, the demonstration of the consequences of the Swedish defeat in Germany, and the imperial and Spanish armies' exploitation of their victory, first towards the Rhine and then towards the Moselle. It is the combination of these factors which gave the war the new character it assumed from the spring of 1635.

When news of the Nordlingen defeat reached Paris, Father Joseph had just drafted instructions for the marquis de Feuquières in reply to Oxenstierna's proposal for an offensive alliance. These had to be amended and completed by other instructions dated 14th September. Richelieu thought that the chancellor of Sweden would be more accommodating over the question of the Alsatian towns, but his prime concern was to prevent the electors of Saxony and Brandenburg concluding unilateral peace agreements with the emperor. Feuquières had to despatch a French agent called Rorté, who was working for him at the time, to convince them of the king's 'urgent desire to see peace re-established under safe and reasonable conditions for the well-being of his allies'. The king, however, believed that the only means of obtaining these 'safe and reasonable conditions' was through a general peace. If, on the contrary, said the instruction, the two electors 'set an example to the others by disbanding their armies and entrusting their states to the emperor, the Spaniards, who to all intents and purposes control both him, his son and his cabinet, will not allow such an advantageous and unexpected opportunity to slip away without exploiting it to suppress German liberties once and for all.' Clearly this was a very strong argument, but it came too late and there is no need to follow Rorté to Dresden.

It was only at Frankfurt that Feuquières could do anything. Oxenstierna was not well-disposed towards France whose constant evasions and ambitions in Alsace had annoyed him, but he could not do without her. As for the cities and petty princes who made up the League, they felt defenceless before the victorious advance of the imperial forces and looked for a swift intervention by France as their only salvation. Richelieu was well aware of this and stated his terms quite categorically. If the king was to declare war on the house of Austria the allies would have to undertake not to make any separate peace settlements or truces. The king would replace the subsidies which he had paid hitherto by troops recruited in Germany and commanded by a German prince. Henceforward he would have a say in the League's political and military management and would be represented on its Council. Finally, he would substitute French for the Swedish or German garrisons in the towns of Alsace which he did not yet occupy, with the main object of 'helping them to reach a quick and satisfactory peace settlement and of serving them as a barrier against a flood tide which might otherwise engulf them before they had time to collect themselves'.

The results of Feuquières's negotiations did not quite meet with Richelieu's expectations. Nevertheless, two agreements were signed, one at Strassburg and the other at Paris. At Strassburg on 9th October the residents of the king of France and the queen of Sweden, Melchior de l'Isle and Richard Mockel, negotiated with Henri Mogg, the syndic of Colmar who thought that he could speak for all the cities of upper Alsace and undertook to obtain their agreement. They were to accept French garrisons; their government, liberties and religious status were to be respected, as well as their obligations towards the emperor; they were to ensure free passage for the Swedes. On the same day a private treaty was concluded with Colmar which placed itself under French protection until peace returned, on the condition that its liberties, the authority of the magistrates, and the religious status of the town should be restored as they were in 1618 before the outbreak of the civil war. In fact the greater part of Alsace was handed over to French occupation in this way, in particular Colmar and Sélestat, which Marshal de La Force immediately garrisoned.

In addition, Feuquières succeeded in having Löffler and Streiff, two representatives of Sweden and the League, sent to Paris where they were authorised to agree to the French occupation of the cities of Alsace, with the exception of Benfeld,[1] but only if there was an open breach between France and the house of Austria. When Richelieu received them, however, he already had his hands on the treaty of 9th October which gave France all the cities of Alsace, including Benfeld, and which made no conditions about a breach. It became impossible for the representatives of Sweden and the League to stick to their instructions, and the treaty they signed at Paris on 1st November was more favourable to France. Her promise of an open breach with the emperor was made dependent upon the electors of Saxony and Brandenburg remaining loyal to the party. Should there be a breach she undertook to raise 12,000 men in Germany, but in this case she would have a seat in the Council of the League. The king reserved the right to grant his protection to any cities or princes on the other side who asked for it, and his Protestant allies renewed their promise to restore Catholicism in all the lands they had conquered as it had been established in 1618. Finally, Sweden and the League recognised the king of France's right at some future date when imperial and Spanish forces had been expelled to garrison all the cities of Alsace (including Benfeld), as well as Breisach, the towns of Brisgau and all the forest towns.

In fact, although the League accepted the Paris treaty of 1st November, Oxenstierna refused to ratify it, nor did Richelieu ask the king to

[1] Between Sélestat and Strassburg.

ratify the Colmar treaty, probably because the conditions of the Paris treaty, which were valid for all the cities of Alsace, seemed more advantageous to him.[1] But neither the lack of Swedish ratification for the second treaty nor of French ratification for the first prevented French troops from gradually taking over the Alsatian towns and remaining in Colmar, which they had already entered. From the end of November 1634 France was in fact mistress of the whole of Alsace except for the Sundgau.

Whilst all this was going on, France had strengthened her alliance with the States-General of the United Provinces as a measure against Spain. The treaty signed by the United Provinces on 15th April 1634 was a purely defensive alliance and was to run for only a year. A closer, more permanent, agreement had not been possible because the States-General and the king of France were unable to agree on the future fate of the Spanish Netherlands. Frederick Henry thought in terms of a partition, whereas Richelieu would have preferred Belgium to 'form separate cantons' once it had been freed from the king of Spain's power. On 8th February 1635 a new treaty was made embodying a defensive and offensive alliance between France and the United Provinces. Two armies, one French and the other Dutch, each of 30,000 men, were to enter Belgium, and the two allies finally reached a compromise over the question of the partition or cantonment of the conquered lands. It was agreed that the two allies should give the Belgians three months to rise against Spain and form a free state under the joint protection of the United Provinces and France. If this happened France would occupy Thionville, Namur and the Flemish coast up to Ostend, while the United Provinces would retain Breda, Waesland and Gelderland. If the Belgians failed to raise against Spain, the country was to be jointly occupied and partitioned according to the conditions in force after the war.

It was not until the very eve of hostilities and in a rather unsatisfactory form that a new Franco-Swedish treaty replaced the one of November that Sweden had not accepted. Oxenstierna had come in person to conduct the negotiations at the court of France and the treaty was signed at Compiègne on 28th April 1635. It embodied the main clauses of the treaty of 1st November, particularly the one specifying the re-establishment of Catholicism, but there was a new clause guaranteeing freedom of worship for the Protestants. Sweden did not give up her claim to the archbishopric of Mainz nor to the diocese of

[1] A further, almost identical, treaty was made with Colmar at Rueil on 1st August 1635.

Worms which she occupied, and possession was guaranteed by the king of France. There was no mention of the Alsatian towns in the treaty. Lastly, the alliance was only to come into force after it had been ratified by Sweden, and this was to be dependent upon an actual breach between the king of France and the sovereigns of the house of Habsburg.

The sum total of those few months of intense diplomatic activity was that France was assured of considerable—if at that stage somewhat dubious—benefits. She occupied the greater part of Alsace but her authority to do so was recognized only by the Heilbronn League, and not by Sweden. The compromise which had been reached between the king and the States General of the United Provinces did not finally settle Belgium's future. The treaty of Compiègne which Sweden had not ratified because the king of France had not declared war on the emperor, could not in its unratified form impose any precise obligations on the Swedes, who were free to abandon the French king when they pleased. Finally, the clauses regarding the archbishopric of Mainz and the diocese of Worms committed Louis far beyond what he would have liked, for they amounted to a complete repudiation of all the work accomplished in Germany for the restoration of Catholicism. The policy of Richelieu and Father Joseph, who had done their best to reconcile their Protestant alliances to the protection of Catholicism, had been largely overtaken by events. The concessions made by France could be justified, but only in terms of a new war, a European war in which Germany was no more than a battlefield, a war aimed at achieving a balance of power between France and the house of Austria. This indeed was the form that the Thirty Years War was going to take during its final period from 1635 to 1648.

The consequences of Sweden's defeat were similar at the imperial court and in Germany. At the imperial court Ferdinand II was torn between two rival movements. The first, represented by his confessor, the Jesuit Lamormain, was towards a policy of Catholic intolerance. Lamormain did everything in his power to see that the emperor did not grant any religious concessions to the Protestant princes, even to the elector of Saxony. He advised that full advantage should be taken of the Swedish defeat to complete the restoration of Catholicism by implementing the Edict of Restitution. The other movement was political rather than religious, but in spite of this it was backed at the court by another Jesuit, albeit a Spanish Jesuit, Quiroga, the empress's confessor. Until then Lamormain had had his way, but it was now that Quiroga's influence prevailed. He considered that there was no immediate prospect of destroying Protestantism in the Empire, and so he advised the emperor to seek closer ties with the king of Spain in order to fight and overcome France. To this end he should offer the Protestant princes, starting with the elector of Saxony, fairly moderate terms in order to persuade them to make peace separately. It was this course of action that the emperor chose.

So it was that negotiations between the imperial court and the elector of Saxony were resumed, and this time the terms which were offered brought them to a speedy conclusion. On 24th November 1634 the elector signed the Preliminaries of Pirna. These preliminaries are particularly important because, apart from the reparations made to John George, they contained general clauses aimed at paving the way for the subsequent acceptance of the Saxon peace by the other German princes. The emperor granted the Lusatias to the elector of Saxony as a Bohemian fief together with four bailiwicks of the archbishopric of Magdeburg which were to remain in the hands of their administrator, a Saxon prince, for life. In return John George cancelled his claim against the emperor, who had promised to repay the expenses of the war in 1619. Other articles in the preliminaries established terms which the elector of Saxony accepted with a view to re-establishing general peace in the Empire if the other Protestant princes in their turn accepted them. The emperor declared that he was ready to proclaim an amnesty for all those who had taken part in the war, and the mutual restitution of all occupied lands. But the restitutions were to be limited to territories conquered or confiscated since Gustavus Adolphus's landing in Germany, with the result that the Palatinate and Hesse were excluded. The religious clauses of the preliminaries were only drawn up after consultation with a college of theologians and the four Catholic electors. Even at the imperial court they met with very stiff resistance. Many Catholics thought that the emperor had no right to determine the religious constitution of the Empire without the Pope's approval, nor would they accept that any final settlement of the religious problem could result from any temporary alignment of the forces facing one another. But without this final settlement peace was impossible, and the emperor, probably with Quiroga's support, overruled the objections. There could be no question either of consolidating the gains made by the Protestants during the Swedish conquest or of restoring the Catholic Germany of the peace of Augsburg. Ferdinand agreed, not to revoke the Edict of Restitution, but at least to suspend it for forty years, which in practice amounted to completely abandoning it. Thus the essential point was the choice of a standard year to replace the one established by the peace of Augsburg. The Catholics secured the year 1627 which was later than a good number of the restitutions imposed on the Protestants by the emperor after his early victories. A number of points of detail relating to the standard year were also settled in favour of the Catholics, particularly the one concerning the administrated dioceses. These were to be returned to the bishops or administrators who had held them in November 1627. Since 1627, however, some of the Protestant administrators who had then been in possession of the dioceses had died. In such cases (and this was true of Halberstadt, Bremen and Verden) the diocese would pass on to the immediate successor of the Protestant administrator who had died after 1627, even if that successor was a bishop. This general provision obviously masked some specific ulterior motives, because as a result the archbishopric of Bremen and the diocese of Halberstadt were restored to the archduke Leopold William, the emperor's son, and the dioceses of Minden and Verden to Francis William, a Bavarian prince. Lastly, the preliminaries provided that the administrators of dioceses would continue, as before, not to occupy their seats at the imperial diet.

The preliminaries of Pirna formed a basis for peace which the Protestant princes could accept amid the confusion which reigned after the Swedish defeat. This did not of course include the petty princes who had nothing more to lose and perhaps everything to gain from the continuation of the war. Princes such as the landgrave of Hesse-Cassel, the duke of Zweibrücken, the duke of Wurtemberg, the margrave of Baden, the count of Hanau and the count Palatine of Simmern could expect nothing from the emperor, and the king of France was able to count on them although they made only a tiny contribution to his forces. Like the elector of Saxony on the other hand, the elector of Brandenburg, the princes of Brunswick-Lüneburg and the free cities might well find the offer attractive. After all was not the substitution of a standard year, even if it was 1627, for the Edict of Restitution, a Protestant victory? And should not all Germans desire a peace which would re-establish the traditional harmony between the princes and the head of the Empire and put an end to the adventures of foreigners, whether they were Swedes, French or Spaniards? It would be premature to speak of patriotism at this period. Nevertheless there are some signs of it, even in a drunken political incompetent like John George of Saxony. He had joined the Swedes in the hope of profiting from their victories, but without wishing them to be in the Empire for ever, and there were many others in the same position. When a little later they were reconciled with the emperor it was partly out of fear or self-interest. But perhaps they also felt in a confused way that the civil war had lost its importance and that, although the powers might continue to wage war in the Empire, Germany was no more than a battle ground for them, perhaps even a victim to their ambitions. The events which followed on the heels of the French intervention had all the appearances of a settlement of the German war.

After the battle of Nordlingen the military operations themselves assumed a different character. Once he had signed the peace prelim-inaries, the elector of Saxony was no longer a force. It was more or less the same in the case of the other members of the League—some were too insignificant for their attitude to worry the emperor, and he hoped that it would not be long before the others accepted the conditions of the Saxon peace. Even Sweden was incapable, for the time being at least, of providing any stiff opposition to the imperial forces' progress. General Horn had been taken prisoner at Nordlingen. Only Bernard of Saxe-Weimar struggled on with his beaten troops at least to delay the advance on the Rhineland by Gallas and Piccolomini. He had to abandon the Main valley and his duchy of Franconia. For a time he held the Rhine between Mannheim and Mainz, but in January 1635 the imperialists took Philippsburg which the French had not had time to fortify. The Spaniards met little resistance in the electorate of Trier which, with the exception of a few towns, had been completely evacuated by the duc de La Force so that he might cover Lorraine against the attacks of Duke Charles and Johann von Werth. Louis XIII stated quite clearly that his efforts on the left bank of the Rhine would be limited to giving the help he had promised to the princes who had put themselves under his protection, but the last few years had brought about a totally changed situation. Everything was happening as though there was already an open breach between the emperor and the king of France, except that in order to avoid being branded as the aggressor, the latter forbade his generals to cross the Rhine. Louis XIII was now acting as an ally of Sweden, protecting the ecclesiastical princes of the Rhine against the troops of the emperor and the Catholic League. Finally, on 26th March 1635 an event took place which put an end to all uncertainties—Spanish troops entered Trier, seized the elector, and took him off to Germany as a prisoner.

In his *Deutsche Geschichte im Zeitalter der Gegenreformation und des dreissigjährigen Krieges*, the German historian Moritz Ritter outlines the changed character of the war after 1635 and wonders whether the rest of the story has any place in a history of Germany. He decides to continue, but only in so far as it is necessary to explain how the powers engaged in the conflict came to call the congresses of Münster and Osnabrück and how they agreed on the peace. In a history of the Thirty Years War we need have no such scruples. However, we are not at the moment concerned with the events of the war, although there can be no question of passing over them. Right to the end, military operations went hand in hand with diplomatic negotiations and influenced them as much as they were influenced by them.

The immediate cause of the breach was the capture and abduction by the Spaniards of Philip of Sötern, the elector of Trier who had placed himself under the king of France's protection, and it is quite possible that the king of Spain would not have sanctioned this act of violence if he had not wanted to force Louis XIII's hand. Whatever the truth of the matter, the king consulted Richelieu at Rueil and afterwards called an extraordinary meeting of the Council on 1st April. What happened there is recorded by Father Griffet in his *Histoire de Louis XIII*.[1] All the ministers were of the opinion that 'the king could not avoid resorting to arms to avenge the insult which he had just received by the imprisonment of a Prince who had put himself under his protection'. Richelieu still delayed matters until 28th April, when the treaty of alliance with Sweden was formally completed; but on 19th May 1635, the king of France declared war in the traditional style by sending a herald to the king of Spain, and to the cardinal-infante at Brussels. In this way Louis XIII respected the fiction that the Spanish Netherlands had been an autonomous state since Philip II had handed over its government to the archdukes Albert and Isobel. Nonetheless they were once again in fact ordinary Spanish provinces by virtue of Isobel's death and the nomination of the cardinal-infante as governor.

The implications and the limitations of this formal declaration must be borne in mind. There was no breach with any other power but Spain. Richelieu's attitude had not changed in any way; his first concern, as always, was the threat from Spain, and his plan for armed intervention related only to the Netherlands, in which respect the alliance with the States-General of the United Provinces was all important. Indeed, the declaration of war against the king of Spain and

[1] Father Griffet's *Histoire de Louis XIII* was not written until the eighteenth century, but documents which have since been lost were available to him and his *Histoire* is a valuable source.

the cardinal-infante was a necessary step in implementing the alliance of 8th February 1635, by which they had agreed to undertake the joint conquest of the Netherlands. On the other hand he was in no hurry to undertake further commitments in Germany, and still hoped that the Alsatian towns he had garrisoned would form a sufficiently strong line of fortifications to keep the enemy armies out of Lorraine and Burgundy. As Louis XIII had no intention of carrying the war beyond the Rhine, there was no need for him to declare war on the emperor. Thus there was no open breach between Louis XIII and Ferdinand II nor between Louis XIII and the Empire, since the latter could only declare war through a diet and Ferdinand had not yet dared to call one. This ambiguous situation allowed the king to preserve his German alliances. It is true that there was a serious danger that the chancellor of Sweden might be dissatisfied and that ratification of the Franco-Swedish treaty might be delayed as a result, but in fact the treaty was not repudiated although the Swedes respected it only so far as it suited them, and the future remained uncertain.

Another characteristic of the war was that the governments involved never stopped talking of peace. They talked about it before war was even declared and went on talking about it afterwards. In this context we should note the untiring, and usually fruitless activities of the Roman Curia.[1] After his elevation to the Holy See, Pope Urban VIII had often intervened in an effort to find a peaceful solution to the conflicts which had set French against Spanish interests in Italy. In 1631 a papal nuncio, Cardinal Bagni, had been one of the chief architects of the reconciliation between Maximilian of Bavaria and the king of France and we have already studied the part played by Mazarini, another papal delegate, in the preparation of the treaty of Cherasco. Urban VIII intervened and preached reconciliation at every possible opportunity. In 1634 he once again took up the idea of a congress which could meet without interrupting hostilities. He first proposed that it should be held at Rome with himself as mediator, but as he refused to have any dealings with the heretics the proposal fell through. He then seized upon an idea which seems to have been suggested by Father Joseph in the course of an interview with the Spanish ambassador. This was that there should be two congresses going on at the same time. In one there would be only the delegates of the Catholic princes who would hold their discussions under the mediation of the Pope. In

[1] Cf. Leman: *Urbain VIII et la rivalité de la France et de la Maison d'Autriche de 1631 à 1635*.

the other, the delegates of the Protestant princes and the king of France would meet the emperor's. The Pope's proposal was accepted in this form by the king of France in January 1635, and by the emperor in March, but it did not prevent war being declared in May. However, this in its turn did not stop the peace talks going on. They continued in fits and starts and were never completely abandoned until the day came when the Pope's proposal for two simultaneous congresses was implemented at Münster and Osnabrück.

But all this only took place after many long years of war, and, despite Richelieu's feverish activity, the first campaign revealed just how far France was unprepared for it.

The popular conception of the situation at that time is one of the great cardinal completely dominating France and inflexibly pursuing a policy whose ends and means he had already chosen. It would seem that the truth was very different. A continual effort had to be made to reconcile the minister's wishes with those of the king in order to achieve unanimity in the government. The king lavished tokens of his affection and confidence on Richelieu and obviously meant them, but he was forever tortured by doubts and scruples, and, although his 'melancholies' made him incapable of exercising his royal authority, he would not relinquish it. This divided command was made worse because neither Richelieu nor Louis XIII could stay put for long, so that they were rarely together in the same place at the same time. This explains the vast number of letters which passed between them and why Richelieu felt it necessary to leave one of his trusted advisers to keep in touch with the king. Sometimes it was the surintendant Bouthillier, at others Bouthillier's son, Chavigny, whom the cardinal nicknamed 'Monsieur le Jeune'; later it was one of the four secretaries of state. Because the chief minister was always on the move and frequently suffered from illnesses, he could not always attend Council meetings and had to leave many of the decisions to his closest collaborators, Father Joseph, Bouthillier and his son, the secretary of state Servien and a few others. So it was that on 23rd April he entrusted them with the task of preparing the urgent decisions which the military situation in Germany demanded. 'Messieurs Bouthillier and Servien,' he wrote, 'to whom all dispatches from the armies and from abroad are addressed, are in a better position than anyone else to know the present state of German affairs, and it is therefore considered to be appropriate that they should meet this very evening with Father Joseph and the Sieur de Charnacé, who is well versed in such matters, to agree upon the appropriate course of action in this situation.'

This little group no doubt prepared the ground for the discussions of the 'council held at the cardinal's residence at Compiègne on 28th April 1635', which Louis XIII seems to have attended and whose minutes—the 'Résultat'—have most remarkably survived among Richelieu's papers.[1] Meeting on the very day when the treaty of alliance between Sweden and France was being signed, and when war, though not yet declared could not be long delayed, the council's decisions provide us with some very interesting information. They show quite clearly that, as each army operated independently of the others, it was only through the council that any coherent direction of military operations could be given, and that nobody in the council had any real grasp of strategy. The efforts of Richelieu and the other ministers amounted to no more than a calculation of the numerical strength of the armies of the emperor and the king of Spain, a guess at their generals' plans and an attempt to thwart them by putting sufficient forces in the field against them. Although Louis XIII was determined only to declare war on the king of Spain, the council seems to have made no distinction between him and the emperor. It is true that the purely defensive role allotted to the king's armies—with the exception of Bernard of Saxe-Weimar's which was not yet a French army— allowed the other side to be blamed for breaking the peace.

One source of concern which cropped up again and again in the discussions was the question of money. The ministers noted that 'by increasing his majesty's forces, which are already very large, it will become difficult for him to pay them all on time'. They could only suggest one expedient: 'his majesty's soldiers', they said, 'can be maintained without giving them a lot of money if instead we give them more freedom than they have had hitherto to live off the country, although not so much that they become completely undisciplined and disobedient.' And they added: 'the rule we will observe in order that the soldiers may live without brutality at the expense of a country's inhabitants will be either to make a very modest charge for all sorts of commodities or to have the troops fed and maintained by the village communities and stop their advances, but give them to hope that they will be made up to them.' The choice between the two methods was left to the generals who no doubt nearly all preferred the latter. So it

---

[1] Min. des Aff. Étr., Mem. and Doc., France, vol. DCCCXIII, fol. 318, unpublished. Only a handful of the 'Résultats' or Council minutes from Richelieu's time have survived.

was that France went to war, her finances in a dreadful plight, her grasp of strategy worse than mediocre, and her high command totally unco-ordinated. There could be no doubt that it was going to be a long uphill struggle and that material difficulties, slowness of communications, and delays in provisioning and paying the troops would play an almost dominant role in it.

It is perhaps artificial to separate the war with Spain from the German war and yet it was the former to which Richelieu attached more importance. In north Italy and the Netherlands it was France that took the initiative. An army commanded by the duc de Rohan entered the Valtelline by the upper valley of the Rhine and during March and April took over almost the whole country. On 20th May, the day after the declaration of war, another army under the marshals de Châtillon and de Brézé was trying to join forces with the statholder Frederick Henry's troops, when it unexpectedly stumbled across the Spaniards at Avein, near Liège, and defeated and dispersed them. Lastly, in the Po valley, Richelieu concluded the treaty of Rivoli on 11th July with the dukes of Savoy and Parma for the joint conquest of the duchy of Milan, but he failed to achieve the wider alliance he was hoping for which would have included the duke of Modena, the grand duke of Tuscany, and the republic of Venice, and the campaign failed almost before it had begun. In the Netherlands things were even worse. Without pay, the victorious army of Avein had to live off the country and committed such outrages that the population rose in rebellion wherever it went. Decimated by desertion and sickness, all that was left after a few months were a few groups of vagabonds, half soldiers and half bandits, whom the Dutch sent home by sea in order that Belgium should be spared. Richelieu's despair at this can be gauged from a note which he sent to Louis XIII. 'My heart bleeds', he wrote, 'to learn of the miserable circumstances in which the army of Flanders has perished. ... This is of greater importance for the king's affairs than one might imagine, for his power is held in low esteem as a result of the miserable state in which his troops are seen to perish.'[1]

Nor were Richelieu and Louis XIII spared any disappointments or anxiety by affairs in Germany during the first year of open warfare. The great Protestant coalition had completely dissolved. On 30th May the elector of Saxony agreed to turn the preliminaries of Pirna into a permanent peace treaty which was signed at Prague, and he went over from the Swedish to the imperialist camp. In September the elector of

[1] Min. des Aff. Étr., Mem. and Doc., France, vol. DCCCXX, fol. 6.

Brandenburg in his turn was reconciled with the emperor, and his troops joined him in swearing allegiance to the head of the Empire. One after another the dukes of Mecklenburg, the princes of the house of Brunswick (except for duke George of Brunswick-Lüneburg), and most of the free cities such as Erfurt, Nuremberg, Frankfurt and Strassburg accepted the terms of Pirna. The Heilbronn League was no more than a shadow of its former self. It still continued, however, as a band of petty princes whose fortunes were indissolubly joined to Sweden's, and it included Duke George of Brunswick-Lüneburg, the duke of Wurtemberg, the landgrave of Hesse-Cassel, the margrave of Baden-Durlach and the Duke of Zweibrücken. Some were only refugees, but others like George of Brunswick-Lüneburg and William of Hesse-Cassel could raise a few troops. The king of France even made a treaty of subsidies with the latter, allowing him to maintain and command 10,000 men who were to be regarded as the army of the League. As for Bernard of Saxe-Weimar, who had lost his duchy, he was more a soldier of fortune than a German prince, but his troops remained loyal to him and his talent as a soldier allowed him to hope that his luck would change. Throughout the summer he had tried to hold Gallas's army at the Rhine, but by August the position in Alsace had become critical and Richelieu was wondering whether it might not become unavoidable to abandon the towns which had received French garrisons, from Sélestat to Montbéliard. Prompted by these disappointments, Louis XIII came to a definite agreement with Bernard in October, undertaking to pay and maintain the 18,000 men that Bernard had been able to keep together, on condition that he commanded them 'under the authority of the king' and employed them wherever the king considered it necessary. In return, the king handed over to Bernard and guaranteed his right to the landgraviate of Upper Alsace and the bailiwick of Haguenau—the Alsatian possessions of the house of Austria. Bernard now had a vested interest in holding out there and in making his occupation more secure by the capture of Breisach which was still in the hands of imperial and Spanish forces.

All that was left of the great coalition, which for a time under Gustavus Adolphus had threatened the house of Habsburg, were two German armies led by the landgrave of Hesse-Cassel and Bernard of Saxe-Weimar, both in the pay of France. The rest of the Empire once again accepted the emperor's authority. The Swedish alliance was all the more indispensable to France who would willingly have directed all her efforts against Spain and left the Swedes to attack the hereditary lands of the house of Austria; but we have seen how precarious the Swedish alliance was. The fact was that France and Sweden did not share the same interests and aims in the war. Richelieu was convinced that France's vital interests demanded a general peace which would include both Spain and Austria, but Sweden was not at war with Spain and Oxenstierna did not think that a general peace was feasible. Besides, he might well have been afraid that it would favour France rather than Sweden, and he would have been happy with a unilateral peace settlement with the Empire if he had been able to salvage for his country something of Gustavus Adolphus's conquests. In fact, so long as he hoped to maintain Swedish domination of the Rhine from Mainz to Worms, he still needed the French alliance, but for him the most important thing was the question of Pomerania, for to abandon it would have been tantamount to the complete abandonment of Gustavus Adolphus's Baltic policy. Despite the rival—and legally justified—claims of the elector of Brandenburg, the transfer of Pomerania to Sweden depended above all on the emperor. Consequently Oxenstierna tended to think in terms of an individually negotiated peace, and avoided too close a union with France so long as there was any hope of obtaining the emperor's recognition of Sweden's right of conquest in Pomerania on the conclusion of peace. However, on the death of Bogislav XIV, the last Pomeranian duke, in March 1637, he had to abandon his hope, and it was only then that any sincere and close co-operation became possible between France and Sweden in Germany. During the whole of the 1635 campaign the Swedes were fighting on their own account in the Empire with no thought for what was happening in the west. The main Swedish army under Baner tried hard to penetrate Bohemia but failed. In the west, Bernard of Saxe-Weimar's ill-fed troops were forced to retreat into Lorraine by the imperial army under Gallas which followed on their heels.

The changing fortunes of the 1635 campaign and even those of the two subsequent campaigns give the impression that Louis XIII's declaration of war against the king of Spain came too early for France to be prepared for them, but too late to prevent the restoration of the emperor's authority in the Empire. In the first instance, the only result of open warfare was to expose France to the dangers from which Richelieu had so long protected her. Furthermore the Protestant party in Germany gained little or nothing. In fact it may be wondered whether there still was a Protestant party in Germany now that the two Protestant electors, Saxony and Brandenburg, the Lutheran and the

Calvinist, had gone over to the house of Austria. The petty princes who still represented the League did not really count, and Bernard of Saxe-Weimar was only a general in the pay of the king of France. The war had now become nothing more than a war between Sweden and the house of Austria combined with a war between France and Spain. There was not even a formal alliance between France and Sweden, whereas the two sovereigns of Vienna and Madrid were working in close co-operation. In these circumstances we should not be surprised by the French army's defeats nor by the Swedish army's failure to capitalise on its handful of successes.

1636 was France's darkest year. The 1635 campaign had convinced the cardinal-infante that France would be in no state to resist a combined attack by the Spanish and imperial troops. He persuaded Maximilian to place Johann von Werth's light cavalry at his disposal and he had Gallas's army, which was occupying Franche-Comté, invade Burgundy. In the meantime he was to march from Artois into Picardy. Neither Gallas nor the cardinal-infante ran into any effective opposition. Gallas advanced towards the Saône from Dôle and besieged Saint-Jean-de-Losne which he expected to take in the space of a few days. The tiny fortress of La Capelle capitulated to the cardinal-infante, thereby opening the road to Paris through Amiens. Downstream of Amiens on the Somme he took Corbie by surprise; the town guarded the main passage across the line of water and the marshes, which was the only defensive barrier to the north of the capital. Johann von Werth's cavalry took Roye and Montdidier and foraged right up to the walls of Compiègne and Pontoise. Considerable agitation in France followed the fall of Corbie. The Parisians daily expected the enemy's vanguard to appear and there were already signs of public disorder, but Louis XIII hastily gathered some troops together and took command of them himself. His steadiness, together with the coolness and industry of Richelieu, who took all the necessary measures in the space of a few days, restored the courage of the people of Paris and order was maintained. In any case, the danger was not as great as it had at first seemed. The garrison of Saint-Jean-de-Losne stopped Gallas in his tracks and protected Burgundy by a resistance which the imperial forces had not expected and which earned the town the name of Saint-Jean-Belle-Défense. As for the Spanish army which had taken Corbie, it met the same fate as the victorious French army of Avein the year before. The cardinal-infante could not ensure its supplies, the troops dispersed, and Louis XIII had no trouble retaking Corbie. The crisis was past. After the recapture of Corbie and throughout 1637 the war lost its momentum, and France's efforts amounted to no more than the siege of a few strongholds. Perhaps the most important event of the campaign was that the young Turenne distinguished himself for the first time.

For Sweden there was no 'year of Corbie' and she did well in the 1636 campaign. Baner's army, concentrated in Pomerania, crossed the march of Brandenburg untroubled by the elector who had fled to his duchy of Prussia, and on 4th October it beat an army of Saxon and imperial troops at Wittstock, to the north of the Havel. Nothing came of the success, however. Baner was unable to penetrate into Bohemia and had to beat a retreat back to Pomerania in the following year.

The years 1636 and 1637 are chiefly important to France and Sweden for the big reorganisations carried out by Richelieu and Oxenstierna. Although relations between the two ministers were not perfect, Oxenstierna was worried about what was happening back in Stockholm, and he resigned himself to allowing France to handle affairs in Germany while he went back to Sweden where he had not been seen for a long time. He knew all about the intrigues of the Queen Mother who had practically imprisoned the young Queen Christina, intending to marry her off to a Danish prince. This would have been the beginning of a complete realignment of policy, but Oxenstierna's arrival in Stockholm put an end to any plot of that sort. Christina was completely freed and the question of marriage was postponed. The chancellor restored the queen's authority and reorganised the finances in such a way that the generals could once again rely on receiving the supplies of men and money that they needed. At the same time Baner, who was ruined by drink, was joined by a new general, Torstensson, whose ideas of strategy soon put him in a class by himself and who assumed command of the main Swedish army.

Richelieu's task was even greater, and not only more difficult but also more necessary. None the less we know very little about it, not for any lack of documentary evidence—for there is a wealth of this among the cardinal's papers at the Ministère des Affaires Étrangères and also in the *Archives Administratives* of the Ministère de la Guerre—but because researchers are discouraged by the very amount of them and the fact that they are scattered, not to mention the frequent difficulty of establishing their value as evidence. Richelieu's latest historians have only given them a cursory examination, so it is only possible to suggest some of the results that a more penetrating analysis would certainly confirm.

There is no doubt that in the years after 1631 the French armies were thoroughly reorganised, but the reorganisation was piecemeal and geared only to satisfy immediate needs. None the less it paved the way for the improved direction of French policy during the last years of Richelieu's ministry. One of the most important features of this was the leading part played by civilians in the military administration and even in the conduct of the armies. The Minister, one of the four secretaries of state, was a civilian; in 1635 it was Servien, and from February 1636 Michel le Tellier's immediate predecessor, Sublet de Noyers. The king's paymasters in charge of the musters were civilians and in every army there was yet another civilian, a legal administrator who had to keep an eye on the distribution of pay and provisions, deliver judgement on soldiers' crimes, and even attend councils of war. Another important fact is that Richelieu continued to raise more troops. In July 1635, after a detailed muster of the troops, the king had no less than nine armies in the field with a paper strength at least of 160,000 men—134,000 foot and 26,000 horse, the latter almost entirely recruited outside France. Later the numbers were even greater. In 1635 Richelieu had tried to call out the feudal levies, the minor provincial nobles who could be called on for military service in times of need, but these conscripted nobles could not be disciplined and, as custom demanded that they serve for only a few months, when Martinmas came along they all went home again irrespective of the military position and without asking anyone's permission. Richelieu did not repeat the experiment.

One of the things that Richelieu kept trying to improve was the supply of bread and fodder, but he only had partial success. He tried the system of having a commissary for each army and also the system of a general contractor entirely responsible for provisions and for supervising the commissaries, but none of them proved very satisfactory. What harmed the armies most was the bad administration of the kingdom's finances. It is quite apparent that Richelieu had a poor grasp of fiscal affairs and was unable to keep an effective check on Bullion, nis surintendant des finances. Able and industrious though Bullion was, he could never do more than undertake an endless succession of temporary expedients, and he was as much concerned with lining his own pockets as with creating the permanent resources essential for the safety of a kingdom engaged in long war.

In any case, all these attempted reforms could only bear fruit later. In the meantime, a series of events took place in 1636 and 1637, some of them quite fortuitous, which created difficulties for the enemies of the Habsburgs, and in particular for France in dealings with Spain. Affairs in Italy had already brought Richelieu a number of disappointments, and in 1637 this was even more true. On the death of Charles de Gonzague-Nevers, the duke of Mantua, in September 1636, power had passed into the hands of his very pro-Spanish widow, since his grandson who was to succeed him was still a child. A year later, on 8th October 1637, Victor Amadeus the duke of Savoy also died. The Duchess Christine, one of Louis XIII's sisters, took over as regent and at first French influence at Turin seemed completely assured. Christine of France, however, had to reckon with her two brothers-in-law, Cardinal Maurice and Prince Thomas, who were both pro-Spanish— the latter even commanded a Spanish army in the Netherlands. Finally, and most important, the duc de Rohan had to evacuate the Valtelline altogether, since France could not manage to pay the mercenaries whom the Grisons had allowed Rohan to raise in their territory. Furthermore, on Richelieu's instructions, Rohan tried to reconcile the Grisons and the inhabitants of the Valtelline, and drafted a treaty which Richelieu modified a little in favour of the Catholics. The only result of this was to alienate the Grisons, who turned against Rohan, isolated him in the fort of the Rhine to the north of the Splügen pass, and forced him to leave the country completely. The French loss of the Valtelline in 1637 was a major triumph for the Spaniards. For a time it made French intervention an Italian affairs quite impossible and it re-opened to the Spanish troops in the duchy of Milan the route through the Austrian Tyrol.

Events in Germany were of a completely different kind and only confirmed the strengthening of the emperor's authority. At the end of the summer of 1636 Ferdinand, whose health was rapidly deteriorating, decided to convene the electoral college at Regensburg. The electors met there on 15th September and on 22nd December they unanimously elected the emperor's eldest son, Ferdinand, king of Hungary, as king of the Romans. He was thus assured of the imperial crown and he became emperor Ferdinand III on his father's death on 15th February 1637. In fact Ferdinand II's death did not alter imperial policy in any way, for the king of Hungary's influence had been predominant for a long time. He inherited a situation which encouraged him to look for an early victory. France, hardly able to defend herself against Spain, seemed in no position to give aid to the Swedes in Germany in sufficient strength to allow them to pursue the ambitious plans of

Gustavus Adolphus and Oxenstierna. By contrast the emperor had rallied practically all the princes of the Empire against Sweden. Even in 1637, however, a year which perhaps marked the height of imperial power, the house of Habsburg, for all its triumphs, had to abandon many of the plans it had dreamed of achieving after Bohemia had been recovered. The princes rallied to the emperor, it is true, but as sovereign princes free to choose their own policies and their own allies. The time was long since past when Wallenstein had thought it possible to turn the Empire into an absolute monarchy. No less serious was the abandonment of the Edict of Restitution. Religious harmony was thereby re-established in the Empire, but at the price of a very important concession, since the return to the status quo of a given date—the so-called standard year—was tantamount to calling off the militant Counter Reformation and the struggle for the bishoprics which had been so bitterly pursued by the emperor and the Catholic League at the time of the Danish invasion. It was another shattered dream. Finally, the imperial victories had been won at great cost. Although it is not possible to give an exact estimate of the loss of human life and the destruction of property throughout Germany, the terrible losses have been fairly accurately established for some regions and no doubt others suffered just as much. In the central region of the march of Brandenburg —Mittelmark and Uckermark—the population dropped from 113,000 to 34,000 in the towns, and from 300,000 to 75,000 in the countryside. The whole march lost at least two-thirds of its population.[1] Germany was no more than a field of ruins. It might even be said that the real masters of the country were no longer the emperor or the princes or even the generals, but the actual armies which for so long had been forced to live mainly by plunder with no concern for what they left in their wake. The soldiery's ravages in Germany during the last ten or fifteen years of the war, and the terrible epidemics of typhoid or plague which accompanied them, present such a picture of brutality and distress that it is hard to find anything more atrocious, even in the darkest periods of the middle ages. Any calculation of imperial victories must take into account the price paid for them.

These victories were in fact short-lived, and the expectations which had been aroused by Ferdinand's activity as king of Hungary were not fulfilled during his reign as emperor. It would seem that his political role was rather unobtrusive and he made the mistake of giving supreme

---

[1] These figures are taken from Albert Waddington: *Le Grand Électeur Frédéric-Guillaume. Sa politique extérieure*, vol. 1.

command of the army to his younger brother, the archduke Leopold, whose military talent did not match up to his appetite for war. From then onwards the imperial court restricted itself to seeking the restoration of peace in the Empire, while European policy was controlled not from Vienna but from Paris and Madrid by Cardinal Richelieu and Count-Duke Olivares. The long duel between the two great statesmen continued, but Olivares found it hard to stay the pace, and his disgrace in January 1643 followed close on his victorious rival's death.

We need not go into any detailed examination of campaigns or diplomatic negotiations. It is simple enough to note the essential events, both military and political, of the years which preceded, not the first session of the congresses at Münster and Osnabrück, but the actual decision to convene them.

The events of 1638 and 1639 showed quite clearly that fortune had changed sides. Oxenstierna had realised back in 1637 that he had to give up any hope of holding on to Mainz and Worms for Sweden, or even of getting the emperor to agree to the maintenance of Swedish control of Pomerania by means of a separate peace. It therefore followed that he should strengthen the bonds of the Franco-Swedish alliance. At the beginning of 1638 he sent an ambassador, Salvius, to Hamburg to meet the comte d'Avaux, and their discussions quickly resulted in the treaty of Hamburg on 15th March of the same year. This time it was ratified by both sides, as it was an offensive and defensive alliance between the crowns of France and Sweden. Louis XIII undertook to regularise the position of the French armies in Germany by declaring war on the emperor, and to determine the rate of subsidies to Sweden. Both allies promised not to make any separate peace treaties or truces. The Swedes were to attack the house of Austria's possessions through Saxony, and the French through upper Germany. No treaty, in fact, could ever prevent France and Sweden from having totally different war aims and so two questions, each of which was of interest to only one of the allied powers, were omitted from the agreement. For France this was the question of Lorraine; for Sweden the maintenance of her control in Pomerania. The thorny problem of settling these points was later to delay the conclusion of peace, but it did not seriously harm relations between France and Sweden. From then on—and this is a point of the utmost importance—the two allies made great efforts to co-ordinate their military offensives and to follow a common policy in Germany.

Two events during the war which had far-reaching consequences were Bernard of Saxe-Weimar's operations on the Rhine and the Dutch naval victory off Dover. Frederick Henry's capture of Breda in October 1637 had brought a band of Spanish troops from their quarters in the Sundgau up to the Netherlands. This enabled Bernard of Saxe-Weimar to return to the offensive. Advancing up the left bank of the Rhine to a point just above Basel, he laid siege to Rheinfelden, one of the forest towns, in order to take possession of its bridge. An imperial army which came to the aid of Rheinfelden was beaten off, and at the end of the battle Johann von Werth was made prisoner. Rheinfelden offered no further resistance. Bernard then crossed the Rhine and went down as far as Breisach which he besieged in June.[1] The fortress resisted for several months, but all attempts to supply it failed and it capitulated on 17th December 1638. Father Joseph, who had been ill for some weeks, was on the brink of death. Legend has it that on 18th December, when his close companion was about to die, Richelieu had no hesitation in announcing to him that Breisach had fallen. The news arrived in Paris by express messenger the following day. For the Austro-Spanish alliances it was an almost decisive defeat. Breisach commanded two routes; the one beyond the Rhine which took the Spanish troops into the Empire, and the traditional route which allowed armies assembled in the duchy of Milan to get to the Palatinate and the Low Countries via Switzerland and Alsace. After the fall of Breisach both were blocked and the Netherlands were completely cut off.

A little later the Spaniards lost control of their sea route too. The Dutch fleet under Tromp drove a very strong squadron from Spain to take shelter in English territorial waters on the coast near Dover. Tromp waited some weeks for it to come out into the open, then, quite illegally, attacked it and almost completely destroyed it in what was his first great exploit. Only a handful of vessels managed to regroup off the Flemish coast to return to the ports of Spain, and Philip IV's finances were in such a state that there could be no question of creating a new war fleet. It was the end of Olivares's old dream of commercial and naval domination of the northern seas, and it was the Dutch fleet which now commanded the sea along the coasts of the Spanish Netherlands. The battle of Dover in October 1639 is a landmark in the

---

[1] The fortress of Breisach formed the bridgehead on the right bank of the Rhine. It was later called Old Breisach when another town had been built on the left bank.

history of Spain's decline during the Thirty Years War.

Olivares did not gloss over the seriousness of the situation. Philip IV had never dared to place too much faith in Belgians or Flemings and he moved their troops about frequently, sending Spaniards to the Netherlands and bringing Walloons down into Spain. As a result of the battle of Dover, however, these constant exchanges of troops were made impossible. Very soon the Netherlands were short of men and money. Franche-Comté was also isolated and help could come only from Germany, but the emperor scarcely seemed to be in a mood to supply it. Olivares became more and more discouraged.[1] For a time he clutched at the hope of coming to an understanding with Richelieu in order to obtain a general truce and thus facilitate peace negotiations, but despite protestations of goodwill by both ministers they did not trust each other enough to reveal to the intermediaries who circulated between Paris and Madrid the conditions under which they would make peace.[2] Perhaps only Father Joseph genuinely wanted to reconcile them; certainly the secret talks stopped after his death. At the same time a rift developed between the courts of Vienna and Madrid. In 1639, much to the annoyance of Philip IV, Ferdinand recalled Piccolomini from the Netherlands for he was unable to get on with either the cardinal-infante or Prince Thomas of Savoy. 'The Emperor,' wrote Philip to the cardinal-infante, 'has not really achieved anything with all the money we have given him. Any further subsidies must be considered a complete waste.'[3] This split between Spanish and imperial policy proved serious for the king of Spain whose military power was becoming exhausted; nor was it any less serious for the emperor, and we cannot overlook its consequences in the development of the war in Germany itself.

France and Sweden were even more successful during 1640 and 1641. In the west these years marked a further stage in the decline of Spain, and the division between Spanish and Austrian policy became final. In August 1640 the French captured Arras after a prolonged siege. This may seem fairly insignificant, but Arras and the part of Artois which was occupied with the town protected the line of the Somme,

[1] The progress of Olivares's disillusionment can be charted from his correspondence with the cardinal-infante such as has been published by Lonchay and Cuvelier Lefèvre in *Correspondance de la cour d'Espagne sur les affaires des Pays-Bas au XVIIᵉ siècle*.

[2] Cf. Leman: *Richelieu et Olivarès* which contains a detailed study of the secret negotiations which took place between 1636 and 1642.

[3] Cf. Lonchay, op. cit. Note of 9th October 1639.

which is why news of the capture of Arras was welcomed so joyfully by the Parisians who had not forgotten the 'year of Corbie'. In 1640, too, serious events occurred within the Spanish kingdom. The Catalans, with their well-known taste for provincial independence, charged the court of Madrid with not respecting their traditional liberties, their 'fueros'. In June the people of Barcelona revolted and appealed to the French, who helped them to resist Philip IV's troops. A little later, in February, the Catalans cut their ties with Spain and proclaimed Louis XIII Count of Barcelona. Another war of independence had begun in December 1640 following disturbances at Evora and an insurrection by the people of Lisbon. Portugal, which had been conquered by Philip II in the previous century and integrated with Spain, proclaimed a prince of the old ruling house of Braganza as King John IV. He concluded an alliance with the king of France against Spain which lasted until Louis XIV's day, when Portugal was completely liberated. The Spanish monarchy was nothing more than a kind of federal monarchy uniting a number of states within the peninsula in obedience to one crown, but without weakening their attachment to their own particular liberties. In 1640 it seemed to be on the verge of breaking up. In any case the imperial court could no longer depend on the financial and military aid which it had hitherto enjoyed to such advantage.

Meanwhile in Germany, other events, quite unrelated to those in Spain, cast doubts on the chances of an imperial victory. At the beginning of 1640 Ferdinand III had decided to convene an imperial diet, the first since the 'broken' diet of 1603. He hoped that it would grant him a heavy contribution to replace the money he had hitherto received from Spain and to enable him to continue the war. At first the three colleges seemed well disposed, but there was a new spirit abroad among the German princes. They had regained their courage after the recovery of France and Sweden, and peace at any price now seemed less important. Some of them began to regret that they had made peace with the emperor so quickly under the terms of the preliminaries of Pirna which they now considered too favourable to the Catholics. They demanded a return to the former standard year of 1618 in any settlement of the religious constitution of the Empire. A chance occurrence soon encouraged them to press their claims. This was the death of George William, the elector of Brandenburg on 1st December 1640. His son and successor, the twenty-nine year-old Frederick William, was cast in quite a different mould to his predecessor. Once he had assumed power, the Catholic prince Adam von Schwarzenberg, who had associated the policies of the elector with those of the emperor, rapidly lost influence, and he died, a year later, on the brink of total disgrace. A little later, in July 1641, Elector Frederick William signed a truce with Sweden and thus recovered his independence. At Regensburg his delegates gathered together all the malcontents and, although the diet did not altogether refuse the emperor financial support, by the time it was dissolved on 10th October 1641 it had fallen far short of Ferdinand's hopes.

In the midst of all the troubles of 1642, the year of the Cinq-Mars conspiracy, Richelieu did at least derive some comfort from the new French victories and the hope of an early peace. On the Spanish front there was the capture of Perpignan and the conquest of Roussillon. In the Netherlands the Spaniards could look for safety only to the domestic problems which weakened France and which they could keep alive at no great cost. In March 1641 the cardinal-infante admitted as much to Philip IV: 'If the war with France is to continue,' he wrote to his brother, 'we have not the means to take the offensive. The Spanish and Imperial armies are reduced to such a state that they can undertake nothing. The only solution is to establish supporters in France and use them to make the Paris government more amenable.' But even this solution failed. In April 1641 the cardinal-infante made a secret pact with the duc de Bouillon, the comte de Soissons and the duc de Guise. It was a failure; the only soldier in the party, Soissons, was killed at the engagement of La Marfée. After the cardinal-infante's death in November 1641, Philip IV welcomed with open arms an offer to betray Louis XIII by his favourite, Cinq-Mars, but Richelieu secured a copy of Cinq-Mars's treaty with the king of Spain and had him executed at Lyons. In Germany war was beginning on a large scale. The untimely death of Bernard of Saxe-Weimar shortly after the capitulation of Breisach had allowed Richelieu to take over his army and put Guébriant in command. He had learned his trade with Bernard and managed to combine the movements of his troops with those of the Swedish army under Torstensson. Very soon, swift, well-managed campaigns began to create disorder in the imperial camp. During the last months of Richelieu's life it is clear that he thought that peace was not far off. At the beginning of the winter of 1641–1642 France and Sweden had proposed to the emperor the calling of two simultaneous congresses in Westphalia, one at Münster and the other at Osnabrück. The emperor had accepted the proposal and had gone so far as to fix the following March as the date for the delegates' meeting. When

March arrived, the opening of the congresses was postponed, but delay in such cases was only to be expected and Richelieu did not seem unduly disturbed. When his life of struggles and suffering came to an end on 4th December 1642, it could be said that he had neither suffered nor struggled in vain.

CHAPTER VIII

MAZARIN AND THE CONGRESSES

By 14th December 1642 France had made considerable gains in the struggle against the house of Habsburg, mainly outside the Empire, but within it as well. Outside the Empire, having been called in to aid the Catalan rebels, the French were able to take Perpignan and to occupy the whole of Roussillon, which has remained French ever since. At the same time this rebellion threatened the foundations of the Spanish monarchy in the Iberian peninsula, and this was even more true of the Portuguese uprising which finished twenty years later in complete independence for Portugal. To the north in the Burgundian circle, which as we have already seen had not been legally detached from the Empire, Franche-Comté was cut off. Furthermore the capture of Artois not only covered the Somme frontier but left the Belgian Provinces open to attack. Finally, within the Empire the fall of Breisach had brought in its wake inevitable consequences for the Spaniards and Austrians. The way into the Swabian lands and the Black Forest across the Sundgau was now closed to the Spanish army, and from Basel to Kehl the course of the Rhine protected Alsace whose defence had formerly caused Richelieu so much concern and which was now occupied by French troops. Alsace, moreover, protected Lorraine, which now seemed safe from the raids of Charles IV and Johann von Werth. So it seemed that the king of France was in a strong bargaining position and that any peace negotiations would be successful if his demands were reasonable. Moreover, international law allowed him to claim not only compensation for the imperial princes and respect for German liberties, but also what was known in diplomatic parlance as 'satisfaction'. This involved the handing over of some territory both for the safety of the realm and to offset the costs of a long war. At a time when states were poor, reparations as they are known today, were made in the form of a territorial indemnity. However, the king of France had undertaken not to make any peace treaties or truces without Sweden, and Sweden was far from being in a position to make the demands she thought she was entitled to. In particular there was nothing to suggest that the dispute over Pomerania would be solved easily or in Sweden's favour. After Baner's death, at any rate, Torstensson's activities and ruthless energy had quickly re-established the position of the Swedish armies in the Empire. During the course of a spring campaign in 1642 he had beaten the Saxon army and had passed through Moravia to within twenty-five miles of Vienna. True, he had soon been forced to re-establish his line of communication with north Germany and had beaten a retreat into Saxony with an imperial army commanded by Archduke Leopold on his heels, but he had inflicted a heavy defeat on it not far from Leipzig. Archduke Leopold lost a quarter of his men either killed or wounded, another quarter in prisoners or deserters, and much war material. The battle took place on 2nd November 1642, a month before Richelieu's death.

It was these military successes as well as the proposed congresses which made Richelieu hope that a return to peace was becoming possible. However, he knew that negotiations would last for a long time and would not interrupt hostilities. How would he have conducted them? What would his war-aims have been? Obviously we can have no means of knowing. The cardinal's realistic and flexible approach never allowed him to make premature decisions, nor was it his wont to reveal his secret intentions. Once the congresses had met, two courses of action would have been open. He might have entered into negotiations merely to appease public opinion, and in particular the Pope, whilst continuing to fight until the house of Habsburg was completely defeated. On the other hand, he might have swiftly negotiated a genuine peace, content merely to ensure the security of the French frontiers and the maintenance of German liberties. It is fruitless to speculate which of these policies Richelieu would have chosen. The most we can do is to recall that in all his public pronouncements he had always shown himself to be firmly in favour of an immediate peace settlement. The question loses its significance, however, because, between Richelieu's death and the opening of the congresses, events took place which created a totally new situation.

Richelieu's death preceded by only a few months that of his 'good master', Louis XIII. The new king, Louis XIV, was a four-year-old child, and the end of the war came before the end of his long minority was finished. By tradition the task of regent devolved on the Queen Mother, the slovenly and greedy Anne of Austria, who had no head for politics and who, as a Spaniard herself, had often worried Louis XIII by maintaining her correspondence with the courts of Spain and Brussels. A complete transformation of the system of government and French foreign policy became possible, and indeed this seemed imminent when the regent lost no time in recalling from exile all those who had opposed or plotted against the cardinal-minister. When Richelieu had lost Father Joseph, who had served as his confidant during the difficult days, he had chosen a successor by recommending Louis to appoint Mazarin who had transferred from the Pope's service to the king's, had received the cardinal's hat, and had become a naturalised Frenchman. On Richelieu's death, Louis XIII, amenable as ever, had made Mazarin chief minister. In fact the accession of the regent left the situation completely open again, since she was free to choose anyone she pleased. Fortunately, Mazarin pleased her, though to what extent we cannot know, and besides it is of little consequence. Suffice it to say that she seems to have had no hesitation in confirming Mazarin's position and his role in the Council. Moreover the decision can be explained without reference to any but political considerations. Anne of Austria was too lazy and too frivolous to saddle herself with the responsibilities of government. She did not feel up to it. She was also terrified of court intrigues. Mazarin had not been involved in any and his innate cunning made him better equipped than anyone to frustrate them. Since he was already in office, was experienced in politics, and nobody could doubt his ability, it was quite natural for Anne of Austria to have placed her trust in him.

One thing which is quite certain is that he very quickly assumed such complete control over the regent that he had a far freer hand in governing the realm than Richelieu had had before him. He was so confident of her approval that he rarely consulted the regent, but merely informed her of his own decisions and the reasons for them. He often dictated what she was to say or do, and the regent acted or spoke accordingly. Mazarin played the part of a prime minister to an even greater extent than Richelieu. He managed the council; he corresponded with ambassadors without consulting the secretary of state for foreign affairs, Loménie de Brienne; he corresponded with generals without consulting the secretary of state for war, Michel le Tellier. Everything confirms what one of Mazarin's contemporaries, the historian Priolo, said of him: 'He rested rarely and slept little and dealt personally with all matters of importance.' When we speak of the regency's European policy between 1643 and 1648, we mean Mazarin's policy.

But what was it? There were two courses open to Richelieu but he had not had time to choose between them: which did France follow under Mazarin's government? His final choice may be explained by the events of the war, the success of French diplomacy, the situation at home, and finally the new minister's own personality.

The events of the war consolidated and extended the successes achieved at the end of Richelieu's ministry. Indeed the first success, the victory of Rocroi (19th May 1643) came within only a few days of the beginning of the regency. The cardinal-infante's successor as governor of the Netherlands, Don Francisco Melo, a Spaniard through and through, had planned a new invasion of France, aimed at Paris, for the spring of 1643. First, however, he had to breach the line of fortresses protecting the head of the Oise valley, and laid siege to Rocroi. Louis XIII had chosen a prince of the blood, the duc d'Enghien, son of the prince de Condé, to command the army which was to check the Spaniards. The duke was still quite young, no more than twenty-two, but this did not prevent him carrying off the brilliant victory of Rocroi. The Spanish infantry was decimated and the losses it suffered at Rocroi could not be made good by an impoverished, depopulated Spain. On that day the famous 'tercios' lost their reputation for invincibility. In any case Don Francisco's planned campaign had failed, and in France the battle of Rocroi was considered as a decisive defeat for Spain, as indeed it was. As such it was an event of the utmost importance, not only in the war between the king of France and Philip IV but also in the war between the emperor and his enemies, because from that time onwards Ferdinand III had to abandon any hopes of Spanish help. In southern Germany the French advance was delayed by the death of Guébriant. His successor, the vicomte de Turenne, a pupil of Frederick Henry of Orange-Nassau, took some time to take the former Weimarian troops in hand, but in 1644 the combined forces of Condé and Turenne entered Freiburg, the capital of the Breisgau, which guarded the southern passes of the Black Forest. In 1645 Turenne's defeat at Marienthal was brilliantly retrieved by Turenne and Condé, once more united, in the victory of Nordlingen on 3rd August, which laid Bavaria open to the two victorious generals. The dawn of the regency was filled with hopeful signs which the end of Louis XIII's reign had never known.

For the very first time diplomatic success and military victory went hand in hand in 1643 and 1644. Mazarin had no more success than Richelieu in his attempts to form a powerful league of Italian princes hostile to Spain, and in Germany he tried in vain to unite the Protestant and Catholic princes in a common defence of their liberties. However, back in 1640, amid great secrecy, talks had been resumed between the courts of France and Munich. They did not reach any precise agreement for a long time, but they were never broken off. Like France, Maximilian wanted a return to peace, and this provided a basis for negotiations. He also wanted his territorial acquisitions to be confirmed and this raised the vexed question of the Palatinate. Even if he did remain faithful to the emperor he felt no affection for the Spaniards. He showed this clearly enough at the diet, and when that body demanded the removal of Spanish troops from the Empire it is possible that it did so at the Bavarian's prompting. It is also possible that the diet's attitude prepared the emperor to accept the idea of convening a congress to negotiate peace. In the meantime Mazarin renewed in the name of the new king the alliance signed with Sweden. On 1st March 1644 at the Hague he at last obtained, not without some difficulty, two new treaties. One was a treaty of subsidies for the continuation of the war, and the other was a treaty of guarantee for the preparation of peace. The latter authorised both allied powers to negotiate individually with Spain on the condition that no agreement would be made, save jointly and with one accord. They were both to do their best to hold what they had conquered and it was understood that their alliance would continue beyond any peace agreement in order to guarantee their territorial acquisitions.

Finally, to all the triumphs of arms and diplomacy abroad Mazarin could add the satisfaction of a solidly based government at home. The opposition which had formed against him was quickly brought down. The 'Cabale des Importants' was no more than a flash in the pan. The minister's power over the regent continued to grow, and though the Parlement of Paris had tried to block his fiscal edicts its resistance was fairly easily broken; after a 'lit de justice' held by the infant king on 7th September 1645, President Barillon was interned at Pinerolo where he died. Among the former servants of Richelieu, Mazarin had found a skilful administrator, a fellow Italian called Particelli d'Emeri.[1] Under the unassuming title of intendant des finances he did the work of a surintendant and, by many expedients, procured all the funds that the minister needed. Mazarin was convinced that he would not be short of money for a long time to come.

How was it that so much easy success did not go to Mazarin's head?

[1] Particelli d'Emeri's role during the regency has not yet been the subject of a study.

8

To explain his policy and distinguish it from Richelieu's we must take his personality into account. It is hard to imagine a more lively mind than Mazarin's, or one more flexible or more prolific in devising stratagems. He was very much a diplomat as well as a statesman. Richelieu was well-acquainted with the subtle game of diplomacy but was unwilling to spend overmuch time on it, seeing it rather as a means to an end. Mazarin's enjoyment was such that he was sometimes carried away. We should also bear in mind that Mazarin was a foreigner, an Italian. At that time no one was surprised that the king of France's chief minister should be a foreigner—although Mazarin's Italian origin was held against him during the Fronde—and without doubt Mazarin served his adopted country faithfully. In spite of everything, his origins made him something of a political adventurer. To use Lavisse's apt phrase, he was something of a statesman of fortune. At any rate he lacked Richelieu's spontaneous and unswerving grasp of France's long term interests. He had been Richelieu's adviser since the death of Father Joseph; he continued the work of his predecessor and brought it to a glorious conclusion. Sometimes perhaps he altered its course a little.

At the very beginning of the regency Mazarin selected France's future delegates at the congress. As was customary the embassy was headed by a person of high rank whose function was chiefly decorative. In this case it was the duc de Longueville, the prince de Condé's son-in-law whom both the regent and the minister wanted away from Paris. Since he would have been incapable of conducting any negotiations as complicated as those in Westphalia were going to be, two experienced and skilful delegates were appointed under him. One of them was the comte d'Avaux, a privy councillor and the best diplomat that France had at the time. He had given ample proof of his ability in Holland. The other was Servien who had just left the office of secretary of state for war. He too was a privy councillor, outspoken at times but none-theless well able to play the diplomatic game with great skill. Later on d'Avaux and Servien clashed with each other, but at Münster they both rendered France invaluable service. When they were selected not a single delegate had as yet arrived at Münster or Osnabrück; when they presented themselves in 1644 they found nobody there and immediately returned to court. There was therefore no need for Mazarin to deter-mine the policies to follow at the congress. Whatever his original intentions, the events themselves decided him not to rush the opening of negotiations and to act without too much regard for future nego-tiations.

In any case he was active both diplomatically and militarily else-where where things were not altogether favourable for France. The death of Urban VIII had put on the papal throne a pope who was ill-disposed towards the French in general and to Mazarin in particular. Furthermore, at the end of the summer of 1634 war had broken out between Sweden and Denmark, who had increased the sound dues without heed to Sweden's interests. Torstensson had to leave the German front to go and invade first Holstein and then Jutland, and for nearly a year the Swedish forces in Germany were too depleted for there to be any combined offensive by France and Sweden. In 1645, however, Mazarin managed to arrange the peace of Brömsebro (13th August) between the two Scandinavian powers and then, by the treaty of Copenhagen on 25th November, he obtained from the king of Denmark the opening of the sound to French trade. In the same year Mazarin's diplomacy paved the way for two other events which acted in France's favour. The king of Poland, Wladislav, married a French princess, Louise Marie de Gonzague, daughter of the former duke of Mantua, and she lost no time in playing an active part in the manage-ment of Polish policy. She had hoped to marry the duc d'Orléans, but at Mazarin's insistence she had resigned herself to seeking a crown far from France. At the same time Mazarin concluded an alliance between the king of France and Rakoczy, prince of Transylvania who laid claim to the throne of Hungary. Thus a ring of eastern alliances was being formed around the territories of the house of Austria at the very moment when the Danish peace, signed at Brömsero, freed Tor-stensson's army once more.

Mazarin then took it into his head that nothing was too much to hope for, and he allowed himself to be drawn into two enterprises which were far too vast. At the very least he should have chosen between them and in the event they caused him a great deal of dis-illusionment.

Least dangerous was an expedition into central Italy, though its outcome was none the less uncertain. Its twin aims were to crush Spanish power in Italy and to force the new Pope, Innocent X, to moderate his hostility towards France. A fleet commanded by the young duc de Brézé and a landing force under Prince Thomas of Savoy, whom Mazarin had managed to win over, were to take Orbitello on the Tuscan coast and then the other presidios held by the Spaniards in the same region. Once in possession of Orbitello the French were to hamper sea communications between the kingdom of

Naples and the duchy of Milan and to present enough of a threat to Rome for the Pope to be forced to change his attitude. In addition the expedition against the presidios of Tuscany masked secret designs on the kingdom of Naples which was the main target of the undertaking. Mazarin was secretly in league with Prince Thomas and urged him, once Orbitello was captured, to take advantage of the Neapolitans' grievances against the Spaniards in order to incite the kingdom to rebellion and have himself declared king. If he succeeded he was to allow the French to occupy Gaeta and another port on the Neapolitan coast. There was even provision for the possibility of Thomas, with the aid of Mazarin's diplomacy, succeeding his nephew, the infant duke of Savoy. In exchange he would hand Nice and Savoy over to France, 'everything which lies on this side of the mountains close to France'.

The second undertaking which was strictly diplomatic was at that time Mazarin's favourite scheme, as Father Bougeant himself affirmed in his *Histoire du traité de Westphalie*. Coming from so unemotional an author this opinion deserves our attention. He wrote: 'The satisfaction with which he outlined his plan leads one to think that he was intoxicated by its beauty.' It amounted to a plan to exchange Catalonia for the Netherlands, with the king of Spain's agreement. Mazarin was well aware that the king of France would not be able to retain Catalonia. He also knew that the king of Spain was very anxious to re-establish his authority there, whereas by contrast the maintenance of Spanish rule in the Netherlands was becoming increasingly difficult, since it tied up a number of Spanish troops and cost a great deal. He fancied that Philip IV might agree to the exchange if the surrender of the Netherlands could be justified by the engagement of the Infanta to the young Louis XIV and be presented in the form of a dowry granted by the king to his daughter. When Mazarin told the comte d'Avaux and Servien of his plan they were against it. They made the point that to negotiate the surrender of the Netherlands with Spain would involve breaking the promise of a joint conquest made to the States-General of the United Provinces. They added that it was a foregone conclusion that Spanish diplomacy would be sure to let the Hague know of the king of France's proposal and would use it to start separate negotiations with the States General. Furthermore the return of Catalonia to the king of Spain would betray the Catalan cause, breaking the alliance, and would no doubt damage for a long time to come the king of France's prestige throughout the Iberian peninsula. But Mazarin was too 'intoxicated with the beauty of his plan' to listen to

Servien and d'Avaux. He thought that he could persuade the Dutch that a French occupation of the Netherlands would be as much to their advantage as to the king of France's, and that at any rate they would be easily convinced if Antwerp and its environs were handed over to the prince of Orange. So Mazarin, amid great secrecy, sent the comte d'Estrades to Frederick Henry. If we bear in mind that at the same time Mazarin, unlike Richelieu, did not conceal his intention to retain Alsace for the king and that rumours of this were rife in Germany, we can see the extent of his hopes in the autumn of 1645.

This is perhaps the only time in the whole history of diplomacy in the ancien régime when we see a minister being influenced by such polemists as the author of Richelieu's *Testamentum politicum*, who would have liked the monarchy to have undertaken to extend the realm of France to the limits of ancient Gaul. That at least seems to have been the opinion of Chéruel in his explanation of a letter from the cardinal to Servien dated 20th January 1646. 'The acquisition of the Spanish Netherlands,' he wrote, 'would give the city of Paris an impregnable rampart and it could then truly be called the heart of France, . . . since the frontiers would be extended as far as Holland and, on the German side from which we have most to fear, as far as the Rhine, by the retention of Alsace and Lorraine. . . . Even our sternest critics would have to agree that so much blood and money were well spent if all the former kingdom of Austrasia were annexed to the crown of France together with whole provinces which in the past have provided the means for individual princes who ruled them, not only to resist France, but to trouble her to an extent which we all know.' For my own part, however, I am convinced that this passage should be interpreted quite differently. It is noteworthy that Mazarin, like Richelieu before him, assigns a purely defensive character to the monarchy's enterprises in the direction of the Rhine; that he had no intention of extending the kingdom to the Rhine anywhere other than in Alsace; that he wanted to consolidate France's frontiers on the German side because it was the side 'from which we have most to fear'; that he was concerned with the former kingdom of Austrasia and the threat presented to the king of France by the foreign princes who had settled there; and, finally, that he does not once mention 'natural frontiers' or the 'frontiers of ancient Gaul', nor do we find them anywhere else in his correspondence although at least one of these expressions would have come quite naturally from his pen. Thus in my opinion Mazarin's imprudent ambitions during this short period should be attributed, not to any would-be policy of natural frontiers but, to use Father Bougeant's words, to the intoxication which overcame him after a series of diplomatic and military victories which had far exceeded his expectations.

In any case, this mood was soon dispersed. The Orbitello expedition was begun too late, the landing force was quickly decimated by fever, and Prince Thomas was not equal to the task. Despite Mazarin's insistence, he failed to start by capturing Porto Ercole which was Orbitello's link with the hinterland. He did not even manage to cross the ditch defending the ramparts of Orbitello. Finally, when the duc de Brézé had been killed in a naval engagement with the Spaniards, Prince Thomas lost no time in raising the siege (July 1646). Apart from this nothing was done to incite the Neapolitans to rebellion. The great undertaking, begun amid so much enthusiasm, finished in complete failure.

Between times the plan to exchange Catalonia for the Netherlands fared no better. It was obviously premature. At the beginning of 1646 the conquest of the Netherlands was hardly begun and the king of France was not yet master of the whole of Catalonia where the Spaniards clung tenaciously to Lerida and Tarragona. Philip IV could not entertain the idea of sacrificing the Netherlands which he had not yet lost in order to re-establish his authority in Catalonia which he expected to reconquer. He would take no part in the negotiations and merely informed the Dutch secretly of the French proposal. So, despite the prince of Orange's goodwill, the mission of the Comte d'Estrades produced no tangible result; the city fathers of Amsterdam, however, were so angry and alarmed that they immediately showed themselves willing to negotiate a separate peace with Spain. Under the cover of the Congress at Münster, secret talks had already been started between Pauw, one of the delegates of the States-General, and the count of Peñaranda, head of the Spanish delegation. Once Pauw learned of the projected exchanges of territory he hurried to the Hague to ask for instructions and returned to Münster. While scurrilous pamphlets circulated by the Spaniards stirred up public opinion in Holland, Pauw and Peñaranda, who were both anxious for a quick solution, began negotiations in earnest. The king of France was in danger of losing one of his chief allies. It needed all Mazarin's energy and flexibility to straighten out the situation which he had unwisely caused. A fresh expedition was sent to Italy before the Spaniards had had time to take advantage of Prince Thomas's defeat at Orbitello. The troops under

Marshal de La Meilleraie, grand-master of the artillery, and Marshal du Plessis-Praslin arrived within sight of Tuscany in September. They laid siege simultaneously to Porto Longone in the isle of Elba and Piombino on the neighbouring Italian coast. On 11th October Piombino capitulated, followed by Porto Longone on the 29th. The defeat at Orbitello had been redeemed and the French were once again established along the sea route which the Spanish galleys used between Naples and Genoa, but Mazarin, learning from his experiences, was henceforth very wary about becoming involved in the complexities of an Italian policy.

From 1646 it was in Germany that the decisive events took place. The great conflict still ran its course, conducted jointly by the Prince de Condé[1] and Marshal de Turenne for the French and Torstensson and Wrangel for the Swedes, but Mazarin was now determined to negotiate sincerely for a general peace settlement. Negotiations of course did not cut short the military operations which coincided with, and sometimes influenced, the diplomats' exchanges; nonetheless, the peace congress (perhaps it would be better to say congresses, since some delegates met at Münster and others at Osnabrück) now became the principal concern of the cardinal-minister, the courts, and all the nations which from the beginning had had any sort of hand in the war. It is the congress therefore which must now occupy our attention.

We have seen that the idea of having two simultaneous congresses had apparently come from a suggestion by Father Joseph and that Pope Urban VIII had adopted it; that it had been put to the king of France in 1641, and that the emperor had backed it in December of the same year; that the meeting of the two congresses in Westphalia at Münster and Osnabrück had originally been set for 25th March 1642 and then postponed; and that the French plenipotentaries had finally gone to Münster in April 1644, and, finding nobody there, had returned to court and had only gone back to Westphalia a little later. Conferences had then been held between the Swedish and French plenipotentiaries, and between the French and the first of the imperial plenipotentiaries who were twice replaced. Long and bitter discussions were held through third parties about the terms of the passports given to all the foreign diplomats and then about the text of their authorisations. It was not until 4th December 1644 that a mass and solemn procession marked the official opening of the Congress at Münster, but the opening itself

---

[1] The duc d'Enghien had assumed the title Prince de Condé on the death of his father on 26th December 1646.

was nothing more than an exchange of preliminary proposals by the various embassies. The French, moreover, proposed that no discussions should begin until the delegates of the princes and free cities of Germany had arrived. As these had been invited to be represented separately at the congress at the insistence of the French and despite strong opposition from the emperor, this was a clever device to secure recognition of their sovereignty, and the French hoped that as a result they would be favourably disposed towards them. In this they were not disappointed. They also demanded at the same time that the elector of Trier who was still held prisoner by the emperor should be set free, claiming that his presence at the congress was necessary to guarantee the full validity of the peace. Negotiations at Münster therefore were once again postponed for a few months, and the situation was even worse at Osnabrück where they did not open until the second half of 1645.

We know every last detail of the Münster and Osnabrück negotiations. They have been pieced together from the plenipotentiaries' correspondence in several great collections such as Father Bougeant's *Histoire du traité de Westphalie*. However, there is no need for us to examine them, even briefly. The only important thing is to understand what sort of Congress it was and how it led step by step, and through many vicissitudes, to the signing of the two treaties of Münster and Osnabrück and the reorganisation of central Europe, which had been thrown into complete confusion by thirty years of war.

The congress of Westphalia was in fact a European congress. All the powers and all the sovereigns were either represented or took an interest in the progress of the negotiations, except for the Czar, the Sultan, and the king of England, who was no longer in a position to intervene in continental politics after the Civil War and the Long Parliament's victories. In fact not all the sovereigns represented were on an equal footing, and men talked frequently of the king of France, the queen of Sweden and their allies, and of the emperor, the king of Spain and their allies. But even if all the important questions were first discussed by the four main belligerents, neither the emperor nor the king of Spain on the one hand, nor the king of France nor the queen of Sweden on the other, had any power to negotiate for anyone but themselves. Their allies also counted. They conspired, plotted, sent memoranda and protests to the mediators and would not allow themselves to be overlooked.

Since it was a European congress great numbers of diplomats were

gathered in Westphalia, each great power sent several, and to these
there had to be added the secretaries, couriers, and a whole army of
servants, because the larger embassies set great store by distinguishing
themselves by their luxury, the magnificence of their carriages and
servants' liveries and by the splendour of their receptions. Münster and
Osnabrück which had been made neutral for the duration of the
negotiations were invaded by a constantly changing host of people who
practically took over the two little towns.

Among such large numbers it was predictable that intrigues should
arise almost spontaneously. There was little goodwill, even within the
individual embassies. The two principal Swedes, Salvius, a skilful and
experienced diplomat, and John Oxenstierna, one of the Chancellor's
sons, could barely tolerate each other. John Oxenstierna had inherited
all the prejudices of his father, who mistrusted Mazarin as he had mistrusted Richelieu. Furthermore he upset his colleague by his arrogance
and even more by his insolent lavishness. He paid all his calls in one of
the queen's carriages followed by a dozen halberdiers, with gentlemen
and richly liveried pages and footmen walking in front of the coach.
Every day he had the times of his rising, his retiring and his meals
broadcast by drums and trumpets.[1] He even managed to make the
French plenipotentiaries jealous. One of the latter, the comte d'Avaux,
spent a large portion of his income on representing his master in a most
sumptuous manner which annoyed his colleague Servien whose more
modest means did not run to such luxury. There were other things too
which caused jealousy between Abel Servien and the comte d'Avaux.
Servien had a justifiably high opinion of himself and it irritated him
that the count d'Avaux, as the senior delegate, should push him out of
the limelight. There was a protracted quarrel between them before
they finally agreed to take it in turns to draw up the despatches they
sent back to court. If divisions such as these occurred within the
embassies it is easy to understand in relations between the different
embassies the part played by personal grudges and irritability. We can
also imagine the extent to which foreign news, whether true or false,
and rumours which it was impossible to confirm or deny, and which
so many people had an interest in fostering, spread among the mass of
diplomats and their attendants. Such news and rumours were avidly
welcomed in their closed world which so often lacked solid information.

The problems which cropped up at the congress were very

[1] These details are taken from Father Bougeant's account.

numerous and many of them were hard to solve. Some could be dealt with individually but many of them could be discussed and settled only in a body. Spain, for example, was concerned with many problems: Dutch independence, Portugal, Catalonia, the territorial changes that had taken place in north Italy, the determination of the ownership of the Lower Palatinate and, lastly, the matter of the French conquests in the Netherlands and Roussillon. As far as the Empire and the emperor were concerned there were all sorts of disputes outstanding. First of all there were the ones which only involved the Empire: to what extent should the princes and states enjoy the rights of sovereignty? What was the religious status of the Empire to be and how would the former possessions of the Church be affected after the succession of different solutions imposed by the religious peace of 1555, the Edict of Restitution of 1629, and the treaty of Prague of 1635? How would the states of the former elector Palatine and the electoral title which had been left vacant by his banishment be finally allocated. Within the Empire a host of individual problems of minor importance but of direct interest to several towns and princes had to be settled. Finally, on the international level, there was the thorny question of the 'compensation' or 'satisfaction' demanded by the foreign powers who had intervened in the German war, in particular by France and Sweden—in other words, the problems of Alsace and Pomerania. It could easily be foreseen that the Congress would need a great deal of time to reach agreement on so many different problems which so often appeared quite inseparable.

It was all the more predictable if we take into account the differing and conflicting interests within the two camps. On the Habsburg side there were often wide differences between the courts of Vienna and Madrid, and between Maximilian of Bavaria and the Habsburg rulers of both Austria and Spain. The kings of France and Sweden differed over their conceptions of the religious settlement which should be imposed on the Empire. Sweden was attached to the Protestant party whose faith it shared, while France wanted to protect the interests of Catholicism, even against her own allies. Finally, as the ill-timed negotiations of 1645 had clearly shown, there were differences between the king of France and the States-General of the United Provinces over the future fate of the Spanish Netherlands.

Above all, the chief reason for the length of the negotiations was the procedure adopted by the powers. There was not one congress but two, in two towns which, although quite close to each other, were nevertheless twenty-five to thirty miles apart and the journey between them took the couriers several hours. It was understood that although the congresses were separate (they should carry out their negotiations simultaneously, keep each other informed of the matters under discussion, and decide nothing without the full agreement of the other.) They were to advance at the same speed towards a common goal. Consequently written proceedings were necessary. At their leisure the various embassies drew up memoranda which, when exchanged, called forth replies, and then replies to replies. And of course these memoranda were drafted less with the object of bringing about a rapid result than to conceal the negotiators' real intentions for as long as possible. What is more, the perpetual exchange of long written notes was not done directly. Everything had to pass through the hands of mediators. In fact at Osnabrück a single mediator had been provided in the king of Denmark who, having signed his own peace settlement at Lübeck, could be regarded as impartial since he had no personal interests to protect. The outbreak of the Dano-Swedish war, however, had compelled him to give up the post and he had never been replaced. At Münster, on the other hand, there were two mediators throughout the congress, Fabio Chigi, a papal nuncio, and a Venetian ambassador, Contarini, who were all the less willing to have their powers prescribed because they were not always completely disinterested in the outcome of the negotiations. How could a nuncio fail to be concerned with the interests of the Roman Church?

Thus, because of the cumbersome nature of the written proceedings and the continual intervention of the mediators, the smallest problem often required long months of discussions.

There is still one more thing to be considered. If negotiations had been speedy the plenipotentiaries would necessarily have retained a fair amount of personal initiative, taking decisions without being able to ask for directives from the regent. But during these slow negotiations governments had plenty of time to intervene while memoranda and replies were being exchanged, and intervene they did. Not only did Mazarin modify or make the French deputation's general instructions more specific, but he often sent completely new proposals to Münster which were not at all in keeping with the ones that the plenipotentiaries had already made. Nor was it only the governments which changed the course of the negotiations. (The movements of the armies also played their part, for the war was still going on and the negotiators were forced to take changing fortunes into account.) Expectations and plans were always determined by victories and defeats. They governed the diplomats' actions(The congress was diplomacy's chosen ground, but diplomacy as it was then understood was a kind of warfare, linked to the military operations and just as dangerous and disillusioning.) Success always depended on the whims of fortune as well as on the skill of the diplomats and the heads of state. Fortunately Mazarin was a past-master at the game.

Since the war was dominated after France's intervention by the rivalry between the house of France and the house of Habsburg, it is appropriate to make a rapid study of the different phases of the negotiations from the French point of view, and of the military operations which accompanied them.

From this point of view the situation during the period when the congresses were gathering and fixing their procedure had been changed by three important facts—one unfavourable to French policy, but the other two favourable.

The first fact was the States General's separate negotiations with Spain. As we have seen, private and secret talks between Peñaranda, Spain's chief plenipotentiary at Münster, and Pauw, one of the Dutch plenipotentiaries, had paved the way for these back in 1645. They moved quickly. When the Dutch learned of the plan to exchange Catalonia for the Netherlands, Pauw received instructions to hurry things along during the course of a rapid visit to the Hague. In fact both negotiators were equally keen to reach an agreement. At the beginning of July 1646 Philip IV, the king of Spain, resigned himself to recognising the independence and sovereignty of the rebel provinces, a very important concession which meant that a peace settlement would soon be reached. The territorial, commercial and religious differences which remained between the former sovereign of all the Netherlands and the provinces which had revolted to gain their independence were settled in no time at all. The king of Spain promised the States General that he would cede them the territories they had conquered south of the Meuse, and after the peace these became the lands of the generality, governed jointly by the seven provinces. He confirmed the closing of the Scheldt, thereby sacrificing the first condition for the restoration of the Netherlands' economy to his desire for peace; and for the Catholics he only demanded the right of worship wherever it was already exercised. In spite of the pressure which France tried to bring to bear on the States-General and the prince of Orange, the Dutch ambassadors at Münster drew up sixty-three articles in December 1646 which they delivered to the Spanish. The only appeasement the Dutch offered

France was to postpone the conclusion of the peace treaty and to sign the preliminary articles only provisionally, subject to France receiving the compensation she was demanding. Despite the illusory precautions, the United Provinces' defection could not be denied. The king of France was losing one of his chief allies. Another result of this was that, once the Dutch question was settled, the king of Spain took little further interest in the discussions of the Münster congress. He thought that from then onwards he would continue the war against France on his own and wait for his luck to change. In fact, a little later when the Dutch peace had been finalised, the Spanish ambassador left Münster.

The two other facts, both favourable to the French court's plans, were two setbacks suffered by the emperor at the congresses themselves. Towards the end of 1645 Count von Trautmansdorf, the chief imperial plenipotentiary, finally arrived at Münster. He was a steadfast, farsighted man, completely upright and good-natured, who enjoyed his emperor's complete confidence. The French plenipotentiaries had already made it clear that they intended to hold on to Alsace as well as the three bishoprics, and Trautmansdorf's instructions were to prevent this. He went to Osnäbruck to try to win over the Swedes and thereby to separate Sweden from France. He also tried to rally the princes and states of the Empire around the emperor in order to win their support against the French claims. But he had no success with either group. None the less he offered the Swedes a solution to the Pomeranian question which might have seemed advantageous to them. He promised to persuade the elector of Brandenburg to make do with the region of Pomerania to the east of the Oder, and accept as compensation a handful of secularised bishoprics. Sweden, by contrast, was to keep western Pomerania with Stettin and the mouth of the Oder, that is the most fertile part of Pomerania with a distinct coast and well situated ports. It might even have been possible to throw in a few imperial lands as compensation for the part of Pomerania that the Swedes would abandon. Trautmansdorf was counting on the frequent disagreements between Sweden and France and a recent one between John Oxenstierna and the comte d'Avaux, but the Swedish court was determined not to change its policy again. Oxenstierna communicated Trautmansdorf's proposals to the French ambassadors and refused to discuss them. As for the princes and states of the Empire, the imperial plenipotentiary tried to persuade them to form a united front in opposition to the French being granted any 'satisfaction' beyond the final transfer of the three bishoprics of Metz, Toul and Verdun, assigned to France in fact as far back as 1559. He saw their representatives and asked them if they thought that France had any right to the 'satisfaction' she was demanding. He expected them to say no, but they had not forgotten that they owed their presence at the congress to French pressure and they said yes, even the representative of the elector of Bavaria, who thought that he needed French backing in order to be sure of keeping the lower Palatinate. Faced with what seemed to be a prearranged stand by France, Sweden and the princes, Trautmansdorf had to compromise. He knew that the emperor did not want to break off the negotiations, so he resigned himself to furnishing counterproposals to the French proposals as a basis for discussion. Serious negotiations were then begun.

They reached some concrete results in the autumn of 1646 and, thanks to the co-operation of the armies, nearly concluded a general peace in the spring of 1647.

The principal area of dispute between the king of France and the emperor was Alsace. The French delegates had decided to ask for full sovereignty for the king over the three bishoprics, upper and lower Alsace ('all Alsace' as the diplomats called it),[1] together with Breisach and the Sundgau and, beyond that, Philippsburg and the forest towns of Freiburg and Breisgau. Naturally they left themselves room for manœuvre. When, after spending two months at Osnabrück, Trautmansdorf was completely convinced that the Swedes had every intention of fulfilling their treaty of alliance with the king of France and would sign nothing without him, and when he was sure that if he rejected the French proposals he would receive no backing from the princes and states of the Empire, he started to make concessions. First of all he offered lower Alsace, but the French plenipotentiaries would not even discuss such an inadequate offer. He finally made up his mind to talk in terms of all Alsace. The French demands and the imperial counter proposals were then examined once more, compared, and amalgamated in a compromise text. This was the agreement of 17th September 1646 which gave France satisfaction on all the essential points. Of course it was still only a preliminary agreement which was subsequently recast before coming into force as part of the general peace settlement, but it raised hopes that the king of France would be able to come to some permanent arrangement with the emperor, especially as Trautmansdorf had added a complete set of peace pro-

[1] When we come to study the clauses of the treaty of Münster we shall see the exact meaning of these expressions.

posals to the articles referring to Alsace, and these seemed to be fairly acceptable.

In any case Mazarin covered himself against the possibility of a sudden change in imperial diplomatic policy. Reverting to Richelieu's policy, he once again resumed talks with the elector of Bavaria, not in the hope of persuading him to change sides, but in order to get him to disarm and stop protecting the house of Austria's states with his own— the emperor might possibly be more accommodating if he felt himself to be directly threatened. Although Maximilian wanted the king of France to guarantee the Palatinate and the electoral title, he continued to hesitate. It was then that the generals came to the diplomats' rescue. Turenne and Wrangel arranged to act in concert. In August 1646 Turenne crossed the Rhine and joined Wrangel in Hessian territory. Their combined armies forced the line of the Main, entered Bavaria and laid it to waste. Finally Turenne entered Munich. The result of this short, victorious campaign was that a truce was made with Maximilian which led to the treaty of Ulm on 14th March 1647. Hostilities between France and Bavaria were suspended until the general peace was signed and Maximilian undertook not to give any direct or indirect aid to the emperor. In return the king of France guaranteed possession of the Upper Palatinate and the electoral title. The elector of Bavaria had only concluded the treaty of Ulm because French troops were occupying the greater part of his states, conceding to necessity, but perhaps he also saw it as a means of persuading the emperor to agree to the general peace which all the German princes wanted so badly. As for the regent and Mazarin, they now had every right to hope that Ferdinand III would at last accept the conditions imposed by France and Sweden and agree to let the Empire rest in peace, even if it did mean making a few more concessions.

But a last reversal of fortune delayed the peace for more than a year. If the belligerents refused to interrupt military operations while the congresses were sitting it was because some saw the possibility of increasing their demands and because others hoped for a change of luck. In 1647 this seemed to have happened for the king of Spain and the emperor. In Catalonia, Lerida, Tortosa and Tarragona were still holding out. Condé, who had been given the title of viceroy and command of the army of Spain, laid siege to Lerida while Turenne and Wrangel were carrying out their combined operations in Germany. He wanted to storm it but he was unable to dig trenches in the solid rock on which the fortress was built. His troops were exhausted by an early spell of hot weather and food shortage. The army crumbled. In June, Condé was forced to raise the siege. In Italy Prince Thomas and the duke of Modena invaded the duchy of Milan with Mazarin's consent and fared no better. In Naples the people, led by a fisherman called Mazaniello, rose against the Spaniards and Mazarin thought that the time had come to take action. A fleet left the coast of Provence, but the rash action of the duc de Guise, who went to Naples without obtaining royal permission, upset the cardinal's plans. The duc de Guise enjoyed a brief popularity. The French fleet cruised up and down outside Naples for a few weeks and then returned to Provence. Once again Italy had brought Mazarin nothing but disappointment. In Germany too the summer campaign of 1647 was marked by some unfortunate events. As operations were moving slowly in the Netherlands, Mazarin sent Turenne the order to take his troops there. Some of them, however, were troops formerly recruited by Bernard of Saxe-Weimar. Poorly-paid and ill-disposed to go and fight in an unfamiliar land, they mutinied in June. Turenne could not manage to regain control until July, and then on condition that they should not be taken out of Germany. Consequently he dared not use them for anything. Maximilian took advantage of this to abrogate the treaty of Ulm and join the imperial cause once more. Finally, Trautmansdorf, who thought that the time was ripe to take back the concessions he had made, suspended negotiations at Münster and Osnabrück and set off for Vienna.

At the beginning of 1648 a peaceful settlement seemed to be further away than ever and no one suspected it was close at hand. Mazarin was faced with ever-increasing difficulties at home where Particelli d'Emeri was continually forced to dream up new taxes. There was the toisé followed by the taxe des aisés and finally the tarif, which annoyed not only the common people but also the bourgeois and even the magistrature. The tarif, which was a duty on all kinds of commodities and merchandise, upset them most; it seemed iniquitous to the members of the sovereign courts, most of whom had houses and gardens in the country where they sent for fruit, vegetables and poultry. The Parlement did everything it could to delay the passage of the tarif bill. The creation of twelve new maîtres des requêtes in January 1648 met with even livelier opposition. The existing maîtres des requêtes met and threatened to withdraw their service—today we would say that they threatened strike action. This heralded the parlementary Fronde.

Unfortunately the Spanish court knew all about this. Hoping that the situation would become worse and that the regent might even be forced to dismiss Mazarin, they were not in the least disposed to conclude a premature peace with France. On the contrary, they hastened to change the sixty-three provisional articles accepted by the United Provinces into a definite peace treaty. It was signed at Münster on 30th January 1648 and confirmed the conditions that had been agreed upon. Spain officially recognized the republic's sovereignty and independence. It handed over the parts of Flanders, Brabant and Limburg conquered by Frederick Henry which formed the lands of the generality; it confirmed the closing of the port of Antwerp. The Dutch had not raised any difficulties over concluding the treaty. They thought that the lands of the generality formed an impenetrable hedge or barrier, as it was later called, against Spain, but that it would not be sufficient to stop the French who were masters of Belgium. The saying 'Gallus amicus, non vicinus[1]' was already current in the States-General. After the treaty of Münster on 30th January 1648, the Spanish army of the Netherlands, which until then had had to fight on two fronts, was free to enter France without any fears of being attacked from behind. From then on there could be no hope of a general peace. It was certain that the king of Spain would continue the war even if the emperor laid down his arms.

But how long could France keep up her efforts? Exhausted by a long war she was already finding it difficult to go on. The exorbitant demands of royal taxation and the people's utter poverty created a state of mind which it is difficult for us to imagine and which neither the regent nor Mazarin could overlook. It spread not only among the country populations whose cries of distress never reached the court, and among the people of Paris with whom Mazarin was in closer contact, but throughout the whole of society, even among the magistrates. The servants of the king, whose job it was to serve the sovereign without criticising his acts, did not escape it either. This defeatism (and I use this word advisedly and in the sense that it is used these days by the people who have coined it) was expressed openly and without restraint, even in front of the regent and the young king. We need only quote from the harangue delivered by the Advocate General during the lit de justice of 15th January 1648. There are various versions of the text extant but they are all broadly the same. The version of the passage I quote comes from Olivier Lefèvre d'Ormesson, a recorder who was present, and it is of particular significance. 'We are told,'

[1] We want the French as friends but not neighbours.

shouted Talon, 'that it is not easy to conclude peace, that it is to the state's advantage not to neglect the king's victories and conquests which have increased our frontiers with new provinces and whole kingdoms. Whether or not this is true, what we can tell your majesty is that his victories and conquests have done nothing to diminish his people's poverty; that there are whole provinces where they live on nothing but a handful of oat-bread and bran; that the palms and laurels that so many people are working for are not counted among the useful plants because they do not produce any nourishing fruit. All the provinces are impoverished and exhausted by providing luxuries for Paris, or rather for one or two individuals. Taxes and duties have been put on every imaginable thing. The only thing that your subjects have left, Sire, is their souls and if they had any market value they would have been put up for sale long ago.'

Talon would not have dared to express himself in this way in front of the king if he had not felt that he was speaking, if not for the whole nation (which is scarcely mentioned again), at least for all the magistrature and particularly the sovereign courts. It was useless for Anne of Austria to call all the maîtres des requêtes to the Louvre and forbid them to enter her councils. It was useless for her to call on the Parlement not to pursue its debates over the fiscal edicts which it had passed only when forced to do so by a lit de justice on 15th January. And the situation became very much worse when Particelli d'Emeri tried to impose the forfeiture of four years' wages on the members of the sovereign courts (though not, it is true, the members of the Parlement) in return for renewing the Paulette.[1] We know that the four courts, including the Parlement, issued a decree of unity in May and intended to talk over together the measures they thought necessary for the safety of the state. Despite orders from the regent in the king's name, they met in June in the Chambre de Saint-Louis, while the duc d'Orléans encouraged their resistance. It was the beginning of the parlementary Fronde.

Mazarin realised that peace—or at any rate peace with the emperor —could not be put off any longer and that one last effort to hasten it was necessary. The best means of forcing the emperor to resume the negotiations which had been suspended since Trautmansdorf had left Münster seemed to be to oblige Maximilian to respect the treaty of Ulm which he had broken a few months earlier. Instructions were

[1] The right to hold government office as a private possession, and then sell or dispose of it by gift or inheritance.

therefore sent to Turenne to prepare for a summer campaign, and Mazarin ordered him to invade Bavaria once more. Turenne took his army there in May, first of all meeting with little resistance and then winning a complete victory over the Bavarian troops at Zusmarshausen. This put an end to Maximilian's hesitation and he had to promise to fulfil the treaty of Ulm and stop the hostilities. In the end, as Mazarin had hoped, Maximilian's defection made the emperor lose heart. Trautmansdorf was sent back to Münster, and did not revive the various arrangements that had been agreed upon at Münster and Osnabrück the year before. At Münster the agreement over Alsace had been recast on a few points. At Osnabrück other agreements had settled the dispute between Sweden and the elector of Brandenburg over Pomerania, the question of the Palatinate and the electoral title, the religious status of the states of the Empire—in fact more or less all the questions which had arisen at the beginning of the civil war or since the intervention in the conflict of foreign powers. The only thing that remained to be done was to include all the individual agreements in one text which would constitute the general peace treaty. Trautmansdorf agreed to this without raising many objections.

In the meantime something had happened outside Germany which had no direct relation with German affairs, but it gave rise to fears that the end of the war between France and Spain was not in sight, and it was an added incentive to the emperor at least to give peace to the Empire. A Spanish army under Archduke Leopold, who had succeeded the cardinal-infante as governor of the Netherlands, had taken Lens which the prince de Condé had been unable to relieve in time. Banking on his superior numbers, the archduke forced the French to do battle and Condé's victory at Lens was as decisive as the one at Rocroi. Between August and October the joint negotiations were completed at Münster and Osnabrück. They had to reach a conclusion since all the contracting powers were equally determined to see them through. The only thing which delayed the conclusion for a few weeks was the need for the complete co-ordination of the clauses worked out individually by the two congresses. It was finally reached on 24th October 1648. That day the two treaties of Münster and Osnabrück were signed simultaneously. Together they formed what we call the Peace of Westphalia, the 'peace so dearly bought', as the German princes said. It finished the long crisis stemming from the Bohemian revolt and was a kind of constitution (the contemporary jurists used this term) for the new Europe engendered by the Thirty Years War.

CHAPTER IX

THE PEACE OF WESTPHALIA

The peace of Westphalia was the first truly European settlement in history. It took the form of two treaties, one drawn up by the Catholic princes and states at the congress of Münster, the other by the imperial ambassadors who negotiated with the Protestant princes and states at the congress of Osnabrück. Both treaties were negotiated and concluded, as the jurists say, pari passu. The plenipotentiaries on both sides had always done their best to remain in agreement. Some of them, such as the comte d'Avaux, had spent quite a long time at Osnabrück, although they were Catholics. Others, like Salvius, though Protestant, had gone to Münster. The chief imperial plenipotentiary, Trautmansdorf, divided his time between the two congresses. Thus both treaties were in full accord with each other. As we have seen, they were made up for the most part of separate agreements signed during the course of the three years before the peace, and inserted more or less without any modifications. A number of disputes settled by the peace affected both Protestants and Catholics so that the provisions for them occurred in both treaties, explicitly in one and referred to in the other. The articles of the treaty of Osnabrück confirming the agreement over Church property and freedom of worship is referred to therefore in article 50 of the treaty of Münster which states that it must also be considered as an integral part of the latter. As a result of the way in which the two treaties were drawn up, they give an impression of disorder, at least in the sequence of the articles. These are not arranged according to any discernible system, with the result that there can be no question of making an analysis based on the order of the contents nor even of studying each topic in isolation. They must of necessity be taken together, and the need for clarity is the only criterion to be followed in grouping the provisions.

However, although the peace of Westphalia was a European peace it was not a general peace, even if we include the treaty of Münster made on 30th January 1648. The king of Spain had recalled his plenipotentiaries before the end of the negotiations and continued his war against the king of France. Until then the Franco-Spanish war had been pursued on the fringe of the German war, but the king of Spain had maintained an interest in the latter and relations between the courts of Madrid and Vienna had been so close that it was impossible to separate Spanish policy from Austrian and imperial policy. After 1648, by virtue of the peace of Westphalia, the alliance between the two branches of the house of Habsburg came to an end. We shall later study how this happened. Apart from the Franco-Spanish war, the peace also failed to settle the quarrel between the king of France and the duke of Lorraine. Just as it had begun and developed in various ways well before the German war had started, so it continued after the signing of the treaty of Münster, which made no provision for it. It was a difficult question and conflicting interests made it almost insoluble. For a start Lorraine's position in relation to the Empire was disputable. Lorraine was referred to as an imperial state and indeed it was included in the Upper Rhine, one of the Empire's ten circles. As the result of an agreement dating back to 1542, however, when Emperor Charles V and Duke Antoine had jointly recognised that the duchy of Lorraine was independent, 'liber et non incorporabilis ducatus' the independent duchy had ceased to be a fief liable to incorporation in the Empire by escheat. It is true that the exact meaning and the validity of the agreement remained under dispute. Besides this, the duke possessed the duchy of Bar as well as the duchy of Lorraine and the former was a French fief owing allegiance to the king of France. Moreover, whatever the legal status of the country, the French occupation continued after the conclusion of peace because the duke had associated himself with the king of Spain's cause. The Lorraine question was only settled in 1659 by the treaty of the Pyrenees, and then only vaguely since it arose again almost immediately afterwards.

For Germany the peace of Westphalia meant an end to all the quarrels which had arisen from the religious revolution of the sixteenth century and the peace of Augsburg of 1555, as well as those which had complicated an already confused situation during the course of thirty years of warfare. Although not the work of an imperial diet, the peace was considered to be an imperial law in the same way as, for example, the golden Bull. So the German jurists called it a constitution, constitutio Westphalica. It served as a basis for the constitution of the Empire until the latter ceased to exist more than a century and a half later.

At first sight it does not seem that the Holy Roman Empire's political status had changed a great deal. We can find the same essential elements in it as before the civil wars, that is an emperor and more than three hundred and fifty princes or states, including a fairly large number of free cities, and an imperial diet representing the princes and states who were split into three colleges. As before we find that the electoral college was the most important, that the Directory of the diet was given to the archbishop elector of Mainz, and that a very important part was played by the electoral union which included all the electors except the elector of Bohemia who was excluded on the grounds that he was king, and indistinguishable from the emperor. However, a new fact had arisen which the civil war had made permanent and the peace of Westphalia sanctioned. This was the almost complete independence of the princes. To a great extent they owed this to the spread of Protestantism which had made many of them heads of churches and thereby had greatly increased their power as heads of state. The peace did not grant them sovereignty for this would have been incompatible with the presence of an emperor as head of the Empire, but it did give them a form of territorial sovereignty known as Landeshoheit, which in practice was the same thing. Articles 64 and 65 of the treaty of Münster defined this Landeshoheit which was thereafter guaranteed to the princes by the peace since it was accepted as an imperial law; their rights were recognised both in ecclesiastical and political matters. This included the right to conclude treaties with each other and with foreign powers for their mutual protection and security. Of course the articles of the treaty of Münster imposed conditions on this which emphasised that a link still existed between the princes or states and the Empire, affirming that 'these treaties may not be directed against the emperor and the Empire nor against the public peace of the Empire', and the contracting parties had to observe the obligations imposed on them by the oath they had taken. This was what Maximilian of Bavaria, for example, had done during the war when he had made defensive agreements with the king of France. However, events quickly demonstrated that the princes could make treaties with foreign sovereigns without breaking the articles by which they were bound, even though the treaties, without being directed against the emperor, took no account of his interests.

It was this increasing independence of the princes that changed the Empire. As they had repeatedly said, it was to achieve this that the kings of France and Sweden had intervened in the German war. They claimed that they only fought against the house of Austria in order to safeguard German liberties from it and from the emperor's ambitions. By 'German liberties' they meant the princes' and states' territorial sovereignty and freedom of worship. Thus a new Germany had gradually emerged, one which was even more particularised and disunited than before. Now that the princes acted as sovereigns, now that their representatives at the diet had become delegates and that together they formed a distinct body, the conception of the unity of the Empire which had existed before the religious revolution was a thing of the past. For the German jurists this was an astonishing change, one, in fact, which completely upset their ideas on the various possible categories of states. When I studied the constitution of the Holy Roman Empire before the Thirty Years War in chapter one, I quoted the description given by the legal expert Pufendorf, namely 'a sort of un-cordinated body politic which might well be compared to a monster'. It had been true then, but it was even more true after the peace of Westphalia, and it was after the peace that Pufendorf had issued his harsh judgement on the Empire's constitution.

Besides this, although the powers of the emperor and the diet had not been modified by the peace of Westphalia, here again innovations appear. The emperor and the diet continued to be entirely powerless without one another. On the one hand the diet could only be convened by the emperor and its resolutions only became law if they were promulgated by the emperor; on the other, the emperor could not force the diet to discuss any particular subject nor could he force it to review any of its decisions which he did not see fit to approve. However two clauses of the peace increased the diet's impotence still further and quickly changed it altogether. The first, article 8 of the Osnabrück treaty, gave the diet an almost indefinite programme of work. The diet was to establish a 'perpetual settlement', by determining once and for all the emperor's powers within the empire, instead of defining them according to circumstances or at the beginning of each reign by successive settlements. In the same way the diet was also to vote a perpetual 'register'; that is, it was to determine once and for all each prince's and state's contribution to the costs of raising and maintaining the imperial army. Finally, it was to complete all business left in abeyance by previous diets. As a result, the treaties empowered the diet not only to pass imperial laws as in the past but also to regulate the very nature of the constitution. Furthermore they gave the diet a task of such scope that it would be unable to fulfil it—nor did it ever manage to—without being permanently in session. This in fact happened a little later, after 1663. Another clause of the treaty of Osnabrück contained in article 5, safeguarded the minority rights within the diet. This had already been affirmed before the Bohemian revolt and had resulted in a 'broken' diet, something with which the Poles were very familiar. 'In matters of religion,' said the article, 'and in all other matters in which the diet cannot be considered to be a united body, the Catholic states and the states of the confession of Augsburg are to be permitted to form two separate bodies and in this case any dispute may only be settled by a friendly compromise (amicalis compositio), without taking the majority vote into account.' This recognised the necessity of a unanimous vote, not only in all matters of religion, but also—and we should note the all-embracing nature of the words—'in all other matters in which the diet cannot be considered to be a united body'. Such a clause would necessarily have led to the dissolution of most future diets, had the diet not anyway begun to sit permanently. The result was that the diet, which could no longer dissolve, often adjourned for fairly lengthy periods and matters which could not be settled by any 'friendly compromise' had to be abandoned. It was these very adjournments and abandonments which spread the idea through Europe that the diet was totally powerless. The peace of Westphalia was blamed for this, not without some justification, but in fact all it had done on this point was to recognise the consequences of many long years of civil war.

The differences arising from the religious settlement of 1555 had lain at the roots of the civil war which followed on the Bohemian revolt in Germany. It might be said that at that period there had been two different interpretations of the peace of Augsburg, the one Catholic and the other Protestant. The great host of questions which had arisen on this subject were settled somewhat differently and, above all, provisionally, during the course of the war, first by the Edict of Restitution in 1629 and then by the treaty of Prague in 1635. The former was an attempt to carry out the peace of Augsburg according to the original Catholic interpretation, that is by fully exercising the so-called ecclesiastical reservation clause which declared any secularisations after 1552 to be void. The second was an attempt to reconcile the two interpretations of the settlement, but favoured the Catholics rather than the Protestants. Swedish intervention and, more significantly, French intervention had given the emperor's adversaries fresh heart and had encouraged them not to be satisfied with the conditions which they had originally accepted out of sheer weariness. As a result the emperor had been forced to abandon the clauses of the treaty of Prague which went the same way as the Edict of Restitution. Instead of being suspended for forty years the latter was completely revoked. Furthermore, Germany's religious status as settled by the treaties of Osnabrück and Münster was even more favourable to the Protestants than the peace of Augsburg.

One improvement over the peace of Augsburg from the Protestant standpoint was the extension to the Calvinists of all the advantages of the peace. The Geneva confession was put on the same footing as that of Augsburg and the right enjoyed by the Lutherans to reform the Church (jus reformandi) within the framework of a particular state was granted to Calvinist princes as well. Calvinists were therefore no longer regarded as an alien group within the Empire with neither rights nor guarantees.

We should not conclude from this that freedom of conscience and worship were established in Germany, since it is quite impossible to talk of toleration in the modern sense of the word. As in the past there was a Lutheran orthodoxy scarcely less rigid than the Catholic orthodoxy. There was even a Calvinist orthodoxy, and we need look no further than the famous quarrels between the strict Calvinism of the Gomarists in Holland and the more liberal interpretation of the faith by the followers of Arminius for proof of the strictness of Genevan Calvinism. There were also many heretical sects, for example the Baptists and the Socinians, which flourished in certain regions, and these gained nothing from the peace. They remained outside the law. Furthermore the principle 'cujus regio ejus religio', formulated in 1555, remained in force. In every state the prince alone was free to choose his own faith, which he could then impose upon his subjects. It seemed both natural and necessary that there should be a single Church in each State just as there was a single prince. Although the jus reformandi was not specifically laid down in any article of the Osnabrück treaty it was never contested, while article 64 of the Münster treaty substantiated it by granting to the princes, among other rights and privileges, the 'free exercise of territorial sovereignty, *in matters both ecclesiastical* and political'. As before, the only right the subject had was to leave the country if he did not want to follow the prince's faith. On this particular point the peace of Westphalia only went so far as to clarify and to a certain extent enlarge the provisions of the peace of Augsburg. It specified that any subjects going into exile would have the right to take their possessions with them, and it fixed a time limit within which they could exercise this right. But the most important provision still lay in the prince's privilege to choose between the Catholic, the Lutheran, or the Calvinist faith and, in the case of the last two, to organise the church as he saw fit. If any flexibility can be discerned in the religious organisation of the Empire it was due to the broadmindedness on the part of certain princes and, above all, to special circumstances rather than to any law. For instance that great collector of lands, the Calvinist elector of Brandenburg, had inherited the duchy of Cleves with its almost exclusively Catholic population, the Lutheran duchy of Prussia, and the march of Brandenburg where the Lutherans were in the majority. Like a good administrator he preferred not to enforce his jus reformandi and within his territories Catholics, Lutherans and Calvinists lived in harmony. Such an example of personal tolerance, however, had nothing to do with the treaties of Münster and Osnabrück.

The Ecclesiastical Reservation of the peace of Augsburg was also made more flexible. The Lutheran princes who had protested against it in 1555 and had rejected the article which defined it, had for many years refused to pay heed to it, and further secularisation had taken place. Indeed they had twisted the law to their advantage over the question of the bishoprics. They had used the cathedral chapters' undisputed right to elect bishops and the absence of any specific condition in the peace as to the chapters' composition. Tempers, however, had gradually cooled. At the congress of Westphalia the Protestant princes did not renew their opposition to the principle of the reservation clause; instead they concentrated their efforts on selecting a standard year, that is the date they would agree to return to in order to regularise for all time an ad hoc situation. Naturally there could be no question of accepting 1552 as the standard year, as originally laid down in the peace of Augsburg. Nor were the Protestant princes prepared to accept 1627, the year established in the treaty of Prague, which left them at too great a disadvantage, because in that year the imperial troops had followed up their victories over the Danish king by recovering a number of secularised territories. They won their case and the treaty of Osnabrück designated 1624 as the standard year. This was before the Danish invasion and the battle for the bishoprics took place, but after the victories of the emperor and the League over the elector Palatine. In addition, the term standard year was given a very general meaning. From this date not only all secularisation of dioceses and abbacies, but also within each Protestant state all secularisation of convents and religious foundations was to be invalid. It was understood that, in the free cities, the state of affairs which had existed in 1624 with regard to the division of property between Catholics and Protestants should be re-established and made permanent. As far as the dioceses were concerned, the composition of the cathedral chapters—that is the numbers of Catholics and Protestants in them in 1624—was also to be maintained in the future so that the Protestants at least retained the positions acquired by that date. Lastly, the dioceses which had had a Protestant administrator in 1624 would continue to be administered and, more important, the administrator was to be invested by the emperor and have the right to be represented at the diet. There can be no doubting the importance of these concessions by the emperor which clearly demonstrated the triumph of the princes. What is more, they demonstrated the cooling-off of the religious passions which until then had made such concessions impossible.

The treaties settled not only the political and religious constitution of the Empire, but also the fate of the princes who had taken arms against the emperor, some of whom, like the elector Palatine, had forfeited all their rights as a result of being banished. Most of them had their lands and possessions returned. This happened for example in the cases of the duke of Wurtemberg, the landgrave of Hesse-Cassel and the archbishop of Trier. Eighteen articles—numbers 12 to 29—of the treaty of Münster were devoted to the settlement of the much more difficult question of the Palatine. All they did was to reproduce a private agreement signed by all the interested parties at Osnabrück in March 1648. By this time Frederick V was dead. His rights had passed to his eldest son, Charles Louis, who demanded the restoration of the electoral title and the two Palatinates, but it was impossible to take the electoral title away from Maximilian since this had been guaranteed by both the emperor and the King of France. It was returned to Charles Louis, but the emperor created an eighth electorate for Maximilian, and so the heads of both the Bavarian and the Palatine branches of the Wittelsbach family were now electors. It was understood, however, that when the Bavarian branch became extinct the eighth electorate would die with it. As for the territorial question, it was settled by a compromise. Maximilian retained the upper Palatinate which he had taken with the emperor's agreement and which bordered Bavaria. The lower Palatinate was returned to the new elector Palatine, Charles Louis. The settlement of the Palatine question had one consequence which interested the whole Empire, or at least the whole of the electoral union. It raised the question of parity—the matter of equal distribution of votes in the electoral union between Catholics and Protestants. The union had three Catholic electors, the ecclesiastical electors and the three Protestants, the duke of Saxony, the margrave of Brandenburg and the Count Palatine. After the creation of an eighth electorate for a Catholic prince the ratio between the two faiths was four to three. The question of parity was discussed at great length after the conclusion of peace and was only settled later by giving each of the Protestant electors in turn a double vote. However, although the discussions were very lively they did not degenerate into open quarrels, and this was one more sign that religious passions had cooled.

The clauses which embodied the internal constitution of Germany were accepted by all the princes and states. They had bought them too dearly to risk compromising the Empire's tranquillity by disputing them. In any case the princes' independence was already of long standing and had nothing to do with any treaties. The emperor himself realised that it was pointless to go on opposing it. Quite possibly the impotence of Germany as a whole was thus ensured to the advantage of her great neighbours and of France in particular, and also, though not to the extent that is often said, the impotence of the emperor within the Empire. The emperor had several times been on the verge of defeating the coalitions which had sprung up to contest his claims to absolute authority. He abandoned the claims but retained his prestige. In German eyes he was still the defender of the German nations against the Turks. In spite of everything he was still the undisputed head of the Empire and the princes turned naturally to him as soon as they felt threatened by a common danger. The emperor no longer claimed the sort of universal power which went back to the medieval dream of a united Christendom, but he was still the powerful ruler of a group of states which the ancestors of Ferdinand III had gradually acquired by marriage or inheritance, and most of them were included in the Holy Roman Empire. He was to all intents and purposes an hereditary emperor since the electors had grown used to keeping the imperial title in the house of Habsburg and more often than not associated the emperor's son with his father's reign by making him King of the Romans. The French delegates at the congress of Münster had tried to introduce an article into the treaty forbidding the anticipation of the election by the creation of a King of the Romans from the same family as the emperor.[1] They had failed. Nor had they managed to prevent

[1] Ne ex familia imperatorum regnantium eligatur.

the emperor from maintaining in the diet his own clientele of many minor princes who thought the electoral college was too powerful and were jealous of its authority. Later, in 1654, when Louis XIV sent a representative to the first diet convened after the restoration of peace, Vautorte, his minister at Regensburg, gave him this salutory warning: 'In future we will not have many interests to look after in the diets and we must hope that this state of affairs continues because the emperor will always be more powerful than the king.' Perhaps young Louis XIV did not think much of Vautorte's farsightedness. Nevertheless, it was Vautorte who was right.

Passions had cooled to such an extent that the religious clauses of the peace were perhaps accepted even more readily than the political clauses. As we have seen, it was not only the question of parity which failed to raise strong feelings, but also the question of the ecclesiastical reservation. It seems that the Protestants considered it quite natural that secularisations should be forbidden in future and even that lands and foundations which had been recently secularised should be returned to the Catholic Church. They were happy that the standard year which was established was one which did not put them at too much of a disadvantage. This is clearly explained by the fact that Protestantism had lost its proselytising vigour. Once the Lutheran reformation had been enshrined within a rigid orthodoxy and organised into a host of petty state Churches bounded by the narrow framework of the principalities, the Confession of Augsburg could no longer extend its sway. Even Calvinism broke little fresh ground since the principle of cujus regio ejus religio prevented it gaining a foothold. After the peace, only the broader and more flexible forms of heterodoxy such as Socinianism continued to develop. The era of great religious quarrels involving entire populations was over. Religious problems certainly played their part in the lives of the nations but never again did they override national interests.

The peace of Westphalia was a German peace which put an end to nearly a century and a half of civil wars, the last of these being the Thirty Years War. It also established the political and religious constitution of the Holy Roman Empire until it ceased to exist. That was why the jurists termed it the Westphalian constitution. But over and beyond this it was a European peace. It settled the partition of the Empire and the satisfaction which the powers who had intervened in the conflict received to offset their costs. It also stabilised relations between the Empire and these powers, notably France and Swed en and certain very general clauses settled the Empire's relations with the rest of Europe. That is why from the middle of the seventeenth century to the beginning of the nineteenth, the peace was considered to be one of the cornerstones of European constitutional law.

The opening articles of the two treaties which constituted the peace re-established friendly relations between the contracting powers. For example, article 3 of the treaty of Münster set out to eliminate all sources of dispute between them and did so in exceptionally precise terms. It runs: 'In order to ensure that a sincere mutual friendship shall in future be preserved between the emperor, his very Christian majesty, and the electors, princes and states of the Empire, it is laid down that none of the contracting parties shall furnish the present or future enemies of another, on any grounds or under any pretext, for reasons of disagreement or war, with weapons, money, troops or supplies, nor shall he succour in any way whatsoever, the troops led by anyone whatsoever against one of the contracting parties to this peace, or grant them shelter, camp or right of passage.' In this article we find a list of some of the obligations imposed on the powers in peacetime and it is no exaggeration to say that this article of the treaty of Münster contains the draft of a new code of international law. Nevertheless in 1648 it was somewhat before its time. Even throughout the whole of the eighteenth century it continued to be normal practice for one state to supply another with rights of passage, quarters, subsidies and even with auxiliary troops of any number in order to fight a third state, and yet not enter the war itself. For example, after the death of Emperor Charles VI in 1740, France fought Maria Theresa for several years without ever declaring war simply by using as a cover the elector of Bavaria, Charles Albert, who became Emperor Charles VII.

Articles 69 and 70 of the treaty of Münster are also very far-reaching. They bear witness to a concern over economic questions which one would not expect from the chancelleries of that period, although provisions relating to trade had previously figured in the treaty of Vervins between France and Spain, and even in the treaty of Monçon under Louis XIII. The treaty of Münster did not merely re-establish peace between the contracting powers; the plenipotentiaries also did their best to give trade a new lease of life, for it had barely survived the extension of hostilities and the setting up of customs posts on most of the roads going in to Germany. The treaty's aim was stated quite unequivocally; article 59 said: 'And because it is in the common interest, once peace has been made, trade should be developed once

more. . . .' It then went on to the means of achieving this. 'All obstacles
created against trade during the course of the war are to disappear and
commercial transport will be free.' It is even more surprising to see for
the first time a provision which a great many peace congresses were to
take up again later. The Rhine was to be freely opened to the trade of
all nations. This in fact is what we call the internationalisation of the
great waterways which pass through several states in succession.

Finally, several articles regularised many matters of long standing
which until then had not had diplomatic recognition, and so this helped
to make the peace of Westphalia the foundation of international law
in Europe before the French Revolution. Article 63 of the Münster
treaty, for example, recognised the complete independence of the Swiss
cantons; articles 72 and 73 granted the king of France sovereignty in the
Three Dioceses he had occupied for nearly a century, recognising the
frontiers which Henry IV and Louis XIII had established unilaterally;
finally, article 74 confirmed the duke of Savoy's cession of Pinerolo
to Louis XIII. It might be added that by recognising the independence
of the United Provinces, the king of Spain had therefore excluded
them from the Burgundian circle, that is to say from the Holy
Roman Empire, and thereby gave legality to an established fact.

Among the territorial clauses, the most important, because of the
effects they had on the history of the Holy Roman Empire and in a
more general way on European politics of modern times, were the
ones which provided France and Sweden with 'satisfaction'. They are
worth detailed study, all the more so because a number of important
ones have remained the subject of dispute and to this day have been
interpreted in a very different way, first by the interested powers and
then by historians.

The counter proposals which the French plenipotentiaries produced
on 24th February 1645 in reply to the early imperial proposals did not
contain any reference to Alsace, since they wanted to gain the confidence of the German princes and states who were reluctant to see any
German territory detached from the Empire. When the regent had
secured invitations for all the princes to send representatives to the
congress, the reason she gave was that they could thereby see for
themselves the frankness and good faith her ambassadors brought to
the negotiating table. Nevertheless Mazarin was certainly quite
determined to retain Alsace and when, on 30th December 1647, he
wrote to Turenne: 'I trust that you consider Alsace a country which
belongs to the king no less than Champagne does', he was not expressing

a new opinion. Moreover, secret talks took place coincidentally with the official negotiations, and by 1645 these had established the claims published in a note dated 7th January 1646. Apart from the Three Dioceses, the ambassadors claimed for France upper and lower Alsace, together with the Sundgau,[1] Philippsburg, Breisach, the Breisgau and the four forest towns above Basle. Of course they were asking for more than they hoped to receive. At first the imperial plenipotentiary refused. He then offered lower Alsace, but it was not until 1646 that he resigned himself to giving up all the house of Austria's Alsatian possessions. It was then possible to draw up the private agreement which was later inserted into the peace treaty, France contributing to the compromise by giving up her claims to the forest towns and the Breisgau.

In order to understand how much the Viennese court agreed to abandon, we must first know a little more about seventeenth-century Alsace. When the French plenipotentiaries had used the term 'all Alsace' in their preliminary negotiations it is possible that they themselves were not really very clear what they meant by it or else that they were only employing a vague term as a basis for further discussions. In any case the expression 'all Alsace' could not apply to any geographical region for its boundaries were not by any means universally recognised. Some would have had the northern boundaries of Alsace finish at the Lauter, the river of Wissemburg; others extended it as far as the Queich and included Landau. The geographical region had long since lost any kind of linguistic, religious or political unity. In a few mountain valleys of the Vosges the Alsatians spoke French; the others spoke German, or more often Alsatian, a special German dialect. Protestantism had spread to Alsace in two forms, as Lutheranism and Calvinism, but only among a third of the population; the other two-thirds had remained Catholic. Alsatian culture was Germanic, but on that frontier of the Empire which faced the barbarians, Roman domination had left a deeper impression than it had beyond the Rhine. Finally, Alsatian territory had been fragmented into a great number of distinct political units which differed greatly from each other. Without hoping to cover the subject completely we must at least give some idea of its composition.

---

[1] The name Sundgau, which originally applied to all upper Alsace, later designated only its southern part below the Thur. The Sundgau became almost synonymous with the landgraviate of upper Alsace whose landgrave, Archduke Charles-Ferdinand, was one of the emperor's nephews.

A fairly large part of Alsatian territory belonged to the house of Austria. In upper Alsace there was the landgraviate of upper Alsace which included almost all the Sundgau and whose landgrave was Archduke Charles Ferdinand, a nephew of Ferdinand III. There were also territories annexed to Austria, such as the lands of Ribeaupierre around Ribeauville. Then there was the great bailiwick of Haguenau on which depended not the town of Haguenau but half the forest of the same name together with some forty villages around it. Apart from the Austrian possessions there were the republics which owed allegiance to the Empire but which in practice were independent; these included Strassburg and Mulhouse, the latter having concluded a treaty of alliance with the Swiss cantons. There were the free or 'immediate' cities (that is, those owing a direct allegiance to the emperor) such as those of the Decapolis to which I shall soon return; there were the little ecclesiastical principalities like the diocese of Strassburg (which should not be confused with the town), and the abbeys of Münster, Andlau, Mürbach, etc. Then again there were the Alsatian estates held by several German princes such as the duke of Wurtemberg who held the county of Montbéliard and Riquewiller, the duke of Zweibrücken who held Bischwiller in lower Alsace, Count Hanau-Lichtenberg, and any number of others. Lastly, on top of all the possessions, we have to take rights into account. There were the emperor's rights (which nobody at the congress was in a position to define) relating to the functions of the 'Landvogt' which he delegated to a prince of his house (the French translated 'Landvogt' by the words 'grand bailli', i.e. bailiff, or magistrate, or in Latin by praefectus). The Landvogt claimed among other things to exercise certain rights over ten free cities which were allied together and known as the Decapolis; four were Lutheran— Landau, Wissemburg, Colmar and Münster; and Haguenau, Rosheim, Sélestat, Obernai, Kayserberg and Türckheim were Catholic. It is easy to understand how a country which was so fragmented politically should have been split by opposing coalitions during the war and unable to offer any resistance to the invaders. This was why it suffered such terrible ravages before most of the cities made up their minds to call on the king of France for protection.

One can also understand how the surrender of territory to France could not be carried out in a simple manner. The country's political constitution would not allow it and it is equally possible that the plenipotentiaries of both sides themselves did not want it. Thus the articles of the Münster treaty relating to Alsace were fairly numerous

9

—articles 75, 76, 79 to 85 and 89. It is difficult to interpret them because they often contradict each other, or at least appear to do so. Later, at the diet, they were the source of interminable discussions among jurists; later still, both in France and Germany—but above all in Germany—they provided material for a vast number of historical studies which, as one might expect, are at variance with each other. Perhaps the most lucid is the one given by Christian Pfister in his *Pages alsaciennes*. That is the one I shall use as a guide.

The sum total of the surrender may be defined by saying that the emperor handed over to the king of France everything he possessed in Alsace as head of the house of Habsburg and all the rights he enjoyed as emperor. I have already listed the Austrian possessions. They became French possessions and it would seem that their transfer should not have given rise to any dispute. This, however, was not the case. There was one ambiguous term in the text of article 75. In the name of the whole house of Austria the emperor handed over to the king of France 'the landgraviate of upper and lower Alsace.'[1] What exactly did that mean? A little later the imperial side claimed that 'landgraviate' referred only to the landgrave's authority and the rights attached to it. Christian Pfister replies that the emperor was not in a position to cede the rights of the landgrave of lower Alsace because the latter was bishop of Strassburg and not an Austrian at all. He concludes that in this case the term 'landgraviate' does not mean the rights pertaining to the title but the land itself. Under this interpretation the emperor ceded both landgraviates, that is upper and lower Alsace, excluding only those lands or rights mentioned in the other articles as being excepted from the cession.

On the other hand it might be argued that since the emperor no more possessed the whole of the territory of the landgraviate than he did the title of landgrave, the only things he could cede were the landgrave's rights. At the very least the article should have listed there and then the lands which were not to be included, but in the treaty there is no connection established between the so-called general cession of article 75 and the list of lands and rights excluded by article 89. So Pfister's theory seems to me to be just as blameworthy as the opposite view of German historians. I incline to the belief that both Servien and Trautmansdorf deliberately put an ambiguous term into the text and waited for an opportunity to arise for them to interpret it in their own ways.

[1] Landgraviatum superioris et inferioris Alsaciae.

There is another similar difficulty arising from article 89. This article is entirely separate from the others and is made up of two parts which are clearly at variance with one another. In the first part there is a clear-cut list of lands and cities that the king of France had to leave 'in the same liberty and possession of immediacy in relation to the Holy Roman Empire as they have hitherto enjoyed'. These include a few abbeys and monasteries, the Alsatian estates held by several counts, palatines and barons, and the ten free cities (Decapolis) which recognised the prefectship of Haguenau. The text adds that it was to be carried out in such a way that the king could not later claim 'any territorial sovereignty but must be content with whatsoever rights that belonged to the house of Austria and are ceded by this treaty to the crown of France'. The text is crystal clear. But straight after this comes a final phrase which more or less contradicts this. It runs, 'in such a way, notwithstanding, that it should not be understood that the right of supremum dominium ceded above is in any way diminished'. So we have lands and cities over which the supremum dominium ceded to the king of France is in no way diminished, as far as the emperor sees the situation, but none the less over which the king is unable to claim any territorial sovereignty at all. There was material enough here for the jurists to argue over and they never did manage to sort out the contradiction. No doubt the answer to the problem (identical to the one posed by the use of the term 'landgraviate') is revealed by something that Servien wrote during the course of negotiations. 'I believe,' he wrote, 'that we shall have to be content that everyone should keep their claims and interpret the treaty as they see fit.' Servien did not want to accept the first part of article 89 under its original form so he had the second part added without worrying about the contradiction between the two. Trautmansdorf did not raise any objections to the addition because he was no more anxious than Servien to break off negotiations. They were agreed that the matter should be left in abeyance. No doubt we should also add that Mazarin did not want Alsace to sever its ties completely with the Empire. It was possible that by maintaining the ultimate sovereignty of the emperor over the Ten Cities and a certain number of fiefs he would have a lever which the king could use to gain admission and a vote at the diet. This was what he had originally hoped for and, if Alsace remained to a certain degree attached to the Empire, it might be possible.

The question of Sweden's satisfaction provoked hard bargaining as difficult and as long drawn out as it had been with France. After holding

out for a long time for a foothold in the very heart of Germany, either
in Silesia or the Rhine Valley, the Swedish crown had limited its
demands to the recognition of its ownership of Pomerania which it
had occupied since 1630. Sweden claimed right of conquest but this
was countered by the elector of Brandenburg who had a contractual
right to the territory. The elector had considered himself duke of
Pomerania since the death of Bogislav XIV by virtue of a family pact,
and there was no contesting its legality. At the outset the Pomeranian
question seemed insoluble, for both the queen of Sweden and the
elector claimed the whole of the duchy. Negotiations hung fire until
the beginning of 1647[1] when the comte d'Avaux took the matter up
on his arrival at Osnabrück. France had just concluded with the emperor
the agreement of 13th September 1646, a kind of preliminary treaty
which safeguarded her own satisfaction, and this left her free to find
solutions for those other disputes which delayed the restoration of a
general peace. The comte d'Avaux got the elector Frederick William
to agree to the principle of Pomerania being shared. Then, as Father
Bougeant says, he 'dragged' from the Swedes their consent to the
agreement of 7th February 1647 which was later inserted in the treaty
of Osnabrück. Sweden had the best of the bargain, namely western
Pomerania with the mouth of the Oder and the port of Stettin, a strip
of territory on the right bank of the river protecting the city and the
Pomeranian islands of Rügen, Usedom and Wollin. It was fertile
country with a well-defined coastline and a number of little harbours.
Furthermore, by way of compensation for giving up eastern Pomerania, Sweden also received the two secularised dioceses of Bremen.
This was a Hanseatic town, and its territory controlled in the west the
mouth of the Weser, and in the east the mouth of the Elbe. These were
the two principal trading routes to the German plains of the Westphalian and lower Saxon circles. In this way the crown of Sweden
retained its foothold on the German coast and continued the policy of
Gustavus Adolphus who had made it master of the Baltic. The elector
of Brandenburg had to make do with eastern Pomerania—which was
less valuable with its low coast-line and lack of natural ports—and the
secularised diocese of Cammin which was included in it. But as compensation for what he was giving up he too received some secularised
Church lands. These were the dioceses of Halberstadt to the north of
the Harz, and Minden on the middle reaches of the Weser. They were

---

[1] Full details can be found in Albert Waddington: *Le Grand Électeur
Frédéric-Guillaume de Brandenbourg. Sa politique extérieure* vol. I.

handily placed, like signposts for the future, between the Brandenburg march and the Rhenish duchies that an elector had acquired at the beginning of the century. Frederick William also received the reversion to the archdiocese of Magdeburg and could take possession on the death of a Saxon prince who administrated it. Magdeburg was of great strategic importance on the Elbe, and a very important stage for river traffic. Furthermore its territory shared a boundary with the Old March. So the elector gave up 6,500 square kilometres of land and received 9,500 in compensation. He had no grounds for complaint. By virtue of this he became known as the biggest landowner among the German princes.

It only remains for us to say how the treaties of Münster and Osnabrück settled two problems which did not concern Germany alone but which, especially the second, had grave consequences for its national life during the period which followed.

The first was posed by the continuation of the war between France and Spain. The French delegates had naturally persisted in introducing clauses in the peace treaties which prevented the emperor from continuing to fight France indirectly under the cover of his cousin at Madrid. The French delegates were also very keen to add stipulations as to the nature of future relations between France, the empire and Spain. These form articles 4 and 5. The difficulty arose from the fact that Franche-Comté and the Netherlands continued to make up the Burgundian circle and were thus part of the Empire. How could they stipulate that the Empire should not defend one of its own circles? None the less this was the object of the articles in question. They declared that the Burgundian circle was to continue to be one of the circles of the Empire but that neither the Empire nor the emperor had the right to intervene in the war the kings of France and Spain were waging there. There was even provision for the future. The text read: 'If, in future, differences should arise between the crowns of France and Spain, the aforementioned reciprocal obligation (a reference to article 3) shall remain in force between the whole of the Empire (that is acting as a body) and the king and kingdom of France.' However, the text made one reservation: 'It shall still be permissible for each state (of the Empire) to give individual aid to one or other kingdom outside the confines of the Empire, but only in so far as this falls within the constitutions of the Empire.' Clearly in this last sentence, which seems to have been drawn up half by Trautmansdorf and half by Servien or d'Avaux, we can see ambiguities and loopholes reminiscent of article 89 relating to Alsace, but the king of France could at least hope that after the conclusion of peace in Westphalia he would no longer be faced by imperial troops backing the efforts of the Spaniards in the Netherlands.

The second problem, which was more serious and rather more far-reaching in its consequences, arose over the peace treaty's 'guarantee'. Mazarin and the regent had hoped that a special article making the king of France sole guarantor might be inserted in one or other of the treaties. As a result the king would have acquired an authority in the Empire nearly equal to that of the emperor, but the princes and the emperor would not agree to it. France had to make do with a general clause which made all the contracting powers guarantors of the provisions they had accepted. France was one of the powers, but only one of many. In fact, since the value of the guarantee depended first and foremost on the power and prestige of the state exercising it, France's was exceptionally important. As guarantor, France acquired the right to keep an eye on the Empire's internal affairs, to follow the differences which arose between the princes and the emperor, and even the right to intervene when she considered that some contravention of the peace of Westphalia had been committed. It was quite common, even throughout the eighteenth century, for France to invoke her position as guarantor. We must also emphasise the consequences that this use of the guarantee had for Germany, since by virtue of the guarantee shared by foreign powers, any question arising within Germany could easily become a European question. Germany was no longer the independent mistress of her fortunes. Her international position might almost be compared with that of the nineteenth century Ottoman Empire which was also dependent on guaranteeing powers. After 1648 the emperor was made keenly aware of the tutelage that France had taken it upon herself to exercise over Germany as a result of the guarantee. We might also wonder whether the way the problem of the guarantee was settled did not help the congress to sidestep Louis XIV's ambition to obtain for Alsace a seat and vote at the diet. The emperor preferred to detach Alsace from the Empire rather than introduce the king of France's plenipotentiary into the diet. However, he granted the king of Sweden (who caused him far less apprehension) three seats and three votes for the duchy of Pomerania and the principalities of Bremen and Verden.

It is not within my brief to study the way in which the peace of Westphalia was implemented, how it was received in Germany and elsewhere, the state of the new Germany which emerged after the peace, or how France and Sweden, especially the former, turned to account the advantages they had been granted. In concluding this study I shall merely dwell briefly on a few points.

Too many historians have emphasised Germany's plight and the extent of the depopulation at the end of the Thirty Years War for there to be any point in my following suit. It is precisely the extent of the ravages caused by the war which explains why contemporaries nearly always qualified the peace which put an end to it by the words 'so dearly bought'. They were strongly attached to the peace, and it lasted. Villages were rebuilt, populations grew up once more, trade appeared along the roads it had abandoned, and prosperity returned. However, a number of social changes which had occurred during the war and which were also inherent in its consequences were to last for some time. I am thinking in particular of the deterioration of the peasant class and their enslavement by the landowners. The main beneficiaries of the peace were the princes and the land-owning nobility, though it is true that once the atrocities of the soldiery ceased the peace brought the country populations a little more security in their poverty.

It would be quite wrong to believe that a new Germany was born out of the peace. While it is true to say that religious feelings did not play the same role in the Empire as before, it must be remembered that they had already died down during the course of the war. As for the political changes, they were of long standing. The peace of Westphalia recorded them and gave them a contractual guarantee, but it did not create them. This does not alter the fact that they had a significance which we can gauge today but which quite naturally eluded the attention of their contemporaries. The result of undermining the emperors' power within the Empire was that the emperor took less interest in Germany's internal life and became more preoccupied with his personal estates and the threat presented to them by the Turks, who were masters of the greater part of the Hungarian plain. The prestige that the emperor still retained and which continued to increase was due more to his imperial prerogatives than to his double role as head of the house of Austria and defender of Christendom against the Ottoman infidels. Austria became the eastern march once again, and devoted herself more and more as time went on to its eastern mission.

Germany did not escape the spread of ideas of absolute monarchy which had already won the day throughout western Europe. But in Germany the reinforcement of sovereign power was not carried out to the advantage of the emperor but to that of a few princes and within the much more limited framework of a few states of the Empire. Bavaria was one such state. Another, made up of detached pieces and belonging to the Hohenzollerns, did not even have a name but it had revealed its vitality during the latter years of the war. In elector George William's time it had been unable to gain the belligerents' respect, and yet, thanks to a new master, the elector Frederick William, it was already the leading Protestant state of the Empire after the territorial acquisitions it had received from the peace. It was the strengthening of the better placed and better governed principalities that paved the way in the eighteenth century for the future of Germany. Another contributory factor was the emergence of a sort of German patriotism. The impotence experienced by the divided princes during the war had caused a number of them to feel a desire for unity. This later expressed itself in the politics of Philip von Schönborn, an elector of Mainz, and in his efforts to organise a common defence for the Empire against foreigners. The Germans did not like foreigners whether they came as enemies or allies. Sweden frightened the princes, especially the Hohenzollerns and the princes of the house of Brunswick-Hanover who were her neighbours. They were even more frightened of the mighty France. These fears, as well as the jealousy and mistrust which set them against each other, killed any hope of unity, but the desire for unity gradually gained the upper hand when Louis XIV's ambitions once again disturbed the peace of the Empire. These fears, and their aversion to the French—a new phenomenon—slowly created a bond among the princes which had been hardly in evidence when they had been able to count on the protection of the emperor and the imperial laws.

In contrast to Germany which in 1648 was still seeking its destiny, France and Sweden appeared as the victorious powers. As has so often been said, Sweden had acquired a position in northern Europe out of all proportion to her strength. It was a little country, poor in men and resources, which until then had lived on its forests, mines and fishing. In the space of a few years she had become a great military power, thanks to the genius and daring of Gustavus Adolphus. She considered herself mistress of the Baltic. From our historical vantage point it is easy for us to say that she could not long sustain so unnatural a role. Contemporaries thought differently. By abandoning its claims to the Rhenish dioceses and Silesia, the crown of Sweden seemed to have given up the unattainable part of Gustavus Adolphus's dream. There was not yet any sign of Sweden's decline. In the early days of his personal rule Louis XIV continued to seek Swedish alliance, and Charles

Gustavus's reign was a great one. It is true that in the aftermath of the peace France, the most densely populated country in Europe and with natural resources of every kind, seemed destined to profit far more than Sweden from Germany's confusion, but we must bear in mind that in 1648 France's internal situation presaged a serious crisis and there was no means of foreseeing the outcome. The king of Spain did not think that he was beaten yet, and fully expected to take his revenge. In that case what would have become of the advantages that the skill of the French diplomats at the congress of Münster had won for their king? When we weigh up the results of the German peace we should be careful not to do so from a standpoint of some ten or twelve years later when they were finally settled by the Spanish peace.

Contemporaries of the treaties of Westphalia did not understand until much later that towards the middle of the seventeenth century a new period in European history had begun.

CONCLUSION

The general conclusion of this long account is quite obvious and can be expressed in very few words.

The crisis which moulded modern Europe out of medieval Europe finished with the Thirty Years War. The Thirty Years War saw the last effort of the Roman Catholic Church and the house of Habsburg to re-establish unity by the triumph of Catholicism over the Protestant heresies and the renewal of the emperor's universal power. Had the Church and the house of Habsburg won the day, the medieval ideal of the Christian republic, jointly governed by the emperor and the Pope, might have been restored. But they could not win the day because new political and religious conceptions were already too developed. They foundered. The peace of Westphalia substituted the idea of a system of independent states, a sort of international society, for the idea of a united Christendom. The peace did not openly express this idea but it did contain the idea of a society which took no account of the methods of government of its component states, whether they were monarchies, principalities or republics. Similarly, no account was made of the dominant religious faiths. On the international plane Europe became a secular system of independent states. It was the dawn of the principle of nationalism.[1]

There can be no doubt that France and, more especially, Cardinal de Richelieu were instrumental in helping to accomplish this complete transformation of Europe, this final break with the past which was completed during the last convulsions of the Thirty years War. We should not think that Richelieu foresaw this or in any way wished it, but he did realise that only a league of Protestant powers maintained and led by his king could prevent the house of Habsburg from establishing its hegemony over Europe. Both he and Father Joseph, his adviser during the struggle, hoped that in this way the balance between the two parties could be maintained and that Catholicism would at

[1] Some of the ideas expressed here may be found in an article by A. Rapisardi Mirabelli, entitled *Le Congrès de Westphalie*, and published in *Bibliotheca Visseriana* vol. VIII.

least be able to preserve the positions it had kept or recovered. In this he succeeded. It is no less certain that in order to succeed he accepted a sort of secularisation of European politics as well as the division of Europe into distinct Churches and states—in other words, a new constitution whose consequences are not yet fully exhausted.[1] By widening the frontiers of the Thirty Years War, French policy, the policy of Richelieu, created the modern Europe which emerged in all its essential characteristics from the peace of Westphalia.

[1] This, I think, is all that can be retained of the otherwise extremely debatable theory developed by Hilaire Belloc in *Richelieu*.

BIBLIOGRAPHICAL NOTE

This history of the Thirty Years War does not contain the results of any new researches in the archives. The unpublished documents quoted relate only to Richelieu's policy and are taken from the Archives at the Ministère des Affaires Étrangères. Reference to them will be found in the footnotes. This is intended to be a personal summary of the present state of our knowledge, although so far as the early period of the war is concerned I have tried to take more account of Czech historical literature than is usually the case in France and Germany. Such a summary in a single volume necessarily entails a number of sacrifices: I hope that historians will be able to forgive these and not regard them as omissions. The main object is to summarize the most widely-held views, and for this reason I have only included in this work a list of the more important sources and not a detailed bibliography. Details of other works will be found in the footnotes.

GENERAL

H. Hauser: *La Prépondérance espagnole* (Peuples et civilisations, vol IX). Paris, 1933.
The Thirty Years War (Cambridge Modern History, vol. IV). Cambridge, 1906.

GENERAL HISTORIES OF THE THIRTY YEARS WAR

Père Bougeant: *Histoire des guerres et des négociations qui précédèrent le traité de Westphalie.* Paris, 1751. 3 vols.
Moritz Ritter: *Deutsché Geschichte im Zeitalter der Gegenreformation und des dreissigjährigen Krieges.* Stuttgart, 1889–1908, 3 vols.
Brandi, Karl: *Gegenreformation und Religionskriege.* Leipzig, 1930.
C. V. Wedgwood: *The Thirty Years War.* London, 1938.

COLLECTIONS OF DOCUMENTS

Lundorp: *Der Römischen Kaiserlichen Majestät und des heiligen Römischen Reichs acta publica, vom Anfang Ferdinand II.* Frankfurt, 1668. 4 vols.

Briefe und Aktenstücke zur Geschichte des dreissigjährigen Krieges in den Zeiten des verwaltenden Einflusses der Wittelsbacher. (Neue Folge, vol. II) 1907.

Richelieu: *Lettres, instructions diplomatiques et papiers d'État* (Collection des documents inédits.) Paris, 1853–77. 8 vols.

Mazarin: *Lettres du cardinal Mazarin pendant son ministère.* (Collection des documents inédits, vols. I–IV.) Paris, 1872 onwards.

Lonchay, Cuvelier and Lefèvre: *Correspondance de la cour d'Espagne sur les affaires des Pays-Bas* (vols. I–IV). Brussels, 1923 onwards.

CHAPTER ONE—Besides the general works: W. Platzhoff: *Geschichte des europäischen Staatensystems (1559–1660).* Munich and Berlin, 1928; B. Auerbach: *La France et le Saint-Empire romain germanique.* Paris, 1912; Édouard Rott, *Henri IV, les Suisses et la Haute-Italie.* Paris, 1882.

CHAPTER TWO—A. Gindely: *Geschichte des dreissigjährigen Krieges* (up to 1623). Prague, 1869 onwards; Ernest Denis: *La Fin de l'indépendance bohême.* Paris, 1891. 2 vols.; V. Tapié: *La Politique étrangère de la France et le début de la Guerre de Trente Ans.* Paris, 1934; Karel Stloukal: *Geska Kancelar dvorska* (on Lobkowitz's policy in Bohemia). Prague 1931; Kamil Krofta: *Majestat Rudolfa II* (The Letter of Majesty). Prague, 1909; Josef Pekař: *Bila Hora* (The White Mountain). Prague, 1922; Ernest Denis: *La Bohême depuis la Montagne Blanche.* Paris, 1903. 2 vols.

CHAPTER THREE—A. Wertheim: *Der tolle Halberstädter Herzog, Christian von Braunschweig.* Berlin, 1929.

CHAPTER FOUR—Josef Pekař: *Wallenstein* (German translation). Berlin, 1937.

CHAPTERS FIVE, SIX and SEVEN—Fagniez, G.: *Le Père Joseph et Richelieu.* Paris, 1894, 2 vols.; Johannes Paul: *Gustav Adolf.* Leipzig, 1932; A. Leman: *Urbain VIII et la rivalité de la France et de la Maison d'Autriche de 1631 à 1635.* Lille, 1921; J. Pekař: *Wallenstein* (see above); H. Srbik: *Wallensteins Ende.* Vienna, 1920; W. Mommsen: *Kardinal Richelieu, seine Politik im Elsass und in Lothringen.* Berlin, 1922.

CHAPTER EIGHT—Chéruel: *Histoire de la France pendant la minorité de Louis XIV.* Paris, 1879; P. Bougeant: *Histoire du traité de Westphalie.* Paris, 1744, 6 vols.

CHAPTER NINE—The (Latin) text of the Treaty of Münster may be found in Vast: *Les Grands Traités du règne de Louis XIV* (No. 1);

and the text of the treaty of Osnabrück in Dumont: *Corps diplomatique du droit des gens*. On Alsace see Overmann: *Die Abtretung des Elsass an Frankreich im Westphälischen Frieden*. Karlsruhe, 1906; Rod. Reuss: *L'Alsace au XVII*ᵉ *siècle*. Paris, 1897, 2 vols.; Christian Pfister: *Pages alsaciennes*. Strassburg, 1927.

INDEX